ONE WORLD

Special Millennial Edition of
WHEN THE WORLD WILL BE AS ONE

Tal Brooke

an End Run Book

Contents

We are in a time of worldwide transformation, and unless a miracle intervenes, we could experience a quantum leap more radical than when the Renaissance appeared, driving the Dark Ages out of history.

A New World Order could arrive almost overnight and be unlike anything the world has ever seen, affecting every life on the planet. Yet it may not be the utopian future of universal brotherhood we are all being primed to expect by today's power players and experts.

ONE WORLD uncovers the deep and often hidden forces behind the sweeping changes taking place right now. It suggests that certain critical turns in the road of history have remained unknown by the public—intentionally. In today's monopolized information gateway there are, indeed, patterns being kept from public view for the simple reason that this radical transition requires a docile and trusting public—a public that is willing to accept the popular reasons America and other nations have been pushed into a national debt equal to their net worth; why the family continues to disintegrate; why male and female roles blur; and why Christianity and traditional values disappear to be replaced by another system. The financial, military, political, and spiritual arms of this powerful agenda have an interlocking purpose that gives the plan almost irresistible power.

Yet it is also true that the growing Leviathan of world government cannot break through as long as America and the free world stand in its way, mindful of their former prowess and virtue. America and the Western world is fighting for its soul. Be assured that it will take your breath away when you suddenly recognize the pattern laid out in this book.

Tal Brooke is the President/Chairman of Spiritual Counterfeits Project (SCP, Inc., www.scp-inc.org), a Berkeley-based research organization. He has authored eight books and his work has been recognized in Marquis *Who's Who in the World*, *Contemporary Authors* (Vol. 93-96), and *The International Who's Who of Authors*. He received an EPA first place award in the critical review category. A graduate of the University of Virginia and Princeton, Tal Brooke has spoken at Cambridge, Oxford, Princeton, Sorbonne, U.C. Berkeley, the University of Virginia, and the University of Edinburgh.

Other books by Tal Brooke:
Avatar of Night, the millennial edition
Riders of The Cosmic Circuit (soon to be reprinted)
Virtual Gods
Conspiracy to Silence the Son of God
When The World Will Be As One
The Other Side of Death

End Run Publishing
1442A Walnut St., #387
Berkeley, CA, 94709

First End Run Edition September 2000

Cover preparation & design by Brian Godawa & Tal Brooke
Photos by Tal Brooke, including: public domain, royalty free, reviewer photos, Corel series, photobank, Corbis, softkey, etc.
Graphics by Tal Brooke, Frank Ordaz & Brian Godawa

Manufactured in the United States of America

ISBN:1-930045-07-7

An Overview

"Today, I say that no nation in the world need be left out of the global system we are constructing," —Madeleine Albright, 1997 Harvard University commencement.

T he public in America and the western nations have been under a mounting barrage of arguments stating that separate nations must enter a federation of world states—a **New World Order**. If such a global system appears in our era, it will be the first time in history that the earth will have a world government. There have been countless tries down history from Alexander the Great, Caesar Augustus, to Charlemagne and Napoleon, but no one has ever been able to pull off "the planetary bargain." The stakes are huge.

To close the deal, the arguments must be compelling enough to convince nations and their citizens to surrender their sovereignty and freedoms for the higher good of the planet. They warn of dire consequences if this does not take place. Descriptions of the good life are then added, ranging from heaven on earth, the end of poverty, war and disease, to the inauguration of the anticipated New Age of spiritual brotherhood, peace and enlightenment. We are told the global state is worth *the sacrifice*. But at stake for Americans, among others, is our history and legacy as we have known it. The anticipated change could be far greater than when history leapt from the Medieval period to the Renaissance. That's why it's a "New Age."

Soon after the first edition of this book came out—almost overnight—the Berlin Wall came down, the American president introduced the term *New World Order*, and the death of communism was declared. The subtitle *The Coming New World Order* appeared a full two years before the term

"New World Order" was known by more than a fraction of the public, yet global change is only in its early phases. Everything that this book anticipated has unfolded on schedule with much more ahead.

The political, military, and economic pillars of this long range plan cannot fully support a World Order without the fourth pillar—a global religion—standing beneath the fourth corner, lest the structure collapse. It is that simple.

Let's briefly consider the spiritual part of this agenda:

Religious differences are seen as the final barrier, separating various ethnic populations. Until these differences are broken down, divergent cultures will never fully meld into a One World Order.

Preparation for religious fusion has been well under way for quite some

time. Recently, things have speeded up with talk of a **United Religions,** a **UR,** mirroring the United Nations.

An international Who's Who of statesmen, intellectuals, and financial leaders met on June 25, 1995 at the UN's 50th anniversary in San Francisco at Grace Cathedral. At the key ceremony, it was revealed that Mikhail Gorbachev, the former head of the Soviet Union, had the backing of world leaders to set up a United Nations sister organization in San Francisco called the United Religions. Modeled on the UN, it would have a 500 member assembly, a 36 member executive council, and a General Secretary. Multi-faith Peacemaker teams would be dispatched around the world by the "UR" to trouble spots, just like the UN. In the summer of 2000, in Pittsburgh, the charter for the United Religions was signed right on schedule.

Is it any mystery, then, that perhaps the most powerful force to move across the church in 2000 years is now trying to prepare the way for such a global religion? The momentum of this ecumenical movement is astounding. From another angle the New Age and Neo-pagan alternatives are perfect fits for this grand spiritual synthesis. When Christianity absorbs the new spiritualities, then it will be ripe for a merger.

The *New York Times* bestseller list for the past decade has been dominated by New Age appeals that embrace the coming global spirituality. For instance, Neale Walsch's *Conversations with God* tells the people of the earth to get ready and trust the process of change as we move into a New Age of world brotherhood (Walsch is on the steering committee of the URI). James Redfield's *Celestine Prophecy* shows religious wisdoms fusing like a Chinese puzzle coming together.

There is another, more sinister aspect behind the New World Order that only a few see. Now and then it pops out like a shifting illusion. The public sees one thing, but something else is taking place. From one angle, there is the beautiful lady reflecting back from a vanity mirror. From another angle, it is a skull. Once the eye sees the hidden form suddenly appear, things never look the same again.

Is it possible that today's masses are being set up with a counterfeit vision of heaven on earth just so they will go along with the plan? What if the coming global system is more like the tyrannical system foreseen by Orwell and Huxley, or the one predicted by the ancient apocalyptic writers? Who benefits and who loses?

The Call by Today's Power Players

On *The Charlie Rose Show*, on May 4th, 1993, the new Council on Foreign Relations (CFR) President Les Gelb told Charlie Rose, "You had me on [before] to talk about the New World Order . . . I talk about it all the time . . . It's one world now. . . Willing or not, ready or not, we are all involved (Note, William Greider's recent bestseller uses the words of Les Gelb in its very title, *One World, Ready or Not*.)... The competition is about who will establish the first one-world system of government that has ever existed in the society of nations. It is control over each of us as individuals and over all of us

together as a community...."

Question: *But under who's control?*

Who will rule us? Without the protection of our Constitution—should it be superseded by international treaties and covenants—will there be anything to protect us from the sort of despotic dictators that our founders created the Constitution to protect us from? American citizens could become like the animals in Orwell's *Animal Farm*, creatures with no real voice and no choice but to accept the cards dealt to them by the higher powers.

Like it or not, America could become a defacto New World Order province. The public would miss this quiet transition with its attention distracted by the illusion of things-as-usual—US flags flying, patriotic rituals of pomp and circumstance, political doublespeak, superbowls, national holidays, ad infinitum—as things beneath the surface shift.

What will life be like under this new system? Where did its structure come from, and who conceived it?

Former Secretary of Defense Caspar Weinberger in the February 15, 1993, issue of *Forbes* magazine wrote that a "New World Order means the U.S. and other nations agree to be governed by a rule of law . . . Applying this on a world scale means that we could gain what we had hoped the UN would achieve but has not: global law, breaches of which will be punished swiftly and with certainty."

This book will uncover some of the deep and hidden forces behind the sweeping changes taking place right now. We may learn that certain critical turns in the road of history have remained unknown by the public—intentionally—while today's politically correct versions of history have reigned uncontested in a monopolized information gateway. There are things that the "ordinary people" are not supposed to know, patterns they are not supposed to see. If they did, they might become like alarmed South Sea islanders watching a tidal wave looming towards them and their village; they would be engaged with desperate abandon. Public distraction has been an important aspect of this quiet agenda.

There is no denying that there are unsettling signs beneath the surface: America has been pushed into a national debt almost equal to its net worth; the family continues to disintegrate, male and female roles blur, and Christianity and traditional values disappear only to be replaced by radical alternatives. The financial, military, political, social, and spiritual arms of this dangerous agenda have an interlocking purpose that gives the plan almost irresistible power. The truth is that America is fighting for its soul, but few seem to really know this.

The emergence of a New World Order requires a docile and passive public willing to entrust their lives and futures to an elite leadership. Only then can this elite get on with the business of managing the planet unobstructedly.

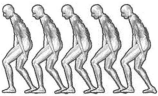

But the Leviathan of world government cannot break through as long as a healthy America stands in its way, its prowess and virtue intact, its citizens vigilant for their hard fought freedoms. That America—its memory and its history—is quickly passing, and that is the real danger.

So should you glimpse this approaching Leviathan of World Order unmasked, the illusion briefly held in check, it will take your breath way, especially when you see how extensive and multifaceted the plan has been. Most would agree that it is better to see it than blindly march down the road to serfdom unawares. But there is another reason to see it. We may have more time than we thought to do more than we ever thought we could! Wasn't that true in the first American Revolution? If our ancestors had lost heart, there never would have been an America in the first place.

1
Contact

Increasing numbers are reporting altered states of consciousness or contacts from beyond with beings of light, cosmic masters, channeled entities, gods, or even "God" appearing in a new form. The elite of these are soon discovered by the media.

What was once faint crackling on America's spiritual Geiger counter has become deafening noise as these messages come in like cosmic telegrams bearing the delicious promise that the human race will transform into an exalted godlike state that will bring in the New Age. But standing in the way of this necessary paradigm shift are the old "prejudices" and beliefs from an outmoded Christian era with its dualistic view of God and man, its moral absolutes of good and evil.

The reigning books on the *New York Times* bestseller list for well over a decade have been books about contacting the other side or experiencing new realities. Betty Eadie's 1992 *Embraced By the Light* by mid 1994 had reached the 66-week mark on the *New York Times* best seller list, primarily holding the number one spot. Then Dannion Brinkley's 1994 *Saved By the Light* got to the top position and toggled between one and two with Eadie's book. By early 1998, James Van Praagh published the bestselling account of his own contact with the other side entitled, *Talking To Heaven: A Medium's Message of Life After Death*, which took over the *New York Times* pole position. Van Praagh was on Oprah Winfrey, Larry King, and *Good Morning America* following the footsteps of Eadie and Brinkley. A little after, Gary Zukav and Neal Donald Walsch entered the stream of media celebrity along with Marianne Williamson, Deepak Chopra, and James Redfield.

These best selling authors have been invading the nation's imagination with their experiences and revelations, creating a psychic and paranormal "Great Awakening."

With these contacts have come messages, and this is the real heart of the matter. What is interesting is that these messages have woven together to form an interesting pattern—indeed, a belief system. The synchronicity of these messages and their divergent points of contact keep suggesting that at least some of these communications are most deliberate and that something is being orchestrated from beyond our known world.

But for what reason? And why is it happening now at an accelerating pace? It did not happen overnight; it has been building up for centuries. Why now? And is there a supernatural dimension to the geopolitical plan?

These messages constantly bring teachings about the New Age and world community. Who can resist such messages, especially when they come from near death experiences?

The Near Death Experience

. . . You watch in awe as a tunnel of darkness suddenly appears before you. In moments it is ready to engulf you. You go flashing down the tunnel at tremendous speed as a brilliant light at the end grows larger and larger. At the end of the tunnel stands a Being of Light. You are about to be shown a "life review" by this being of light who seems to know you through and through.

You have entered the Death plane.

Then you glide above a vast jeweled city filled with bright and luminous "wise beings" who can now talk to you telepathically. They have a message that they want you to convey to the rest of the world. You descend to some vast courtyard surrounded by pillars reminiscent of the Parthenon. Standing before them, these beings show you the earth's

future, a time of coming changes when luminous masters, world helpers, will guide the earth through upheavals into a time of world peace and harmony.

Suddenly, you realize that billions across history have crossed this threshold. Only up until now, this has been a shrouded secret, one that could have remained sealed forever. Soon this glistening region retreats from view.

You hover between "clinical death" and resuscitation during this "near death experience." As you come back into the world, crossing the threshold of heavy matter, you enter your lifeless body as it lies on a stretcher. Your "astral body" descends into it like a hand plunging into a glove. In the process you invisibly pass by physicians and orderlies working frantically to bring your body back to life. According to modern instruments, you were dead, and all vital signs had ceased.

You have returned from the dead. When you open your eyes, those nearby look on dumbstruck. You are both sad and grateful to have more time on earth.

You the viewer have been watching the televised account of a now famous figure who has had a "death experience." Special effects reminiscent of Star Wars have turbocharged the television portrayal of what lies behind the mystery of death. You relive what happened through the eyes of the subject. It is powerful, real, and immediate, and because you have been made to identify with the dying subject, you also sympathize with the account.

In truth, program is the pinnacle of media endorsement—a lavish prime-time special on major network television that is exclusively devoted to the amazing account of a death experience. This televised account is actually a composite of two famous accounts—that of Betty Eadie, and Dannion Brinkley. Their separate accounts have also been recreated on prime time network specials since the generic "synthesis" just watched.

Dannion Brinkley had his near death experience when hit by a bolt of lightening. Recovery was long and agonizing, but this former trouble-maker had a tale to tell from his higher masters and spirit guides. His account is one of future glimpses of a unified world and messages from the Wise Beings. Christ does not really fit the picture. With Eadie, Christ is portrayed as a being of light.

Betty Eadie had her experience after she decided, after a "multitude of problems" following the birth of a seventh child, to have a hysterectomy. It was performed on November 18, 1973, at Riverton hospital (now Highline Specialty Center) in Seattle, Washington.

Eadie recalls being given sleeping pills before and after the surgery, making her "groggy." In this groggy state, she remembers noticing it was

9:30 p. m. before she fell back asleep "chilled and weaker than I had ever felt before."

She claims to have died for over four hours. How does one know? Were there any doctors, nurses, or anyone in the room during these hours? No, because when she revived, there was still no one in the room (except demons and angels). There was no sheet over her face.

The only way she knows that she died is because during her experience she claims Jesus told her she had died—prematurely. Medical records are sketchy, and to this day she refuses to release them.

She soon takes the reader on a vivid recollection of a journey out of her body into heaven. She describes in detail her many encounters with Jesus, old friends from her preexistence, ministering angels, and other beings.

The content of this experience is filled with mixtures of historic Biblical Christianity, Mormonism, New Age philosophy, occultism, and Catholicism. Especially prevalent are the trappings and direct teachings of folk Mormonism and official LDS doctrine.

Upon "leaving her body," Eadie was met by three men curiously dressed in traditional Catholic monk's robes. They had been with her for "eternities." Eadie begins to recall images of her preexistence, her pre-earth life, recognizing old spirit being acquaintances, and that her "death" was a rebirth to greater understanding and knowledge (Eadie, pp. 31, 34-35, 68, 73, 82, 97, 100).

Eadie communicates with her "ministering angels" through something more than "telepathy." She claimed to be able to feel "their emotions and . . .experience their feelings" (p. 32). This was the beginning of several allusions to an undifferentiated oneness of eternal intelligence, of all things (pp. 31, 55, 57, 76, 79, 81, 87, 93). This is the Eastern spin.

Eadie claims that every particle, every element comprising matter has spirit and an eternal intelligence. Later while in a garden in Heaven, Eadie claims to have seen a rose and could "feel its spirit. . . such intelligence within that petal. . . I felt God in the plant, in me, his love pouring into us. **We are all one**" (pp. 79-81). Since her first book, this account has evolved and her teachings have drifted toward some of the Earth Consciousness of her native American ancestry.

From New Age groups to church groups, eager readers circulate Betty Eadie's book basking in the gushing positive affirmations from the other side. It is a picture of a universe so tender and mild that you could almost wander around blindfolded and never so much as trip. (Try doing the same thing in the real world in a Detroit ghetto or Harlem.). That's the thing about Eadie's message, she gushes and it's all good. It is like she found a massive Oreo Cookie for the world. The same can be said for now deceased New Age channeler, Helen Schucman, who channeled *A Course in Miracles* from some cosmic Christ-spirit. It all sounds far too good to be true.

Not every near death survivor nor every medium has such a positive report. Some channelers go into a danger zone that has clear warning signs—warnings that all may not be well. Some reports tell you that you have to absorb both the good and the evil because they are all one.

Seth Speaks

Jane Roberts, now deceased, has remained among the most prolific of all contemporary channelers. Her books have sold abundantly since the mid-70's. Rather than the usual fluffy afterlife affirmations, not only are her revelations more demanding and complex, they occasionally become quite unsettling, indeed, more blatantly evil.

It is an object lesson that what gets through is not always like a cheery cartoon character, but a dark and resourceful intelligence that is after something. Her experience contains, in dramatic form, all of the earmarks of a genuine medium being reached and controlled from the other side. It is a very compelling tale and throws light on more recent, attention seeking channelers such as J.Z. Knight, who channels Ramtha, or Van Praagh, for that matter, who is the latest sensation. In today's sanitized spotlight, you rarely see the twitches in the dark, the groans, the strange faces that tell you that maybe something abnormal is going on here — something that men were not made for. Perhaps there is a monster hiding in the darkness, and the reality is closer to an ancient vampire tale than the sanitized New Age explanations.

Jane Roberts became the channel for an entity named Seth. It started on an early September day in 1963. In her apartment in Elmira, New York, this aspiring novelist suddenly began to have some very strange experiences. Her encounters changed her life as well as the lives of thousands of people who have since read her numerous bestsellers that fill the New Age/Occult sections of countless bookstores.

In her book *The Seth Material*, Roberts tells her story. She portrays herself as a liberated graduate of Skidmore University who was an honest seeker of truth. One day, she and her husband decided to write a book on

ESP. To prime the pump, they used a Ouija board the night of December 8, 1963. After a few sessions, they were able to receive messages from someone who initially identified himself as "Frank Withers." Soon, however, it claimed to be more than this, and no longer wanted to be known as Frank Withers. "To God, all names are his name." Then it said, "You may call me whatever you choose. I call myself Seth; it fits the me of me."

Jane soon reached a threshold where she went from being able to race the pointer all over the board to being able to anticipate the whole words in her mind before the pointer spelled them out. At that moment the pointer paused, and she felt as if she were standing at the top of a high diving board. It was as if she were trying to make herself jump as spectators below egged her on. She took the leap and immediately began speaking for Seth. Jane Roberts was now a full- fledged channel. Seth initially acted like a jocular, wise, paternal old friend from some past life, yet it made no mistake in showing that it was fully superhuman. Among other things, it had a mission to get across to our world the wisdom that it was only now ready for.

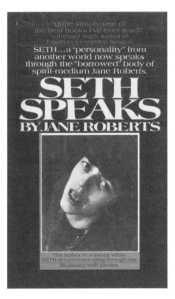

Jane decided to conduct a seance for her ESP book. Her tone was that of a high school girl following a cooking recipe. She got her money's worth; Seth stunned Jane, her husband, and friends: he transmogrified her body. It was not exactly a thing of beauty, but it was, after all, a supernatural manifestation. Those at the seance table were told by the voice to concentrate on Jane's arm. One witness, Robert Butts, said that the hand began to change in appearance and resembled a paw. It gave him an eerie feeling. He said the hand became stubby and thick for a moment. Then it resumed its paw-like appearance. Seth told Butts to reach out and touch the hand. He touched it cautiously. It felt very cold, wet, and clammy, and seemed unusually bumpy. After that, Seth made the whole forepaw glow before the stunned table.

If this gesture were not enough, Seth had another sign for them. They faced a mirror, and Seth told them to look at their reflections in the mirror. As they watched, Jane's image was suddenly replaced with another image. The head dropped lower, and the shape of the skull and the hair style changed. The head in the mirror leaned down even though Jane was sitting erect, looking straight ahead. Naturally, it would take the three people a while to acclimate themselves to such bizarre antics, but they would soon triumph and transcend their visceral horror.

The Seth sessions continued. The next breakthrough in the taking over of Jane's body was the appearance of a deep masculine voice, which issued from her body. Seth told Jane's husband that he had been an extremely vain woman in a former life. Seth also started calling Jane "Ruburt," a male name. Then Seth commented philosophically that the name "Jane" would sound rather unmelodious as a man's voice.

Jane, who was by now called Ruburt, observed that they did not realize she would receive what was known as the Seth material through "the psychic structure." She acknowledged a sense of great power in Seth's voice. It made her feel very small, as if surrounded by a great energy. In time she would learn to remain in a deep trance while being able to talk, walk, and gesture. She would even learn to sip wine at times when Seth spoke through her.

But there was an incident that almost ended the sessions. Jane, who by now had had a series of out-of-the-body experiences, said she was in her bedroom when she suddenly became aware of a dark, looming figure menacing her. She had not previously believed in demons, but changed her mind when the attacker dragged her around and even bit her hand. Finally the thing tried to kill her, and she screamed.

Seth explained it all away. It was merely a projection of her own mind, the energy of hidden fears. Seth assured Jane and her husband, who transcribed the sessions, that the evil that Ruburt imagined did not exist.

Later, a fairly well-known psychologist interviewed Seth to see if it was a double personality. It was his opinion that Seth had a "massive intellect" and did not seem to be a secondary personality, as in the case of multiple personalities. This was further borne out by a number of telepathic and clairvoyant tests. Seth, in a ten-year period, produced over 5000 typewritten records and analogues of higher esoteric truth. Some of this material was most subtle indeed, though much of it was a redundant weaving of semantic spells, as Seth formulated the same ideas again and again. Invariably it was in abstract and often abstruse, erudite, and elusive language, with as much scientific and technical jargon as possible. In this sense Seth's material greatly resembled the earlier teachings coming through Edgar Cayce, who was the most prodigious channeler of the modern era. Seth's teachings are almost identical with those of one of the most famous "entities" of the 1980s, "Lazaris," who channels through Jach Pursel.

What are some of Seth's revelations to the world?

God is an "energy gestalt" who has passed through human stages, and in a Hegelian sense is still evolving. This energy forms all universes. Seth names God "All That Is." God is not personal but is the sum of all consciousness. Humans are co-creators who contain this God within them; they evolve through reincarnation. Apparently Seth evolves, too.

Channeling Seth

Something came along named "Seth II," an ancient friend of Seth I who gave Seth I a punt out of Jane, as though he were a soccer ball.

Ruburt, or Jane, tells what happened one night in April 1968 during the fifth year of the Seth sessions. By then Jane had been forbidden by Seth to read "religious books."

With massive power the voice started to break through, and Jane was hurled off into a void. The voice sounded clear though distant. Jane felt as if a cone had come down over her head. The voice claimed to come from an alien dimension—so alien that the contact was almost a miracle.

Two months later, the pyramid effect started again. Now the voice was plural, speaking of itself using the royal "We." They described themselves as an entity which existed before our own time frame, and which was instrumental in building the physical cosmos—this entity helped form pure energy into physical matter.

Jane said that under this new Seth's influence, her body became like a puppet and her face expressionless.

After the visitation Jane encountered difficulty getting back into normal consciousness, and Seth had to help her.

When Jane went back into a trance, she had a trauma. She had been not only the recipient of words, but of direct spiritual revelations and experiences as well. She says that the entity referred to individuals returning in the future to peer into physical reality like giants upon the floor. At that point she saw a giant's face peer into her living room, its face filling up the entire window. Then her body, the room and its contents all grew to enormous size. She screamed and began to tremble violently.

Jane had one more bout with the higher Seth, Seth II, but she became so shaken that the regular Seth did not allow it to continue for a long time. Again she felt the cone above her head and saw the giant looking in at her. At this point she struggled to get in touch with her vocal cords. She was beginning to feel violated by this being, a problem she had never felt with the lower Seth. The unpleasantness of the experience, she conjectured, could have been due to her lack of evolution of consciousness.

The last statement from Seth II was a godlike declaration; it claimed to have given man the mental images from which man formed the known world and his own physical self. By 1984, the pluralistic Seths had written a compendium of revelations for the human race. Today these teachings are readily available to anyone who walks into just about any bookstore.

"Ruburt" has gone on to be with Seth, and newer channels have come on the scene to replace Jane Roberts (Ruburt). New entities have in turn replaced Seth—such as "Ramtha" and "Lazaris"—who feature among the bright new stars of Shirley MacLaine's autobiographies such as *Out on a Limb* and *Dancing in the Light*.

These newer entities have arrived with exquisite timing to a world in waiting. The advance work has been done. Unlike Seth, who only muttered in dark rooms before a handful of observers, other entites have spoken before millions. Compared to Seth, they have achieved superstar status.

The media have mentioned the enormous gate fees of these entities and their channels, an indicator of the surging popular interest. J.Z. Knight, who channels Ramtha, "on an average weekend draws up to 700 participants at $400 apiece ($280,000); she admits to earning millions of dollars from 'Ramtha,' "[1] and James Von Praagh quickly surpassed that.

Alien Encounters

Whereas Jane Roberts was out there eagerly fishing for entities with a Ouija board, offering herself as a willing vessel, this was not the case with several others who have gained notoriety recently. Some of the things they have hooked into have been a little more strange and a little less friendly than some of the more famous entities. This would be a little hard to take for Harvey Cox, a noted Harvard theology professor, whom *The New Age Journal* quotes as saying of such entities as Lazaris, "They're so cuddly and friendly. They seem to be yuppified versions of the demons and spirits of another time."[2] Some contactees seem less fortunate.

In the case of one of these "victims," a well-known author by the name of Whitley Strieber, he has parlayed his chilling encounters into the number-one spot on *The New York Times* bestseller list twice—first as a hardback and then, in January 1988, as a paperback, earning more than he ever did writing horror novels like *Wolfen*. In fact it makes you won-

der if his present bestseller, *Communion*, is not somehow his ultimate horror novel. He is certainly the right man for the job as "a chosen one," according to the aliens that abducted him. Who else is better suited to report on the sheer terror of such an encounter than a horror novelist?

Strieber has changed his mind a number of times about who these aliens are. In early 1988 Strieber was on the Larry King Show and was formative in his speculations about the origin and purpose of these beings, but he remained vehemently defensive about the authenticity of his encounters. One could say he looked almost paranoid about them and with good reason: according to what he learned under hypnotic regression, these beings have been spying on him from the time he was a small child.

Whitley Strieber, on the night of December 26, 1985, was in his secluded log cabin in upstate New York with his family. In the early hours of the morning, he had a visitation. Small, terrifying humanoids crept up to his bedside. They mentally controlled him by paralyzing him. Then they quietly carried him out of his house naked. They seemed to levitate him to an examination theater in the sky from some spot in the snowy woods.

Once in the small, round theater, he felt like an animal in a medical experiment, one of those monkeys whose skullcap has been sawn off and replaced by diodes. He sat nude and helpless. This was by no means a positive experience:

> The fear was so powerful that it seemed to make my personality completely evaporate. . . . "Whitley" ceased to exist. What was left was a body in a state of raw fear so great that it swept about me like a thick, suffocating curtain, turning paralysis into a condition that seemed close to death. I do not think that my ordinary humanity survived the transition to this little room.[3]

The gray-and-brown-skinned creatures closely resembled the two types of aliens that emerged from the saucer in Spielberg's film *Close Encounters*, except that these were fierce. There were the three-foot variety and the elongated, delicate, and spindly five-foot variety. But unlike the creatures in the film, there were two other types as well. The massive eyes of these creatures seemed like infinite shafts, black abysses. They had an insect-like quality, almost an exoskeleton. The smallest ones moved with rapid, ugly mechanical movements as they sped around Whitley Strieber.

As he was examined, one creature in particular—the spindly leather-skinned, five-foot variety—observed him: "She had those amazing, electrifying eyes . . . the huge, staring eyes of the old gods. . . . They were featureless, in the sense that I could see neither pupil nor iris."[4] In her presence he "had no personal freedom at all." When he looked into her eyes, "It was as if every vulnerable detail of my self were known to this being. . . . I could actually feel the presence of that other person within me—which was as disturbing as it was curiously sensual." Their eyes are often described as "limitless," "haunting," and "baring the soul."

Later on, Strieber would think of this creature as being like Ishtar, the ancient Mesopotamian "Eye-Goddess" with the huge staring eyes. He would observe that the closest he could come to an unadorned image of these beings was "the age-old, glaring face of Ishtar. Paint her eyes entirely black, remove her hair, and there is my image as it hangs before me now in my mind's eye, the ancient and terrible one, the bringer of wisdom, the ruthless questioner."[5] Like the ancients with their goddess Ishtar (or Ashtoreth), Whitley Strieber cited a sexual side to the encounter.

The examination room was untidy, even dirty. The creatures had a bad smell. A probe was jammed into his head. Then the hideously sexual aspect of this examination unfolded: "I was being shown an enormous and extremely ugly object, gray and scaly, with a sort of network of wires on the end. It was at least a foot long, narrow, and triangular in structure. They inserted this thing into my rectum . . . at the time I had the impression that I was being raped, and for the first time, I felt anger."[6]

During this period the "Ishtar" creature asked him why "it" was not fully hard. Under deep hypnosis Strieber was questioned in detail about this event. He was horrified, later likening the event to a human copulating with an incubus or succubus.

The creatures couldn't have cared less about his rights; all they told him was that he was chosen for something—perhaps to be a messenger to the world. But were these creatures space aliens? Not necessarily so. At times they have seemed to be more like the ancient pagan gods and goddesses, or spirits, or incubi and succubi. Strieber has been confused. Maybe the ancient spirits were dressing up for our contemporary culture as space aliens. Their outward form only seemed like shells, anyway.

Whitley Strieber conjectures about them:

> As the ages roll along, it could be that what changes is not our visi-
> tors but our way of installing them in the culture. Maybe they did
> not come here in 1946, 1897, 1235, or even a.d. 300. I have report-
> ed that the being I have become familiar with looks like Ishtar.
> Maybe she is: she said she was old. . . . It would seem that our civi-
> lization is not paying attention to what may be the central archetyp-
> al mythological experience of the age. If so, then this is the first
> time that man has simply refused to respond to the ghosts and gods.
> Is that why they have become so physical, so real, dragging people
> out of bed like rapists in the night—because they must have our
> notice in order to somehow be confirmed in their truth? . . .
> Something is out there and it wants to get in.[7]

Before we can let them in, they claim we must be prepared. Some peo-
ple claim that not only are they being prepared individually to be fit for the New Age, but so is the whole human race. Only the worthy will make it all the way and it depends on the ability of individuals to absorb the new teachings and the new models of reality. They also must abandon the old negative programming for the great evolutionary leap.

2
The Rainbow Bridge

In his visionary blockbuster *2001*, Stanley Kubrick had the edge 15 years before Marilyn Ferguson ever portrayed where things were going in her bestseller *The Aquarian Conspiracy*. By the mid-'60s, Kubrick was both a change agent and a prophet who spoke through the medium of the giant screen. He created whole new realities before audiences of millions. Long before New Age terms were popularized by the masses, Kubrick showed the world what a "paradigm shift" was in his portrayal of Arthur C. Clarke's mystical science fiction epic *2001*. It was quite an experience sitting in a huge cinerama theater, in a packed audience, while the vast screen engulfed us with this new vision of reality.

Quantum Leaps

Kubrick had us sitting in his Darwinian time machine as the vast solar orb rose slowly to illumine the dawn of human intelligence in reddish-golden light. Simian packs roamed the scarred primitive face of a prehis-

toric world. Some of the ape-man faces were less monkey-like and more human. The camera angle seemed to show intelligence in the eyes. Grunts were on the verge of becoming words. Then one type of simian tribe began to move in on another. They moved in place for battle. Mounting shrieks

became physical attacks. It was a war between the species. Suddenly, one of the more intelligent ape-men picked up what was to be the first weapon in history, a large thigh bone. That gave him the critical edge. He beat the opposing simian to death. Others of the same species, with their greater intelligence, imitated what their leader had just done. Then they all held large bones and started smashing their enemies, the more ape-like creatures.

In the silence after the battle, the winning species yelled in exuberant triumph. Ape-like screams filled the air. One superior species suddenly replaced another, but something far more significant was going on than one species replacing another. What was really happening was the indwelling faculty of consciousness suddenly leaping to a greater magnitude on the earth, from one type of simian to another. In reality it was a moment of pure Hegelian consciousness evolution. It was a glimpse at the real subject behind the shifting actors. **Consciousness** was the true timeless protagonist of the vast epic—"the eternal charioteer," to use an expression from the *Bhagavad Gita*, and apparently, it "was up to something."

Then came Kubrick's supreme moment of genius. The humanoid ape leader then hurled his large thigh bone into the air in triumph. The bone filled the screen as it spun in slow motion. It kept ascending, and then suddenly its same basic shape became enormous, filling the whole sky. It had suddenly become a vast space ship as it drifted in outer space. Below it

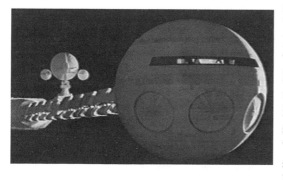

shone the huge, bright, bluish-green planet earth. It was no longer a bone. The leap of intelligence had dwarfed time and turned the simian bone into an interplanetary vessel whose inhabitants— "evolved human simians"—were a quantum leap beyond the ape creatures. Soon the third quantum leap would begin when this vessel reached Jupiter and its human inhabitant crossed the next catalytic threshold into some kind of supermind, represented by the star baby.

This epic is not about creatures but about evolving consciousness reaching what New Agers call *critical thresholds* for the next *transformation of consciousness*. Kubrick's vision is indeed the stuff out of which pantheism, monism, and cosmic humanism are built. As old as the Vedas of India, consciousness is portrayed as ascending up the evolutionary ladder in the act of becoming godlike. The leap in conceptual understanding is called a *paradigm shift* by the New Age movement.

Stanley Kubrick's paradigm shift represented the new myth. The biblical monotheistic view of existence had become eclipsed by the pantheistic-mystical view. It was dazzling, electric, and seemed hauntingly insightful. A generation was wooed. Opinions and lifetimes of thought were shifted in a few brief hours on the screen. It was almost like magic. To many in the audience, this film was a seed which would work away in their minds on a deeper level. In time it would emerge as a worldview. Those on the mystical fringe of the 1960s had already caught the vision.

The New Consciousness

In the sixties there were many apostles of the new consciousness. One avenue for the new consciousness to manifest itself was through mind-altering drugs. Personal experience was key. Beliefs could easily be attached to experience, especially with mysticism. As it happened, Doctor Albert Hoffman, a pharmacologist, discovered one of the most potent mind-altering drugs ever known: LSD-25. It was in Switzerland in the late forties when, by accident, a few millionths of a gram lodged under Dr. Hoffman's fingernail. The resulting mystical experience was soon reported to other elite 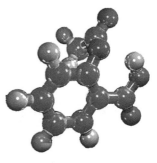 scientists. Not long after that Aldous Huxley, famed British novelist and intellectual, tried his fortune with mescaline and psilocybin, eliciting mystical experiences from these natural hallucinogens. Various shamans had been doing this for thousands of years.

If thousands of years ago ancient Hindu rishis could ingest a plant called soma and write the *Upanishads* in their altered states of consciousness, the same scenario could work again. But it would require finding the right mind-expanding drug, as well as respected members of society to sanction the drug. Well, the drug was in place. LSD had entered the world.

The idea of chemically altered states would have to receive further sanction from the intellectual elite to reach the critical threshold of public experimentation—and it did. Harvard professor Timothy Leary began to administer hundreds of doses of LSD-25 to his graduate students. His assistant was Harvard psychologist Dr. Richard Alpert. They were a team, and their psychedelic road tours across the United States were famous. Meanwhile, another Harvard professor, Dr. Alan Watts of the Oriental Religions Department, had previously taken LSD and written *The Joyous Cosmology*, discussing his own mystical encounters while "tripping" on a New England farm.

By the time Leary and Alpert left Harvard, they were packing university auditoriums, conference centers, and civic centers with their exciting alternative to the straight society. This new secret, which defied the present system, carried the potent sense of mission that the early church had as it met in the catacombs beneath Rome to receive the startling message of the Christian faith. Now again there were harbingers of a new reality. The West was like Rome, ready to crumble under its old system represented by the futility of Vietnam, the banality of Lyndon Johnson's "Great Society," traditional moral do's and don'ts, Pentagon marches, and protest rallies which all seemed to culminate in the Kent State Massacre.

Leary had become the academic celebrity-turned-guru. His cause was in high fashion among the vanguard of the counterculture. *Playboy* interviews popularized his views, and countless cover stories featured Leary's broken smile. He was a bodhisattva in tennis shoes and white chinos who merged psychedelic mystical experiences and modern psychological theories with timeless Eastern holy writ.

In the mid-1960s, I encountered Timothy Leary for the first time in Washington, D. C., in a large church sanctuary overflowing with my contemporaries. In the dim light of center stage leaning against the podium

was Tim Leary, his face creased with a strange wisdom. His soothing voice soon drew us in. It was evident that he had found a key to terrible power and knew that when it was used the world would not remain the same. Whether through flower power or mass ecstasy the world would be transformed, and nothing that the "straight society" did could stop the momentum of the truth they had found. Leary began talking under the spotlight, opening a major doorway into the New Age:

"LSD does not produce the transcendent experience; it merely acts as a chemical key. It opens the mind, frees the nervous system of its ordinary patterns and structures, and releases an enormous amount of awareness-energy. Understanding, describing, and using these released energies intelligently has puzzled scholars for thousands of years. Yet here is a key to the mystery which has been passed down for over 2,500 years; the consciousness expansion experience, pre-mortem death and rebirth. The Vedic sages, the Eleusinian initiates, and the Tantrics all knew the secret; in their esoteric writings, they whisper the message. They figure out the pathways and landmarks. It is possible to get beyond ego-consciousness, to tune in to the neurological processes which flash by at the speed of light, and become aware of the treasury of ancient racial knowledge welded into the nucleus of every cell in the body. Psychedelics can open this door."

We were dazzled. Leary then asked the audience, "Are you aware of the complexity of the human nervous system? For us, the voyagers, the following neurological numbers take on the significance of *mantras* (sacred Hindu words). The human brain receives one thousand million signals a second.

We possess between ten and thirteen billion brain cells. Each neuron is connected to, on average, twenty-five thousand neighboring neurons."

Leary paused, an amazed look on his face. His tone became confidential, almost a whisper, as he went on to share profound secrets.

"During an ecstatic experience these billions of signals, which are normally registered and decoded, are no longer hindered by the conscious-logical-censor. Without the censor, we become unable to describe our experience because the mechanisms of language cannot contain the experience. It all happens too fast." Leary's tone of amazement was that of the explorer finding the secret Egyptian vault. It came from his personal experience.

What was our twentieth-century reference point in relation to this huge new discovery? Leary gave us a means of comparison as he flew through psychological and neurological models. He had walked us from Carl Jung's archetype theory to modern neurology. Now he was about to show us how language—a descriptive and conceptual medium—had limits similar to attempting to drive a Chevy, which performs reliably on land, through the Pacific Ocean depths where only a submarine can go. It was hard to argue with the full clout of Leary's credentials as an Ivy League, indeed, a Harvard psychologist. Our academically competitive generation held intellectual accomplishments in awe. ("Getting into the Ivy League is hard enough. Try being a professor in that league!")

Leary resorted to anthropological and linguistic comparisons: "Picture in some barren, primitive region of Australia an aboriginal tribe that has been completely screened off from present-day civilization. They have not seen the world beyond a 20-mile radius of their cave dwelling; they have never seen a two-dimensional picture, and when they are shown a photograph, they are unable to decipher it, even if it is of something from their surroundings. They have never seen the wheel or woven cloth. Their only implements are stones; their only garments are animal skins and leaves. They have not even seen a truly straight line, a metallic or glassy surface. Their language possesses fewer than a thousand words, and none of them has abstract meaning. Their food is not cooked; it is wild and so depends upon the moods of the forests and the generosity of the seasons.

"Now picture the savage standing alone in the woods, then suddenly hurled into the very center of Manhattan, in front of the United Nations building or Park Avenue. Unless the savage has a stable grounding in some form of religious truth, he will experience utter terror.

"If he is later teleported back to his own culture, hopefully sane, he still has to cross the gulf of semantics to tell his tribesmen of his amazing experience. To do this, he must invent a completely new language. Yet even this is not enough. For even if he has catalogued memories of sensations into new words, he has still failed to understand the new sensations in their own context. The chances are his memory will be scrambled since his nervous censor is used to only a fraction of all that input, unlike those used to a modern city. He will be in a chaos of car horns, sirens, construction jackhammers, jukeboxes, underground subways, jets and helicopters, rumbling cars and whining engines. And while hearing this cacophony, he will be seeing millions of tons of glinting glass and steel, shining metallic objects traveling at frightening speeds, colored lights and glowing neon as evening sets in. He will smell anything from Aqua Velva and Chanel No. 5 to ozone, propylene, phenylhydrazine, chewing gum, super detergents, germicides, gasoline, synthetic flavors and all manner of esters and ketones, methane and assorted sewage gases, exhaust and restaurant smells.

"After an LSD experience we emerge just as overwhelmed, intrigued, frightened and ecstatic as the savage transported to New York City. But our task of finding a language and creating a road map may well be even more difficult than his." A stroboscope flickering in the auditorium seemed to punctuate Leary's statement. The blinding flashes turned everyone's movements into an insect dance.

Leary closed the session with the parting admonition: "Remember that throughout human history, millions have made this voyage. A few whom we call mystics, saints, and Buddhas have made this experience endure and communicated it to their fellowmen. The experience is safe. At worst, all you will do is return as the same person you were before."

Only months after Leary's talk, I had the mystical experience of my life after taking ten times the normal dosage of LSD-25 (pure Swiss Sandoz LSD). I experienced a transformation of consciousness that would take me years to understand in its true context. For the moment, everything seemed to be going my way.

Leary and Alpert (who himself was yet to go to India and become Ram Dass, a New Age celebrity guru in his own right) soon transliterated *The Tibetan Book of the Dead*, a Mahayana Buddhist text on the rite of death. They turned this ancient rite into a manual for taking LSD and entitled it *The Psychedelic Experience*. It further popularized the Eastern mystical teachings of reincarnation, karma, and the self being a spark of the divine.

Strawberry Fields Forever

Meanwhile, LSD had come a long way from that original molecular sample under Dr Albert Hoffman's fingernail. In Kool-Aid "acid tests" in Golden Gate Park during the "Summer of Love" in 1968, gallons of spiked Kool-Aid were handed out to thousands during "Be-Ins" and rock concerts. Youth chemists such as Stan Owsley in Berkeley became famous for taking an esoteric molecule like LSD and synthesizing it for the masses. Now there were new batches coming off the production line like colored candy: mellow yellow, blue cheer, and blotter acid. Leary's dream of nirvana from a pill for the youth culture was becoming a reality overnight. Indeed, much of the labor force for building the Rainbow Bridge came from the counterculture, which exuberantly explored new modes of living.

Hippie communes suddenly appeared on America's historical horizon. They creatively explored new alternatives for abandoning civilization and going back to nature. Men and women, boys and girls cohabited communally in the countryside. Colored Indian tepees, tents, geodesic domes, and other innovative structures suddenly filled the landscape as old farms and ranches were bought. Other groups invaded the woods. Bright scarves and headbands, bell-bottoms, and beads appeared in all patterns and shades. It was Thoreau's *Walden Pond* set to psychedelic communalism from Vermont to Marin County.

The ideals of marriage, college, and striving for a successful career in order to fit into traditional society were replaced by semi-Gandhian values: aesthetics, pacifism, nonviolence, and anti-materialism. But the move for more freedom became obsessive—for sexual freedom, for freedom from all restraints on personal choice. "Be bound by nothing." Freedom from responsibilities and commitments meant the freedom to explore, to fly like a bird. When the hero in Neil Simon's *The Graduate* was advised to go into "plastics," the sixties generation saw that as a cue to sneer collectively at such dull and myopic advice. Their collective response was, "What a compromise of the human spirit . . . what a sellout . . . what a way to spend your life."

Underground journals such as *The Berkeley Barb, The East Village Other, The Village Voice*, and *The Rolling Stone* proliferated the radical new viewpoint from coast to coast. A terrific sense of solidarity and mission resulted. It was almost a conspiracy, the generation gap became so vast. The counterculture had what seemed almost unlimited energy, and their mystical ideals would remain as the sixties generation replaced their peers by the 1980s and became corporate leaders and college professors.

Meanwhile, it is doubtful that Dr. Hoffman in the late 1940s, apart from his wildest acid visions, could have pictured *Woodstock Nation*, where a half a million youths invaded upstate New York for a Super Rock concert, ending the decade of the sixties stoned on his discovery of LSD and similar psychedelics. Their rock bands reflected drug synesthesia with names like: Jefferson Airplane, Big Brother and The Holding Company, The Strawberry Alarm Clock, The Grateful Dead, Iron Butterfly, Blue Cheer (a name for acid), Quicksilver Messenger Service, The Doors, Pink Floyd, Led Zeppelin, The Cream, Riders of The Purple Sage, The Moody Blues, Tangerine Dream, Buffalo Springfield, Credence Clearwater Revival, and so on—all names that are metaphors of psychedelicized perceptions of reality or a return to ethnic innocence.

Acid had even touched music. Every chord seemed to be played for the first time ever, with no repeats. Fresh and original lyrics and images filtered through millions of minds. The tunes were incredibly diverse, whether mystically blissful, erotic, haunting, celebrational, or defiant.

Psychedelic rock became the collective theme song for an explosively radical era that entered the world stage like a musical extravaganza. It made the era of the fifties, with its straight society, its decency, and its gray churches look flat, like a Lucky Strike wrapper lying on the ground. Who wanted to turn back the clock? No one from the youth culture, that's for sure. America had never seen an era like this. Unlimited horizons seemed to flash into view now that this incredible bridge of consciousness was being built. New materials had suddenly appeared on the world scene to help build the Rainbow Bridge from our present world to a New World Order. This growing structure, like the tower of Babel, would likely span from one type of civilization to another. It was a paradigm shift, indeed, and it promised to bring us to the shores of a New Age. Delicious expectations filled the air.

3
Opening the Third Eye

The Jedi prodigy Anakin Skywalker learns that he has the whole universe inside of him. Like Luke Skywalker—his future son—of *Star Wars* fame, Anakin has to connect with and trust the Force. The characters in the Lucas epics are "living myths" existing within all of us, according to direc-

tor George Lucas. Lucas' epics are to inspire the unleashing of these inner realities. Yes, they have a spiritual aspect.

Joseph Campbell, the spiritual teacher of George Lucas, has said that myths are representations of inner realities and truths. Joseph Campbell spelled this out in his book *Hero of a Thousand Faces*. When I read this book before going to India, it hit me the same way it hit George Lucas. It was outrageously seductive. It was compelling and ingenious. It stated that we carried the sum total experience and knowledge of the race. We were walking microcosms; we had the universe within, and carried the inner secrets to our own unfoldment into higher consciousness. The challenge was consciousness expansion through confronting inner and outer worlds, escalating to ever higher levels of energy and consciousness.

Many of us on the pioneering edge of the sixties were pursuing this path. We were persuaded that total awareness about nature, the cosmos, and man—from the spiritual to the mundane was possible. We wanted simultaneous access to supramundane planes and dimensions and command of occult realities that only a fraction of our world even knew about. In short, my contemporaries and I believed in the reality of cosmic consciousness, or superconsciousness, or enlightenment. I felt that life's greatest jewel was to attain it, and that finding this great secret was the real reason we were here. Was there outward evidence for superconsciousness? It seemed so. Leary had spoken about it—but so had Joseph Campbell, Carlos Castenada, and many others going back centuries before them. Analogies already existed.

It was already plain to see that the elevator shaft of consciousness went from the lower floors of the animal world to the incredible levels of man's greatest achievements. If this shaft continued to the vast levels of angels, higher beings, and beyond, then by speculative extension the mystics were right and human potential did not stop until it arrived right at the seat of godhood. We were in a continuum that implied we could ride the elevator to the top floor. Lower rungs of consciousness could be used as an argument for extension.

Even among people there was a huge range of consciousness. In the same way a savvy internationalist can adeptly work through London from Belgravia to Kensington to Soho or Mile End or Hammersmith on one day, Paris the next, from the Left Bank of the Seine to Saint Cloud, then midtown Manhattan the next, and 50 other cities with equal adroitness—flashing through a million nuances of language and culture, mastering customs and cuisine—as compared to an unschooled and unsophisticated villager living in an adobe hut or a backcountry hillbilly farmer, who would be helpless at any of these supercosmopolitan points. The same analogy points to the full range of human differences in consciousness—from a fully empowered yogi and master to someone with the depth awareness of a Formica countertop, living in a world of Wheaties and McDonald's hamburgers. The span from idiot to genius had upper and lower floors to which we were only beginning to wake up; indeed, the elevator shaft broke through new levels all the time.

There were other analogies. If insight could increase a little, it could increase massively. There were a number of ways I pictured superconsciousness. One was by taking the process of insight and extending it with no upper limits. I recalled the time that I wrote a university paper on Plato's cave allegory, and had sudden breakthroughs of insight into the meaning of the concept "abstract." My awareness changed in a moment of time and would never go back. Then when I studied Jean Piaget, I realized that the mental development from childhood to adulthood had tangible barriers that were approached and transcended as growth continued. A child at the "concrete operational level" was incapable of the gear shift of more mature abstract thinking, and so on. It was like the evolutionist's maxim, "ontogeny recapitulates phylogeny." In the microcosm of the womb, the human organism, they claimed, seemed to mimic prior stages in animal evolution. Consciousness had stages as well.

"Heaven and Hell and all the gods are within us," Joseph Campbell suddenly told Bill Moyers. Yet if Joseph Campbell became the guru of George Lucas of *Star Wars* fame, Carl Jung was the source of inspiration and the teacher of Joseph Campbell. Jung's "depth psychology" was the source of almost every major insight that Campbell ever had, and during the six-part series by Bill Moyers on Joseph Campbell, Campbell payed homage to Jung repeatedly.

Campbell

Jung talked about consciousness. The famed Swiss thinker was an important key for many of us in the sixties.

Jung had revolutionary ideas about the mysteries of the self. He believed that man contained the universe within: the entirety of racial knowledge was welded within every cell. Within the mind lay the vast collective unconscious containing every type of character in every Shakespearean play, every mythological figure, and more. These were the inner archetypes. Jung stated that the supreme voyage—and Jung was a mystic, having written the introduction to the Evans-Wentz Oxford translation of *The Tibetan Book of the Dead*—was to boldly encounter and absorb every archetype within, to come to terms with the forbidden, the inner shadow, and ultimately to discover the higher self. To Jung, when this huge collective unconscious, this microcosm within, was fully searched out and no longer a mystery, then one was "individuated." This was a form of enlightenment.

Jung's framework did not merely go beyond Freud's psychoanalysis, but Jungian depth psychology anticipated the eventual merger of the new psychologies of the mid-seventies with Eastern thought. Jung was 50 years ahead of Esalen and the transpersonal psychologists of the New Age movement. Indeed, Jung was the true grandfather of transpersonal psychology. In the sixties another fan of Jung, Alan Watts of Harvard, an orientalist, wrote *The Supreme Identity*. The supreme identity, of course, was the divine inner nature that Watts had learned from studying Zen Buddhism which he then melded with modern psychological theories. For opposites to be resolved and to merge, they had to be encountered: good and evil, male and female.

The male, Jung said, had to come to terms with his opposite valence, the feminine within—an archetype known as the "anima." Where did Jung see this archetype manifesting itself? In Renaissance paintings, novels, and a thousand other places. But there was one novel in particular that Jung felt most fully portrayed the anima, H. Rider Haggard's *She*. The shrouded feminine nature had to be encountered by males, especially those who had all the "defense mechanisms of modern culture." The male archetype was called the "animus" and women had to come to terms with it. The cosmos held the interplay between these universal forces, and Jung turned to Taoism to explain the interplay of opposites. The masculine and feminine polarities were but one aspect of the cosmic dance. The goal was individuation of all opposites within.

Jung's pathway through the mysteries of the self seemed to us in the sixties to be tailor-made for the taboo-ridden Westerner who had such an ordeal looking within, especially when it came time to facing "the shadow" and one's "inner demons." Evil was now relegated to areas within the individual that were projected out; it was the other half of good. To Jung, there was no really absolute evil. It was merely one more opposite out of which the cosmos was composed—light and dark, male and female, good and evil, and so on. As Taoism stated, all life is an interplay between these opposites until they finally merged into one.

This was an attractive universe indeed. In a way, it made that irritant of a continually gnawing guilty conscience now obsolete and irrelevant. That carryover from Old Testament morality, the Pentateuch within, could now be "outgrown." There were times when my conscience weighed me down greatly. I welcomed a way to be rid of it, if it could be transcended as taboos and fears, the dragons at our inner gates, were defeated. Thus, as the myth of the ego dissolved, our inner potential would increase exponentially as we worked toward superconsciousness. No wonder they called it "liberation."

Superconsciousness went way beyond the range of merely intellectual knowledge. The superconscious individual could look into people and read them like a book. He was equally able to adeptly frolic through any fields of knowledge like Horowitz at the keyboard. Such a mind could picture DNA or glycolysis at a glimpse; inhale Wittgenstein or Kant's *Critique of Pure Reason* (appreciating why he evolved the solipsism he did, in T. U. A., in answer to Hume); or see all nuances of literary brilliance in James Joyce,

William Blake, or Tolstoy. But beyond all this, the superconscious one was able to know all these things with an infinite depth after having attained full awareness of "the Self." It was this latter achievement that gave full scope to this awareness. It is this mystique that Westerners see in a Krishnamurti. They represent the mystical masters of superconsciousness.

It was easy to romanticize the potentials of human consciousness and its evolutionary expansion into superstates of being. Hegel had talked about it and so had the ancient writers of the *Upanishads* of India as well as myriads of more recent voices. This challenge made the church on the corner seem dead, irrelevant, and boring. On the other hand, I felt a thrill of enthusiasm each time I thought of the possibilities of consciousness expansion just waiting around the corner.

Then one day, I apparently experienced it all—in a glimpse, a split second in eternity. This experience radically changed the course of my entire life, ultimately sending me to India on a quest for full enlightenment.

Encountering the Ground of Being

It was a balmy evening in the late spring of 1966 when I rode my motorcycle deep into the countryside of Virginia away from civilization. The meadows seemed like a vast armchair as I sat atop a smooth, warm, grassy knoll, slightly higher than hundreds of acres of surrounding fields and woods. My knapsack and sleeping bag were propped against a lone tree that arched into the night sky like a giant ganglia reaching into the cosmos.

I took ten times the normal dosage of LSD-25—3000 micrograms—then soon watched my own consciousness explode open as the celestial powers seemed to speak to the deepest core of my being. The LSD I took was the purest you could find in the world—Sandoz LSD made in Basel,

Switzerland, right out of the labs of the inventor, Albert Hoffman. The result of the experience is that I was sure that I was a mystic and had seen things only privy to a few. I was a master in the making, an adept. In order for me to show the lure and power of this type of experience, I shall record what happened to me as it is written up in my book *Avatar of Night*::

My Leap Into Cosmic Consciousness

At a fraction past midnight, I swallowed the capsule. I accepted the fact that I was, in effect, sitting on top of an atom bomb and would either come out on the level of Gautama Buddha or the coyote in the Roadrunner cartoon.

An hour later, what looked dead was conscious, as all of creation crackled in dialogue with itself. Meanwhile, my thoughts and perceptions began to fuse. Stars joined like drops of mercury across the night sky forming multicolored webs—breathing and arching across the heavens, across galaxies and onto the very ground where I perched. Grains of sand, pebbles and trees, ebbed and flowed with this impersonal consciousness.

If my own consciousness was layered and branched in a million places like a banyan tree, it was now as though the rest of my being had squeezed what was most essentially me into the top stem of the uppermost branch. Down to the deepest root, there were a thousand astral levels at war within me, as my uppermost self was fighting to stay aloft through the aid of a million subordinate parts that were straining and tugging. Even below these, there were endless rumbles and shifts, like a subterranean city, while every archetype that I had ever encountered was presently being held at bay.

Soon I was above even the dazzling beings and demigods that were so special before. The celestial cities and realms were like the lower strata of a pyramid whose fascination I had sacrificed—things great enough to inspire the master poets and painters—in order to approach the level of the of pure thought, pure knowing, pure being. If I did reach the purest state, I could diffuse like a drop of Mercurochrome throughout the ocean of thought.

Every second that passed, one of my million parts was answering something comparable to the riddle of the sphinx to propel me on to the level of super-consciousness.

A new truth came. I, like every man, was a hierarchy of men, a living society, a kingdom and a nation, and before I became enlightened, I would have to bear the weight of all truths, to encompass the total history of my nation within a fraction of time. After a thousand other thoughts, I passed on to the next level of realization.

Momentarily, I shrank and became so small that "humbling" does not describe it—I became insignificant. Far less than a blade of grass that has just been given the brief consciousness to realize what it is. It might hear the voice that shakes the mountains of the worlds and announces, "You thought you were a god and you stir only to find that you are but a blade of grass lying helplessly on the forest floor. Even the ants walk over you. How tiny you are. Your delusions end. Can you bear this, and yet live?"

Then the sheer jet-like force of what was happening to my mind became too great. I became a twig riding a tidal wave. I clutched that Virginia meadow as though clutching the rigging of a hurricane-swept deck of a Galleon. It seemed that something other than the drug had taken over, something supernatural perhaps.

As a force drove my mind at a speed greater than thought, I could feel something far older than I suddenly start navigating my course. I passed ten thousand cross-roads per second and took the proper turn on each one of them. I feared that if I tried to grind down the gears at this point, I might wake up on the outer edges of the galaxy not much higher up on the phylogenic scale than a cucumber. And after all the billions of years it took me to work my way up to becoming a human being, I did not want to blow it now, and enter a form of loneliness that was unthinkable.

My speed increased even more, as I became a diamond wedge cutting the finest possible arcs, from one juncture to another. Then it occurred to me that on some level I was being asked questions in which a correct turn could only be made by means of a totally spontaneous truthful answer. Anything else would veer me off course. Like the Day of Judgment, a lie would be impossible damnation, because there was not an atom of time to deliberate. Anything but the truth, it seemed, would have fragmented me all over the cosmos.

Then something happened: I lost all grasp of language and thought. I saw a doorway into a new universe. It was a pinpoint of light. To fight the acceleration required to approach it was to fight the mass of the entire universe. I could not tell whether the distance within the pinpoint of light was as minuscule as the angstrom units between atoms, or almost infinitely huge, as the distance from one side of the universe to the other.

At the barrier of the pinpoint of light

I enter the eternal present. All thirteen billion brain cells within me seem to turn inside out, as though jumping to a higher gestalt and forming into a higher struc-

ture that was previously latent. Each cell recites one of my former names, and I as a nation hear the thirteen billion names of my subjects and former earthly identities on the wheel of reincarnation. Once I enter the pinpoint of light, all ties with the world vanish. I enter the Unborn.

A caterpillar cannot experience the butterfly transition and remain a caterpillar. One structure cannot be smuggled across into the other, that is impossible. You are either one or the other. That also applied to me. At most, my experience could be paralleled from one universe to another, but nothing could cross the barrier.

I have never been able to completely summon what happened to me during that stretch of time after entering the pinpoint of light. Months later, I assumed that I had entered into the ocean of being . . . "the void, also known as the clear light or the Ocean of Brahman," that I had been allowed to experience the highest mystical state that the Hindus call *Nirvikalpa Samadhi*.

By the time I went to India three years later, I had absorbed thousands of pages of the greatest mystical revelations. I understood these writings as though I had written them myself—from the writings of Sri Aurobindo to the ornate descriptions of Sri Ramakrishna; from Shankaracharya to Patanjali; from the ancient *Upanishads* to the *Bhagavad Gita*. They made complete sense of my mystical experience, putting flesh on it with new language.

Another change happened. My life took on a thrust of manic joy that felt unstoppable. I was in the currents of a vast positive wave directing my life. I felt like some Boddhisatva in the making. Inevitably, I had to take the leap the classic way and could do none other than sell all that I owned and head East in the manner of the great yogis of the past. I spent several years in India as a close disciple of Sai Baba, India's greatest miracle-working super guru. This experience was beyond anything Leary had described the day I heard him (fully written up in *Avatar of Night*).

I was a New Ager before the term ever came into public use. My beliefs were a composite of the East blended together with the most radical breakthroughs in the West—the new physics, new forms of psychology, psychic research, channeled information from such psychics as Edgar Cayce, Theosophy, and creative ideas coming from the psychedelic subculture. The drama of life was to ride the wave of destiny and "trust the Force."

4

The Coming Changes

A mystical experience can blow the mind wide open and change one radically. It did me! After my powerful mystical experience under LSD, I was walking to the beat of a different drummer. I began to tune into things that I had never noticed before. I felt part of a great pattern. Suddenly I sensed that history was unfolding according to a deep plan. Perhaps a hierarchy of advanced adepts were pioneering the coming of the New Age and I was among them—ancient souls cast into the world for the coming earth changes. Overnight, my conceptual universe had altered radically. Perhaps similar changes could happen on a mass scale to the whole world—a global alteration of consciousness.

Before I took that leap to India, I felt new experiences beckoning me on, preparing me for new leaps in consciousness. I had to leap off the diving board of uncharted experience. I had to explore new thresholds beyond the mindset of our materialistic culture which had demystified the universe. America, by the end of 1950s, had become a society of people whose intellectual curiosity rarely ranged beyond the mundane and the prosaic. It was intimidated by the unknown and seemed to easily settle for a McDonald's spiritual diet and a K-Mart lifestyle. The grand summits of ancient wisdom towered above our distracted and busy culture which had lost its roots with eternity. We were ants absorbed in disposing of some small speck of waste food at the base of a grand edifice. The vast and splendid columns of the Parthenon dwarfed us into insignificance. We never looked up.

The challenge for me and the pioneers of my generation was to plug back into the ancient secrets of existence that our modern world had cast away. Yet in this alien and uncharted universe, I also needed some sort of compass. Like most of us in the army of mystics, I felt that my ultimate navigational instrument was my deepest intuitive promptings. Now a new door appeared, and I had to open it.

The Astral Traveller

On many a freezing winter's night in 1968, I motorcycled down the rustic wooded lanes weaving from Charlottesville, Virginia, to the spectral ranch house of Robert Monroe, author of *Journeys Out of the Body*, poised on its many acres and beaming multicolored lights like an airport control tower. We often met several times a week. Monroe was gaining increasing fame across America among connoisseurs of the underground new-consciousness movement as a legitimate astral projector—one who was able to leave his physical body. Twenty years later, Monroe's writings were to become among the most recognized of New Age advocates, and he would be a key conference speaker at New Age conventions.

At the time Dr. Charles Tart and an array of notable parapsychologists had run a whole gamut of double-blind tests on Bob Monroe. Skeptics were invariably baffled each time by Monroe's unaccounted for powers. Robert Monroe would whoosh out of his body at midnight and travel to an anechoic chamber beneath Stanford University, the University of California at Berkeley, or the University of California at Davis, where Tart and others awaited. On the West Coast, it was only nine in the evening. Monroe would look around the room, noting people, conversations, and furniture arrangement. Then he would whoosh back to his body in Charlottesville, Virginia, and give them a long distance telephone call describing what he saw. He was right on target repeatedly, astounding these scientists with the fact that there are other forces operating behind the machinery of the physical universe that they had barely scratched. But what was really important to Monroe and me were not these trips around the country, but trips somewhere else.

Monroe and I met regularly to make sense out of the whole phenomenon of astral travel, catalyzing one another in the process. He was approaching the subject in terms of the "higher teachings" he had received while out of the body in his encounters with "higher beings," astral masters, and other entities. Monroe combined this with his diversified readings in yoga, Eastern thought, and scientific theory. I approached his bizarre exploits and spirit encounters from the viewpoint of Indian monistic philosophy syncretized with a new emerging "mystical Christianity" that came

through channeled teachings of Edgar Cayce, Levi Dowling, and others combined with Carl Jung, Paul Tillich, and Teilhard de Chardin.

From Monroe's perspective, perhaps my most important credential was that I, too, had been able to leave my physical body sporadically. It had started when I was a ten-year-old battling the mumps in London, a little after I had started toying with a Ouija board. Half asleep in bed in our old Victorian house in Knightsbridge, I would become paralyzed, hear the sound of jets, and go ripping through the roof to hover above our house. The same thing happened during my teens occasionally and it was starting again in college. Monroe's out-of-the-body symptoms matched mine point for point.

Monroe and I were also working on the technology to elicit astral experiences in ordinary people. Monroe was getting his ideas from his "contacts." This became known as the M-5000 program, a complex, multi-channel recorded tape which the subject listened to on going to sleep. Cables and sound equipment trailed through Monroe's house from central command, an isolated geodesic chamber of pyramidal glass which rippled with colored lights, while pulse generators whirred and hummed to the syncopated beat of a synthesizer/organ. Bob Monroe had been the child prodigy of a medical doctor father and college professor mother, spending much of his life dabbling with inventions. Much of what we were doing now with sound equipment came from his era as a vice president of Mutual Broadcasting in New York City.

What was most momentous about this was that we were on the pioneering edge of occult technology. We were not closing the gap to enter the spiritual dimensions by blindly putting together the machinery. Rather, the powers on the other side had bridged the gap, with Monroe as medium, and they were telling him what to do. Monroe cited a long list of technological breakthroughs that came from the other side to various inventors, including the benzene ring and the Xerox copier.

We pictured the transformation of America into a spiritual technology. The story of Atlantis came to mind. Channelers such as Edgar Cayce stated that Atlantis had risen to great heights until it destroyed itself. This time, hopefully, we were wise enough not to let the power get out-of-hand. But there was something even more profound than getting millions to have occult experiences by a new technology. There was, on a deeper level, a number of revolutionary spiritual implications behind astral travel; namely, these experiences implied a whole metaphysical reality that was completely new to the West— America above all.

Implicit in soul travel among the living—those who have bodies to leave—is soul travel among the dead, whose souls can freely range through other planes without need of bodies. Implied in this is soul travel from life to life, incarnation to incarnation—or *reincarnation*. Further implicit in all of this is the concept of "old souls" who have an almost endless history of reincarnations. And what is the reason for reincarnation?

The answer is central to Eastern mysticism itself. We reincarnate up the evolutionary ladder for the purpose of ultimate perfection and self-realization into pure consciousness. When consciousness realizes its identity with ultimate consciousness, and the mystery of being is over, then the separate ego-self ceases to exist. Then the "true self" unites with the ocean of being, the godhead. In short, as the Hindu masters have stated all along, the self or *Jivan Atma*, merges with God or the *Paramatma*, thus attaining eternal liberation or *Moksha, Nirvikalpa Samadhi, Sat-Chit-Ananda*. As our past records of karma are worked away, we evolve spiritually and climb the ladder of being. We are a composite of millions of former characters in the cosmic play, and some of us have very long dossiers of former lives.

This brings up the question of past-life speculation. For instance, if Monroe and I had been in Atlantis at the same time, playing around with dangerous cosmic devices, perhaps we helped blow up the whole works then. Our karma, therefore, was to correct now what we had blown up then when the ancient civilization of Atlantis went up in a vast explosion so great that there is no longer any record of it (this eliminates the archeological question, by the way). I remember, after all, at 13 years of age going to the great pyramids of Egypt with my parents and later doing drawings of how they were built using anti-gravity "Atlantian" technology; colossal blocks hovered in the air above the Sphinx en route to Cheops.

I also remember an epiphany I had in the Egyptian city of Alexandria at the age of 14—I suddenly felt this blissful sense of connectedness, total belonging. As we took a horse-drawn carriage through the royal gardens of Alexandria, I had this overwhelming nameless emotion, a timeless yearning.

Tal at 13 with his parents in Cairo

Later in India I was told such signs in my early childhood indicated I was an advanced adept on the edge of remembering a former life. (I speculated about my own past lives as some insiders do in today's New Age circles. Picture a Hollywood cocktail party where all kinds of incredible past lives are spoken of with this sense of profound knowing—heroic lives from King David to Abraham Lincoln, to Atlantian priests and great Indian sages. Now the Hollywood incarnation—perhaps playing a werewolf in some horror movie—is a former pupil of the Buddha. How did he get to Hollywood? He is working off some last traces of karma.)

There was an aspect to some of Monroe's encounters with the other side that threatened any notions of a peril free universe void of absolute evil. Some of these spirit encounters had a brutal, almost demonic concreteness. This cut away at the stereotype I was forming of an almost symphonically gentle and peace-pervading cosmos whose evil was so wispy and illusory that apparent evil was little more than good English humor turned up to a cosmic scale.

A weary looking Monroe one morning described how he had been assaulted by alien beings that night. I was absolutely fascinated by his report at the breakfast table.

"I felt about as significant as an ant compared to these two beings," Monroe confessed. He said he had perceived clairvoyantly two massive beings of light, brighter than stars and of vast power, drifting deep in the heavens like two meteors. Then they stopped their drift and honed in on him, beginning a terrible drilling down upon him like huge, sparking hornets. They descended with great speed while Monroe remained in the paralyzed "buzz region."

These beings soon reached his room and went through the hidden records of his mind like speed-readers flipping through a card file. After about ten minutes they evidently had gotten what they wanted—or as he suggested later, implanted what they wanted—and then pulled away, much like a huge hypodermic being pulled out of a patient. This experience brought up the question of victimization and cosmic bullying, and individual worth and privacy, but we preferred to theorize more in the direction that the incident was an act of charity, that the two beings had probably left a subtle implant which would germinate when Bob Monroe was ready, perhaps years in the future.

In a guarded manner, Monroe said that these two beings might have had some connection with UFOs which he believed were not necessarily machines, but celestial beings rather like angels.

Since that time in 1968, Robert Monroe wrote several sequels to his bestseller, *Journeys Out of the Body*. They follow up on his experiences and contacts with the beyond. He also entered the New Age movement as a sort of guru—as have several past friends of mine from that era, such as Raymond Moody, who wrote the bestseller *Life After Life*.

India

After my psychic dabbling, I realized that my first love remained the sheer genius of India's spiritual break- 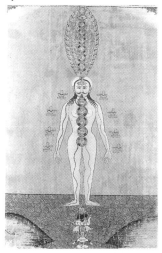 throughs. Its depth and range were light-years ahead of what I considered to be our psychic hobbies in the West.

The West was just discovering spiritual realities that Indian sages had exhausted millennia ago. We were exulting over novel toys that the ancients had abandoned as tokens of spiritual infancy. Astral travel to a rishi is like the neon lights of Broadway to a native New Yorker who looks on in disdain as some visitor from the Third World stands with his mouth hanging open over the blips and flashes of neon at Times Square or some techno-trinket at Toys-R-Us—say a dayglow robot that follows you around the store speaking in metal-voiced banalities. The Western counterpart is to go into silent awe before some Indian yogi who makes deep penetrating insights into our character or family history. These are party trinkets to an *advaitin*, the cream of the crop of India's spiritual elite, who admit of no subject-object distinctions in the universe including between self and God.

In truth, Monroe's contact teachings did not reach what I considered to be the highest truth of all: the ultimate oneness of all things, which is at the kernel of India's perennial philosophy. To me, his contact teachings from astral classes seemed little more than the low-level pyrotechnics that the Indian masters had been warning against all along. His teachings were fragmented interpretations of reality taught by demigods and entities which, though higher up the evolutionary scale than your generic citizen, still fell vastly short of the absolute. These entities were way down the scale of consciousness compared to an enlightened master who had reached unity with the godhead. Even the hierarchies of celestial beings were subject to such a one—so said India's most ancient shastras.

Indeed, Seth or Lazaris are to sit at the feet of such a master, not the other way around. Why ask a disincarnate Tibetan priest or "entity" a question that only a full master can answer? Why, I asked, bother hooking up with space visitors or drifting entities who are still learners themselves?

Inevitably, the next major door to open in my life was India. But as always, there were dragons at the gate.

En route to India, I met the head swami of the Ramakrishna Mission in London. He walked with me through Holland Park to quiz me on my

understanding of India's non-dual philosophy known as *advaita*. I was considering joining the Ramakrishna Mission in Bengal. Yet I knew only a handful of Westerners ever made it. Then, the day after our initial encounter, the swami amazed me. He gave me a letter of recommendation. I had apparently passed his tests. I knew that my awareness came only partially from reading the great mystical books. The main source of my understanding came from that massive mystical experience I underwent.

The swami's parting words were very encouraging: "Your understanding of advaita philosophy is as advanced as the best young Brahmin men I have seen in India. I will write a letter of recommendation to the Ramakrishna Mission in Calcutta recommending you for *sanyas* (initiation as a renunciant and monk wearing the ochre robe). I believe you are sincere and have real understanding." Those who read Christopher Isherwood, a well-known author, orientalist, and follower of Ramakrishna, will learn from his own testimonial that I was given a very rare appraisal and invitation for a Westerner. But other things awaited me in India than ordination into the Ramakrishna Vedanta Society.

Within six months of my arrival in Delhi, I was rewarded by the powers that be for my costly leap of faith. I became, after some months of wandering across India, the top Western disciple of Sai Baba, India's most powerful miracle-working godman. His following numbered over 20 million in India alone. I lived with him in South India for two years, gaining a rare residence permit in the process. I meditated and practiced a range  of yogas under Baba. I also became a privileged spokesman under Baba. A number of times I joined Sai Baba onstage at his massive ashram, *Prasanthi Nilayam*, to speak before vast crowds.

Before I had left for India, I realized that Edgar Cayce's contacts with the Akashic Records were the ultimate endorsement of Eastern mystical revelation. They brought me to the shores of India, to the heartland of Vedanta, but no further. There was another purpose.

Western psychic revelations were preparing the West for a leap in evolution as new paradigms of the ancient wisdom were needed to reach that critical threshold of people sent to catalyze "the time of changes." Some of us were among the predicted higher souls to incarnate in our time to help bring in the New Age. Cayce described a mid century "descent into the earth plane" of advanced souls.

Many of the sixties pioneers would abandon their mystic attire, join the establishment, and become yuppies. But their understanding of reality would infiltrate the world. They would remake the corporation. They would fill the ranks of influential occupations and, from their prestigious vantage points, they would then parlay this new belief system into acceptability as it descended down the slopes of the pyramid into the average living room of middle America.

These embryo mystics of the sixties were destined to grow up and take over the gears of society: publishing, movies, news magazines, television shows, schoolrooms, government agencies, science labs, academia, banking, even Wall Street. It was a *coup* of quiet succession, of one generation replacing another. A whole new world was waiting in the wings. It just needed time.

It also needed a line of credit from some quiet insiders behind the scenes. There were many players in this drama of shaping global history. Some were actors in the parade, some were movers and shakers. The plan for a New World Order was not a new one. But certain things needed to be aligned before it could even be discussed. The spiritual structure of this was absolutely crucial.

As a spiritual system, naturally it must have its human agents—its mouthpieces—in contact with powers beyond this world. They themselves look to higher guidance and then transmit this guidance to others. Clearly a plan is unfolding, and it has everything in the world to do with the New World Order.

5

Higher Guidance

"Higher guidance" is crucial for the process of spiritual transformation from normal consciousness to cosmic consciousness. This axiom is universal among New Age luminaries. Neale Donald Walsch, Gary Zukav, Betty Eadie, David Spangler, Fritjof Capra, Marilyn Ferguson, and other well-known figures emphasize the need to be guided by higher powers. They have been foremost among the new wave in letting go and letting the process of guidance from beyond take hold in their own lives. There are many forms of guidance. It is an open field. Any technique that works is fair game in this new renaissance, whether it has come out of the ancient mystery religions, India, or the very newest experiments in producing altered states.

To the zealous mystic, the smallest perception or event can be loaded with significance. Intuition alone can go a long way. Then there are higher octane methods such as the tarot, visualization, meditation, shamanistic techniques, drugs, the Ouija board, astrology, and the I Ching. The higher powers can use these things as mediums through which to guide inquiring minds. Things did not start to happen to the famed channeler Jane Roberts until she started using a Ouija board—that opened the door. After that, her life was never the same.

Certainly in my own life, once I crossed the threshold, I quietly watched for signs from the cosmic gatekeeper to direct my course. I knew the higher sources could break through into our material domain to direct spiritual adepts such as myself—of that I was positive. I gambled my life on it.

Once I gained the ability to see things "from the plane of the gods," I was able to look back and suddenly see meanings behind events in my early life. I could detect patterns of "guidance," such as when I got a Ouija board at age ten and subscribed to a spiritualist newsletter when my father was a diplomat in London; or when I left my body for astral travel at the same age; or when I became obsessed with the wider field of psychic phenomena at 12. Invisible hands were directing my course.

It was, therefore, no accident that I met a classmate when I was 13 who was psychic. He would receive mental pictures of distant events like a cosmic television station. He blanked out his mind and in they would come. He also received images from people's minds that we called "pictures." We engaged in a kind of psychic voyeurism. We sat at the back of the class, eyes closed, waiting for impressions to come from the prettiest girls in the class. What usually came through was fragmented and odd. But we were compelled by the sheer fascination of the unknown.

By high school there was a lull as new interests filled the gap, yet cosmic tidbits did come through. I was in an advanced English class under a teacher who had just come back from Oxford. J. D. Salinger was required reading. There it was, another tidbit—the short story entitled "Teddy." It was about an "embryo mystic," a precocious ten-year-old boy crossing the Atlantic on an ocean liner (at age ten I, too, crossed the Atlantic on an ocean liner). I walked home rehearsing Salinger's story in my mind. It brought back my fascination. One passage in particular between ten-year-old Teddy and an adult had great impact:

> "From what I gather, you've acquired certain information, through meditation, that's given you some conviction that in your last incarnation you were a holy man in India, but more or less fell from grace."
>
> "I wasn't a holy man," Teddy said. "I was just a person making a very nice spiritual advancement."
>
> "All right—whatever it was," Nicholson said. "But the point is you feel that in your last incarnation you more or less fell from grace before final Illumination. Is that right, or am I? . . ."
>
> "That's right," Teddy said. "I met a lady, and I sort of stopped meditat-

ing."

. . . Nicholson was looking at him, studying him. "I believe you said on that last tape that you were six when you first had a mystical experience. Is that right?"

"I was six when I saw that everything was God, and my hair stood up, and all that," Teddy said. "It was on a Sunday, I remember. My sister was only a very tiny child then, and she was drinking her milk, and all of a sudden I saw that *she* was God and that the *milk* was God. I mean, all she was doing was pouring God into God, if you know what I mean."[1]

It kept echoing in my head on the way home from high school: ". . . all she was doing was pouring God into God, if you know what I mean."

The Big Picture

When I was a bit younger than Teddy, we lived in Georgetown, Washington D.C., not far from Dumbarton Oaks. One day I wandered down to the Georgetown theater after school. I used to go to movies alone so I could concentrate without interruption. On the marquee it read: *The Day the Earth Stood Still*. I was haunted, invaded by the film. It touched a primal nerve in me. There it was, the earth in chaos, a hostile planet whose nations were at war. Suspicion and weaponry were everywhere. The earth was like a big ship out-of-control, with no one at the helm to steer it. People battled and tugged on the wheel—frightened, warlike people with hair-trigger responses to threats, real or imagined. At any moment the ship might collide with any number of things and that would be it—down it would go. So, too, with an earth run by unenlightened people who were always on the brink of war.

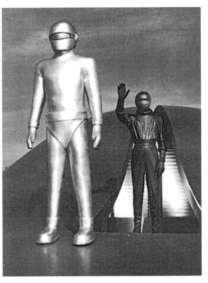

In *The Day the Earth Stood Still*, a saucer fills the sky and glides down into the park behind the White House. The alien visitor, played by Michael Rennie, is an infinitely noble-looking man whose handsome, refined, and

intelligent face is grieved by people who cannot handle their own affairs. The earth is
given an ultimatum. If it wants to survive and
join the planetary confederation, it must
abandon national rights, surrender to global
government, and immediately disarm, otherwise the earth will be reduced to cinders.
An elite of the world's top intellectuals, of

course, understood this like the ABCs. Presumably they would be among
the elite of the global government. But military men and politicians needed a show of power, which they got. Gort, the robot with the one eye, a
supertitanium cyclops, could melt anything in sight if he so chose, from
Sherman tanks to the entire planet.
Idiots with guns finally got the point
and backed off after he vaporized numbers of them.

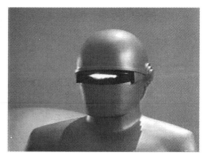

The alien visitor was what all earth-
lings needed to become: an infinitely
noble and wise being with a cosmic
outlook and who detested violence,
valued all things—including the
sacredness of life—was impartial,
peace-loving, and who held an air of unshakable superiority. He was among
the enlightened. He was the ultimate role model. The producer, Mr.
Blaustein, made a deep point to my tender young mind in a post-World-
War-II world. After the afternoon matinee, I walked through Dumbarton
Oaks—an ironic act, though I did not know it at the time.

Indeed, I used to love exploring Dumbarton Oaks, the
beautiful estate where a handful of intellectuals, some who
were acquaintances of my father, had held strategy meetings preceding the formation of the United Nations. It was
also the meeting place of another group of intellectuals,
physicists such as Robert Oppenheimer, Enrico Fermi,
and Edward Teller, who had met eight years before the

Oppenheimer

first group. Their purpose was to explore the feasibility of
building the world's first atomic bomb—what was known as the Manhattan
Project. All this was just around the corner from where I lived—a peaceful
and innocent-looking place with stunning fountains, flower gardens,
woods, and red-brick buildings, and where global war and global unity had

been discussed and planned. It implied a planet in chaos, without peace and order, where perhaps an elite group of men might intervene to keep a great tragedy from happening. All someone needed was to go along with the plan. It was democracy in action. In those days, all I could see glinting within the walls of Dumbarton Oaks were the bright coins shining at the bottom of the fountain.

The truth seemed simple then and many years later: all the world needed was a change of consciousness, of mindset. That was it. Then people could put down their arms and live in peace, sharing selflessly the resources of the world. Indeed, a new viewpoint was needed—a sense of the cosmic and, of course, a change of self-orientation so that universal love could take root. This didn't seem to be asking too much.

By the time I went to India I was convinced that there was a fundamental and supreme basis for unity that few people saw or understood. It was a unity that we already had in our very deepest natures—that if we were all sparks of the divine, then to be anything but united in global peace and love was a miscarriage of highest truth. "I am you as you are me" sang Lennon and Harrison of the Beatles in "I Am the Walrus." If I am shooting a fellow human being, then I am shooting myself—that is what the mystic finally realizes. Once you can see the divine within, then you can see the divine without—because it is within others. Then boundaries of the ego dissolve, and only love can exist. This was "cosmic love" for all people about which the yogis of India and the mystic masters spoke.

This was also an essential tenet of New Age thought. Peace is a by-product of our realizing our mutual divinity through planetary evolution of consciousness. This was the true cement for global unity—a change of consciousness. New Agers use the term "planetization." Until we did that, the threat of a planet in chaos capable of destroying itself almost any time in nuclear fire loomed on the horizon. This is the platform of Greenpeace and a thousand other New Age groups.

But there is a hidden work: networking groups have to reach a critical threshold of people, a minimum number required to catalyze the New Age planetary *transformation*. This is viewed as a necessary evolutionary event without which the planet might not survive. The catalytic threshold occurs when that minimum number of people experience "consciousness-raising."

Events like Earth Day, Hands-Across-America, and the Harmonic Convergence are events that the public can role-play which have far deeper significance than they realize in acclimating them for globalism and the new consciousness. It is like getting millions of people to recite a mantra on a TV program; the act itself is an unconscious invocation. Hands-across-America was the seeding among the people of a mindset. It was a dress rehearsal for universal brotherhood, gearing the public for world cooperation. It is the fishnet approach. First you identify and then catalyze those among the masses who will be future beacons to help steer this process of public influence.

The film, *Close Encounters of the Third Kind*, carried this message—the gathering together of those from out of society who were receptive to higher guidance. They were ready for change and ready to take the leap to leave the old world behind.

Again, it involved alien intervention. It included a seeding process and a gathering process. By the late seventies, people were ready for aliens who did not need to look like the ultimate role model. We could now accept things that were more dehumanized and alien. This time Spielberg replaced Blaustein as the director of a landmark film about aliens arriving.

In *Close Encounters of the Third Kind*, a giant mental pulse goes out worldwide in the form of a primal melody, almost a nursery rhyme. The experts are baffled. Those that are being called learn to surrender to a deeper impulse behind the tune. They zone out, trance out. The chosen few around the world chant the melody as the experts look on. Ochre-robed Brahmins chant the cosmic melody in Rajasthan while little Johnny plays it on his xylophone. It is a global Rice Krispies commercial.

Guidance continues. The meeting point is Devil's Tower, Wyoming. Many have telepathic images of it. Only the chosen will get there, and that includes little Johnny. Awed faces drift along. The same faces that were once awed at Christ in *Ben Hur* and *The Robe* will soon shine with reverent awe at the strange-looking aliens that they meet at Devil's Tower. But this new awe has taken a left-hand turn; it is zoned out. The players in the game look like a long line of Rajneesh disciples star-

ing at their guru. Something in them is missing.

The aliens coming out of the saucer greatly resemble what Whitley Streiber reported in his contact. It is a cosmic omelette of mixed emotions—"love the alien"—not the powerful romantic love of Zeffirelli's *Romeo and Juliet*, where your guts are on fire. No, this is different. This is the zoned-out grin of the Zen master or a member of a transpersonal encounter group—not always a thing of beauty, but cosmic.

Spielberg and Lucas were able to hammer this message home again— love the alien—when they made *ET*. People wept over a creature with messianic powers that looked like a reptilian foot upside down. Its poignant moments of helplessness made the hideous creature endearing—the koala-bear effect.

The message was *"Love that which is strange, breaks convention, is unacceptable, monstrous, even grotesque; and only those who are ready can experience such cosmic love."* In the words of the Indian yogis, "Learn to love all—including things which are ugly or may even appear evil—by seeing the unity in all, the divine in all." Again, as Luke Skywalker was told, "Let go. Trust the Force."

6

Voices from Out of the Rainbow

On prime time television, an articulate Indian named Deepak Chopra, a multi-million copy, bestselling author of 27 books, tells an amazed host about the God-Consciousness within: "Our ancient Vedanta states that 'the Divine Consciousness is in everything' (Pantheism) and that 'all is One' (monism)." With easy confidence Chopra forcefully describes how the ancient yogis and rishis of India made breakthroughs of "Self-Realization" only now being discovered by New Agers in the West. On another channel New Age bestselling author Marianne

Williamson describes the "divinity within" from a contemporary Western perspective as a wide-eyed Oprah Winfrey nods in a moment of total woman-to-woman rapport. Oprah offers her latest book on the Oprah Book Club.

Such messages have been getting special media consideration with the ease that privileged members enter an elite club. Then the ideas resurface powered up in prime time TV or in movie blockbusters.

Again the messages are like cosmic telegrams bear-

ing the delicious promise that the human race will transform into an exalted godlike state that will bring in the New Age. But standing in the way of
this necessary paradigm shift are the old "prejudices" and beliefs from an
outmoded Christian era with its dualistic view of God & man, its moral
absolutes of good and evil. It is a pervasive message, and I was on the forefront of this wave for a time.

By the late 1990s, esoteric spiritual paths that I had explored for years,
at one time placing me in a distinct minority, were almost the consensus
view of America. Perhaps the few are becoming the many as New Age
blends and moves into other movements such as Neo-paganism, Wicca,
and other spawns.

Planetary Events

In 1987, over a decade back, millions gathered in convention halls and
stadiums and even churches to invoke the New Age by means of various global events such as International Meditation Day for World Peace.
Hundreds of organizations in 60 nations sponsored this event. New Age
leader John Randolph Price called the event:

> A planetary affirmation of love, forgiveness and understanding involving
> millions of people in a simultaneous global mind-link. The purpose: *to
> reverse the polarity of the negative force field in the race mind, achieve a critical
> mass of spiritual consciousness, usher in a new era of Peace on earth, return
> mankind to Godkind.*[1]

By mid-January of 1987, famed actress Shirley MacLaine had finally
found "the truth," and she was telling the world in her autobiographical
miniseries *Out on a Limb*. Fifty-million-plus American homes were treated
to such scenes as:

Shirley MacLaine walks Malibu beach. A slightly crooked, all-knowing
smile passes across the face of Dave, her New Age teacher. "Now open out
your arms, face the ocean, and repeat after me. 'I am God.' Go ahead, say
it."

Shirley looks awkward, embarrassed. Tentatively she mouths the words,
"I am God." Inhibitions keep her from a full-hearted acclamation.

Dave persists, "Come on, yell it out. Don't be chicken, say it convinc-
ingly. 'I am God.'"

Shirley's chant mounts in volume. She forces herself to act out the con-
viction. "I am God, I am God, I am God." David has chimed in, helping

her to build up steam.

She is breaking through the resistance, the cold barrier. "Hey, it isn't so hard. Just say it." By the end of her repetitions, Shirley is celebratory, liberated. That wasn't so painful. Wow! What a lesson.

Fifty million Americans get the message: "Hey, we are God." That is the cornerstone of the New Age movement: *Man is God.*

Shirley soon becomes aware that a non-physical hierarchy exists and is waiting to intervene in the affairs of the world. It is New Age lesson number three. Celestial beings, "Walk Ins," are waiting to walk into prepared bodies of surrendered subjects who have obeyed the *impulse.* America now knows that they are out there as well. We just need to get ready to surrender to the intuitive impulse.

The summer of 1987 also celebrated another mass invocation, the Harmonic Convergence. Scores of people worldwide invoked the higher powers from the spiritual realms as they flocked to the Great Pyramid in Egypt, Stonehenge in England, Machu Picchu in Peru, and Mount Tamalpais in California's Marin County, plus thousands of other "sacred" places.

Mass rituals were indeed increasing, rituals that would have been as alien to the America of the 1950s as an alien invasion. These were huge signs of change.

The Nexus of The New Spirituality

The core beliefs of the various Western spiritual hybrids such as the New Age Movement, Neo-paganism and Wicca can be found in the basic tenets of Eastern mysticism with some modern ideas added from the West.

Eastern Influences

1. *THE IMPERSONAL GODHEAD.* God is the *Brahman* of Hinduism. It is impersonal, like the Force in *Star Wars*, or the ocean of supreme consciousness. It is the Ground of Being and non-being, the static eternal, the overmind, the consciousness within all things and sustaining all things. Hence, New Agers talk about the *sacredness of all things.* It is beyond all attributes and all polarities.

The yin/yang symbol of Taoism expresses the One as being beyond all polarities. It is indeed composed of them: light and dark, masculine and feminine, good and evil, etc., for all polarities are composed of the godhead. White light going into a prism comes out as differentiated colored rays on the other side. The phenomenal universe is like the differentiated colored rays. They are no longer unified. But if you examine the unified white light, the source of all color, the colors can no longer be differentiated. Blue, red, yellow cannot be seen in the white light. There is not even a hint of their existence without the prism. This is how consciousness emerges from the godhead and forms the phenomenal universe.

On the other side, within the ocean of pure consciousness, all seemingly separate forms are perceived as being the One. It is their appearance of differentiation that is the illusion. An impersonal god has no forgiving grace, no personal love, no higher morality, and is not the transcendent personal creator of the universe. To an impersonal consciousness, the lives of struggling individuals rate no higher on the scale than ants being swept off a tree trunk in a summer thunderstorm. Older cultures, such as the Hindus of India who have lived under this perennial philosophy for many centuries, understand the downside of an impersonal godhead, and it can be a source of great despair as they struggle to escape the great wheel of karma.

2. *THE DIVINE WITHIN.* The mystery of man's ultimate identity is finally revealed as his divinity within. It is the basic tenet of pantheism, the core belief of Hinduism: All things are One, since all energy is divine consciousness "frozen" into matter. Since all things are made of God, man in his deepest self is none other than God. But without "enlightenment," he does not know this and, in effect, lives as an amnesiac. The purpose of man is to realize that he is God, thus ending the "illusion" of separation.

3. *THERE IS NO DEATH.* As parts of God we are immortal, and death is only an illusion as we evolve throughout eternity. Death is only a veil between one lifetime and another. Reincarnation is one element of this scheme. Others speak of continuation on other planes; the Tibetans use the term *bardos* in Mahayana Buddhism.

4. *GOOD AND EVIL ARE ILLUSIONS.* Evil is just the reverse side of the coin of good. It is the back side. Each is incomplete without the other. In effect, both good and evil are part of the illusion of existence. Good and evil merge at an upper threshold, and both are necessary in the phenomenal universe. Indeed, both are parts of the godhead, as polarities that unify in the One. An aspect of the godhead is evil, as we see represented in Kali and Siva who wreak death and destruction as the dark underbelly of reality. Because of this, sin is ignorance. Both polarities are to be transcended; they are not absolutes in the biblical sense.

5. *ALL PATHS LEAD TO GOD.* Through a higher understanding, it

can be seen that all world faiths point to the same spiritual reality and are all paths up the mountain to the godhead. The goal is to show that all religions are saying the same thing. Syncretism is a central goal of the New Age movement.

New Western Hybrids

6. *SPIRITUAL EVOLUTION.* The New Age view of history is one of spiritual evolution, almost in Hegelian terms. History is seen as a kind of cosmic genetic code that unfurls the divine dimensions of man as consciousness evolves. Consciousness, in the act of self-discovery, must answer the riddle of its true nature. The cosmos is purposeful as it moves inexorably toward its final goal: global enlightenment and the deification of man. New Age theoretician Ken Wilber says, ". . . if men and women have ultimately come up from amoebas, then they are ultimately on their way towards God."[2]

7. *SHIFTING PARADIGMS.* This is the shift in the way reality is perceived due to the inevitable momentum of the evolution of consciousness. Virginia Hine, the respected sociologist, has mentioned this shift as our leaving the Faustian myth of scientism. And Ferguson spoke of the need to shatter the confines of the present "crust of custom." In short, New Agers anticipate the collapse of the Old Age and the birth of the New Age by means, in part, of the paradigm shift in the way reality is perceived. Rationalism and Christian monotheism will be supplanted by mystical monism, as the intuitive right hemisphere of the race is brought into equal footing with the long-reigning logical left hemisphere of Western consciousness, as Peter Russell observes.[3]

8. *OPTIMISM.* Though New Agers are deeply aware of the precariousness of human existence due to such things as the nuclear threat and the ecological and population crises—from which they cite dire statistics such as the Global 2000 Report (to show how the old paradigms have failed)—they nevertheless brandish a positive spirit, rising above contemporary despair. With Marilyn Ferguson this mood of optimism is almost a manic expectancy. Former Secretary General of the United Nations Robert Muller exults, "The next stage will be our entry into a moral global age—the global age of love—and a

Robert Muller

global spiritual age—the cosmic age. We are now moving fast towards the fulfillment of the visions of the great prophets who through cosmic enlightenment saw the world as one unit, the human race as one family, sentiment as the cement of that family, and the soul as our link with the universe, eternity, and God."[4]

9. *CRISIS AS TRANSFORMATION.* The dark and foreboding horizon of impending global holocaust is an important catalyst that will help thrust the planet into a new awakening, breaking down walls of resistance like a tidal wave crashing through a seacoast village. Man stands at the crossroads about to make a quantum leap forward. Such things as atomic threat raise the global temperature to the boiling point where human ego structures are forced to break down in the manner that hostages trapped in a hijacked airplane suddenly feel the futility of worrying about their belongings. Outward necessity forces the dire realization and the transformation.

10. *HOLISM.* We must relate to our world from the viewpoint of the solidarity of all reality, the "all is one" of Eastern thought. When we do, things that are presently out-of-balance will be restored—whether ecological, political, or geophysical. Human health will be restored and earth itself will reach a kind of planetary consciousness that Cambridge-educated New Age apologist Peter Russell calls "Gaia Consciousness."[5] In short, for those who are ready it will be a new heaven on earth, a New Age millennium.[6]

Triggering The Grand Event

Alice Bailey spoke of "The Externalization of the Hierarchy" (also the title of her major work) to help bring on the New Age. It would be a broad-range release of forces on every level of the continuum of consciousness, from ascended masters to impulses coming from deep within "the godhead." These were all seen as manifestations of the One in a grand concert.

In a talk in Geneva, Switzerland, before the Arcane School, which she founded, Alice Bailey thrilled her audience with descriptions of this release of forces:

> The decision to release the Shamballa force during this century into direct contact with the human kingdom is one of the final and most compelling acts of preparation for the New Age.
>
> The Shamballa force is destructive and ejective . . . inspiring new understanding of The Plan. . . .

It is this force . . . which will bring about that tremendous crisis, the initiation of the race into the mysteries of the ages.[7]

What were once the "mysteries of the ages" are now being revealed before the world. We have seen them in bestsellers, movies, and television specials. Most central of all is the discovery of the divinizing of man. Not just the discovery of the divine within—the heart of pantheism—but a global process of objective and conscious divinizing of the race that will change the entire earth.

If true, it is a titanic event, and it cannot help but affect all and everyone. Those that go along with it are told that they will apparently experience heaven on earth as they become gods. Those that resist it because of outmoded beliefs will apparently have some rough lessons in store for them. And why should it be any other way? The brutal facts of evolution, they point out, have told us this. Life is a spectacular passing show of variant creatures, from bright-green frogs to behemoths. But invariably some species are discarded as they are replaced by more evolved species. It is just one more a cappella note coming from the voices from out of the rainbow.

7

The Eye of the Earth

In December 1968 the Apollo 8 spacecraft hung above the earth and suddenly man looked down upon the earth from space for the very first time. Marshall McLuhan's Global Village metaphor became a reality as TV sets around the world showed the earth *live* from space for the first time in history.

There it was, this immense pristine ball of living green hanging in the heavens. Viewers beheld an undivided planet without arbitrary man-made boundaries.

A kind of global patriotism filled the heart. As Ross West observed in *New Realities*, "Something small and tribal in our understanding died that day; something larger was born. The genie of planetary unity had slipped out of the bottle." Public sacraments such as Earth Day would soon appear along with a host of consciousness raising events. Such things as global rock concerts would strike up a sense of planetary unity, often paying homage to the sacredness of the earth.

In the 1980s another idea emerged: the earth was more than a dead planet that just happened to have life crawling on its surface—an outdated concept from the mechanistic and modernist past—but was in fact an awakening planetary consciousness. James Lovelock, a NASA astrophysicist, popularized the idea that the earth is a meta system of consciousness in the process of becoming self aware. He called this the *Gaia Hypothesis.*

In describing this consciousness, Lovelock returned to an ancient concept, **the goddess**—that the earth is a goddess who is rapidly awakening in our time. Thus human communities were merely neural nodes in this larger life form. Before Lovelock came on the scene, I had anticipated the same "breakthrough" in a poem I had written in Mysore, South India, likening the awakening planet to Kali. The idea was in the air to be seized by the right visionary. And it is here today, including the downside of a planetary goddess capable of wrath (rather than moral agents being judged by God, we are now ants being judged by a goddess).

Lovelock rediscovered the Design Argument: that the infinitely variegated equilibrium of the global ecosystem was just too staggeringly complex to have happened by accident (a classical evidential argument for God now applied to Gaia). The old scientific cliche that randomicity and time can create order was impossible to believe. The only sensible answer was that an intelligence was at work. And that intelligence was life itself teeming across the earth's surface and forming a more complex meta-intelligence, indeed, a planetary intelligence that was able to fine tune its atmosphere and temperature to become optimal for life within narrow limits.

Lovelock cautiously revealed his deeper convictions in an interview in ***Orion Nature Quarterly:***

> Gaia is Mother Earth. Gaia is immortal. She is the eternal source of life. She is surely a virgin. She does not need to reproduce herself as she is immortal. She is certainly the mother of us all, including Jesus. . . .Gaia is not a tolerant mother. She is rigid and inflexible, ruthless in the destruction of whoever transgresses. Her unconscious objective is that of maintaining a world adapted to life. If we men hinder this objective we will be eliminated without pity. (Ross Evans West, 1989, "Gaia—She's Alive: A Conversation With James Lovelock," Orion Nature Quarterly 8:l, p. 58.)

Lovelock's Gaia hypothesis was perfect for the ecology movement, giving it a spiritual and moral foundation that could replace the reigning biblical one. Global architects meanwhile could envision human consciousness reaching a unitive level of sensitivity to the earth rivaled by only the most romanticized notions of plains Indians. Reaching "planetary servanthood" Gaians might some day tiptoe across the earth's surface under the higher mandate of mother earth. As "earth servants" (abandoning the view of being creations of God appointed as stewards over creation) they could now have an alternative spiritual context to willingly lay down their individual rights for the higher planetary and ecological good.

If Gaia should become a religion, it would fit handily into a centralized international order because it is collectivist and anti-individual as opposed to the biblical view. It is also generically spiritual, and compulsively environmental, gathering up a broad variety of traditions. Gaia will boast of a broad-mindedness that includes Wiccans, Neo-pagans, New Age groups, pagans, meditation groups, astrologers, gay and lesbian spirituality, and Eastern religions. It will be far less tolerant of Christian and conservative groups. Should Christians refuse to fit in, a new generation of Salem Witch Trials—this time with the Christians on trial by the witches— could come about, signalling a grand historical reversal. America's pioneers and forefathers might then be sentenced retroactively for crimes of deforestation. While Temples of Diana  and Artemis replace the deteriorating churches and cathedrals of the old order—which for most people would probably go unnoticed.

New Agers and sectarians who gleefully rejected God would be only too eager to become Gaia's children in servitude to Mother Earth. Wearing green leaves, they might do wild things, nature things. Mother Earth's moral permissiveness could be fun as long as her subjects blocked out the other side of the goddess—the cruel arbitrary side demonstrated by Hinduism's Kali.

Orwell could not have conceived of a better means of mass socialization, a parallel but alien value system to the Christian one. The human race could be radically redefined. Suddenly, people—as earth servants— under the dominion of "mother earth," could also be seen as expendable as ants. Their acts of deep ecology could be earth sacraments. Unlike their ancestors, the Genesis overlords of nature, Gaians would define themselves as subjects of nature, without rights. It is a creed that goes far beyond people in grey suits picking up Styrofoam cups. Fuelling this Gaian revival would be various compelling ecological arguments that nobody can deny.

The strategy is recurrent in bringing in the global era: focus on a legitimate problem, reinterpret it, then devise a solution that will further demolish the old order and introduce the new. Gaia and Deep Ecology are perfect instruments for this process. The starting point is our natural and inevitable love for nature against the backdrop of the harm that industry has brought since the industrial revolution.

The Ecological Great Awakening

Few things thrust us to the upper limits of our capacity to feel awe as when we behold the splendor of natural beauty (that's why theologians for hundreds of years have called the natural order the fingerprint of God).

From Springtime at Victoria Falls, Africa, to Autumn in England, from the tropical and lush shores of Maui to the grand summits of America's West, the facets of the earth's beauty appear boundless. The initial and primary human response is to love and cherish nature, to want to protect it. That is why the sense of polluting the earth feels like a crime for those of us with any conscience at all.

The marring and defacing of any sort of beauty—natural, artistic, architectural—we instinctively know is wrong. Arbitrary, wanton, and wasteful destruction and defacement is hideous and we recoil from the thought; Nero burning the city of Rome (an ancient eco-crime) and blaming Christians for it to deflect the blame, then burning them as human torches while they were tied up on wooden stakes in his royal gardens. The Emperor Caligula carved up the faces and bodies his subjects at will, like a child making halloween masks.

Equivalent villains of ecological destruction have remained in the shadows till the industrial era at the mid point of the 1800s. The industrial era created tycoons who would pillage vast regions just to make money. But the masses looked the other way in their desire of the goods and services that these new industries provided. There was so much pristine nature out there that it seemed endless with more to spare. It was a kind of boundless blindness. All were culpable in this give and take.

For every notorious "eco villain" such as Sadam Hussein, who ignited over a thousand Kuwaiti oil wells to poison and incinerate the skies of the Gulf region, there are myriads of lesser offenders defacing our collective inheritance. Culpability keeps widening when we consider that each individual adds to the world's problem of pollution. You toss a styrofoam cup and it becomes a problem as you become an accomplice in *earth-crime*. If those in high places establish collective guilt, then they can devise a collective solution. Yes, it's another piece of the globalist puzzle.

When we exchanged our once pristine wildernesses for factories, progress brought terrible rewards. Is any modern convenience worth it, or was it a shortsighted bargain? That is the collective question of the ecological era. The call for Gandhian simplicity goes out, a lowering of standards. The great fear of the present is that what took only *decades* to pollute, such as Europe's great rivers, could take *centuries* to clean up and detoxify at the earth's natural recovery rate.

It seems like a devil's bargain. Our technological prowess has multiplied our power to pollute a million fold. It gives us a terrible, perhaps irreversible, power over the planet. This is the high point of the Malthusian argument that cries out for a simpler world of natural ornaments and cottage industry goods and lifestyles that harken back to earlier eras on the earth. It is the call of the ecology movement and the New World Order. "Get ready for less, be willing to give it all up, to be downsized in your way of living."

Real And Imagined Crises

In 1972 the Club of Rome published its famous *Limits to Growth*, on the earth's impending crises. It was based on Club of Rome member, computer genius, and MIT professor Jay Forrester's elaborate computer models. This early report was one of the flagship doomsaying treatises which gave the environmental movement its teeth for social and political action.

It painted a stark and menacing future. Its basic theme was that the earth was running out of key resources while economic growth had a ceiling because of such non-renewable resources, inadequate food supplies, pollution, and over population. It was a manifesto by an elite of planetary managers. Among its predictions was that the world would run out of gold by 1981, mercury by 1985, tin by 1987, zinc by 1990, petroleum by 1992, and copper, lead and natural gas by 1993.

Limits to Growth was dead wrong on every point. In fact, prices of these metals and minerals have fallen by 50 percent since the book was released, according to the World Resource Institute.

Ronald Bailey, in *"Raining in Their Hearts,"* (National Review, Dec. 3, 1990, p. 34.) says of Forrester's fourth limit to growth, pollution, that we are not choking on our own wastes quite yet and that "the quality of air and water in the United States has improved markedly over the last twenty years. For instance, Lake Erie, which both Ehrlich and Forrester pronounced dead, is once again being fished commercially."

We face the challenge of dividing *actual* environmental crises from *contrived* crises (formulated to alarm the public?). The latter may not depict the state of the world after all — as has been shown with **all** of Forrester's dire projections as well as Paul Ehrlich's scenario in *The Population Bomb* (released in 1968). Bailey notes, "Twenty-two years after *The Population Bomb*, the fact that none of Ehrlich's predictions have come true has in no way harmed his career or his credibility." (P. 33). (Ehrlich's doomsaying exercise, *The Population Explosion,* echo the predictions of the first book.) Another threatening prediction of the 70's was Carl Sagan's idea of a *nuclear winter* predicting that life on earth would end from even a limited nuclear exchange.

We are witnessing how legitimate public passions are being directed by the rhetoric of war—propaganda. The public is challenged to make the sort of sacrifices expected of a nation when it is under the threat of annihilation. Such challenges only carry weight with convincing crises and nothing less.

What better way to get people to surrender their freedoms, their way of life, than to use such a crisis as a means to a radical solution? One wonders if the people would still end up with the same ecological problems but minus their freedoms in the exchange. This is the kind of Jacob and Esau counter trade that appears beneath the rhetoric of today's ecological leaders—as in Al Gore's *Earth in the Balance*—who speak in the compassionate tones of public servants but whose intent might more closely resemble the techno-tyrants in Huxley's *Brave New World*.

Leaders and social planners have often relied on crises to herd the cattle. They need a problem, a perpetrator, a source of guilt and a ready scapegoat for blame, in order to implement truly drastic solutions. Finding and directing blame is a critical concern if social change is behind the real objective.

Interestingly, the body of much of today's ecological doctrine allegedly emerged in secret meetings in the 1960s when a think tank was set up to look for an alternative to war as a means of keeping history on course. The think tank had its introductory meetings in upstate New York deep inside the earth at Iron Mountain. News leaks exposed the reality of what was going on—insiders in a kind of James Bond underground hideaway conspiring—but like most things of this nature, its existence was buried with denials and soon forgotten by the media. Some self described intellectuals prefer to believe the spin artists who have labeled the report "a satire." If so, so was Karl Marx's *Das Capital* a satire. "We can let our guard down, it was only a satire."

The Report From Iron Mountain

Accounts of the secret think tank emerge in a book whose full title is *Report From Iron Mountain on the Possibility and Desirability of Peace.* The

REPORT FROM
IRON MOUNTAIN
ON THE POSSIBILITY
AND DESIRABILITY
OF PEACE

". . . The Special Study Group, as the
commission was fondly called [by Washington]
met and worked regularly for over two and a
half years, after which it produced a report . . .
they concluded [that] lasting peace . . . even if it
could be achieved . . . would almost certainly
not be in the best interest of a stable society."

author is identified only as "John Doe," an obvious pseudonym (most think it is John Kenneth Galbraith, Harvard economist). The author claimed to be a member of the think tank of 15 experts. The author describes it:

> The cloak-and-dagger tone of this convocation was further enhanced by the meeting place itself. Iron Mountain, located near the town of Hudson, is like something out of Ian Fleming . . . It is an underground nuclear hideout for hundreds of large American corporations. Most of them use it as an emergency storage vault for important documents. But a number of them maintain substitute corporate headquarters as well, where essential personnel could survive and continue to work after an attack . . . .[1]

They must have known the cold war would not last forever. Ahead, some day would be World Order. Wars so far had been the engine to break and remake nation states. If an era of peace broke out, how could they perpetuate this process with a substitute for war?

In the words of Brooks Alexander, "In accord with its mandate, the Special Study Group had approached its subject with a calculated detachment from ethical standards and a profound rejection of moral considerations. Its moral nihilism ultimately endorsed war as the cornerstone of social order and the foundation of social institutions. Equally cynical — but more manipulative — were its proposals for long-range social engineering."[2]

The Report affirmed history's options for equilibrium:

war . . . human sacrifice, slavery, genocide, racist eugenics (including
the substitution of artificial insemination for normal human procre-
ation), a planned economy, fascist partnership between business and
government, planned government waste, official opposition to medical advances, globalism, environmentalism, and even the new pagan
Mother Earth religion.[3]

The Group decided that if no workable substitute for war can be
found or created, then the coming of peace could mean destabilizing
chaos and dissolution (or loss of control of a well established elite).

> However unlikely some of the possible alternate enemies we have
> mentioned may seem, we must emphasize that one *must* be found, of
> credible quality and magnitude, if a transition to peace is ever to come
> about without social disintegration. It is more probable, in our judg-
> ment, that such a threat will have to be invented, rather than devel-
> oped from unknown conditions.[4]

Alexander observes, "Of all the possible substitutes for war that the
Group surveyed, it thought environmentalism to be among the most
credible and effective. However, while an eco-threat served the functions
of war very well, it was (as of 1964) not fully credible yet, and thus not
ready to be invoked." Iron Mountain stressed that our environmental
problems needed more time to mature, and to reach a more obvious danger point

> It may be, for instance, that gross pollution of the environment can
> eventually replace the possibility of mass destruction by nuclear
> weapons as the principle apparent threat to the survival of the species.
> Poisoning of the air, and of the principle sources of food and water is
> already well-advanced, and at first glance would seem promising in
> this respect; it constitutes a threat that can be dealt with only through
> social organization and political power. But from present indications
> it will be a generation to a generation and a half before environmental
> pollution, however severe, will be sufficiently menacing, on a global
> scale, to offer a possible basis for a solution . . . [however], the mere
> modifying of existing programs for the deterrence of pollution could
> speed up the process enough to make the threat credible much soon-
> er.[5]

The ideas broached in Iron Mountain soon broke the surface in mainstream publications. The CFR magazine *Foreign Affairs*, in April 1970
(just in time to coincide with the first Earth Day), contained an article
entitled "To Prevent a World Wasteland — a Proposal," written by
George Kennan, an eminent government policy planner.

Kennan's article made three points:

1) The eco-crisis a global threat so great that it endangers life on earth;

2) The crisis should be controlled by a partnership between government and business, operating under a central, international Super-Agency to regulate environmental issues; and

3) The new crusade "must proceed at least to some extent at the expense of the . . . immensely dangerous preoccupations that are now pursued under the heading of national defense." In other words, the military threat will be phased out, and the eco-threat phased in, while national sovereignty is whittled away. Kennan's "Proposal" does more than "echo" Iron Mountain's precepts— it turns them into a concrete program.

Al Gore's *Earth in the Balance* essentially promotes Iron Mountain's program for transition from war to peace. It adds some detail, but otherwise takes the Report's purposes for granted — especially its globalism and its assumption that national sovereignty is expendable. Gore's book exhibits a remarkable, point-for-point adherence to the Report's strategic agenda. Perhaps Gore's book is the greatest evidence that the Iron Mountain meetings took place.

The same can be said of The Earth Charter, Gorbachev's World Forum, The Earth Summit, the World Wilderness Conferences, and the Conference in Rio. And this is exactly where the rubber meets the road in world order thinking. Once the compelling arguments are backed up by international law, then we have a system that has enough teeth to change lives at will.

Today's ecological charters and treaties—armed by the rule of law— are the means for providing these teeth.

Controlling Despoilers

Turn the clock forward thirty years from the Iron Mountain meetings in the '60s to the present ecological conferences and tell me if it is not all coming true to the letter. It is. That alone substantiates *The Report from Iron Mountain* more than any single piece of evidence. It is all taking place as masses of people watch TV sitcoms and other television distractions, their lives drifting into the future guided by other hands.

When the Parliament of World Religions was held in Chicago, 1993, one key declaration was called, *Towards a Global Ethic*. Keynote speaker

Gerald Barney (the lead author of the Global 2000 report for the Carter administration) announced, "Five billion of us humans must prepare to die to 20th century ways of thinking and being.... Every person must learn to think like earth, to act like earth, to be earth."

Barney helped create 'Global 2000 Revisited: What Shall We Do?' The appendix contains an invitation for heads of state and religious leaders to convene in Thingvellir, Iceland, on January 1, 2000. There, in a tent, surrounding a stone alter, the gathered leaders would present handwritten covenants pledging loyalty to *Gaia*. This event would constitute what Barney calls 'a ritual death to and giving up of the old 20th century and its ways of thinking and being.'"

The Rio Declaration

The United Nations Conference on Environment and Development met at Rio de Janeiro from June 3rd to the 14th 1992, and reaffirmed the Stockholm accord, namely "the goal of establishing a new and equitable global partnership through the creation of new levels of cooperation among States, key sectors of societies and people, working towards international agreements which respect the interests of all and protect the integrity of the global environmental and developmental system, recognizing the integral and interdependent nature of the Earth, our home."

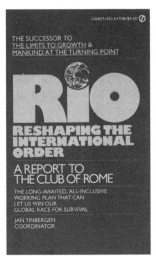

In Rio, world government, utopianism, and ecology would all fit together as a subset of the Charter of the United Nations, all in earth-friendly language:

Principle 7

States shall cooperate in a spirit of global partnership to conserve, protect and restore the health and integrity of the Earth's ecosystem. In view of the different contributions to global environmental degradation, States have common but differentiated responsibilities. The developed countries acknowledge the responsibility that they bear in the international pursuit of sustainable development in view of the pressures their societies place on the global environment and of the technologies and financial resources they command.

Principle 8

To achieve sustainable development and a higher quality of life for all people, States should reduce and eliminate unsustainable patterns of production and consumption and promote appropriate demographic policies.

To repeat, "States should reduce and eliminate unsustainable patterns of production and consumption and promote appropriate demographic policies." You have just read part of the Marxist platform. If that means nothing to you, you are already sheep to the slaughter. For a higher world body to actualize principle 8—mandating "sustainable development—could mean a scene right out of *1984*. America's good life is nothing less than "unsustainable patterns of production and consumption." China allows only 1 child per couple. That could become the way for America, as it shifts into a third world protectorate.[6]

What about *the Earth Charter?*

The Earth Charter

Green Cross International argues the case that despite repeated efforts, the international community of nation states has not yet been able to agree on "an effective international treaty which guarantees the rights of the Earth."

The creation of international law is seen by them as being a slow and tedious process. In a 1997 interview with the *Los Angeles Times*, Gorbachev said:

> We also need a new international environmental legal code rooted in an Earth Charter - a covenant similar to the United Nations Declaration on Human Rights. The idea of an Earth Charter was first conceived at the Rio Summit. During the Rio evaluation meeting this March, the Earth Charter Commission, which I chair, drafted such a document with the aim of presenting it to the U.N. General Assembly for approval by the year 2000. 'Do not do unto the environment of others what you do not want done to your own environment,' reads one charter item. 'Adopt modes of consumption, production, and reproduction that respect the regenerative capacities of the Earth,' said another. My hope is that this charter will be a kind of Ten Commandments, a 'Sermon on the Mount,' that provides a guide for human behavior toward the environment in the next century and beyond."[7]

Mikhail Gorbachev, in case you did not know, is President of Green

Cross International. He and Maurice Strong, Chairman of the Earth Council, met in the Hague in April 1994 and agreed to launch The Earth Charter initiative. The key points for an Earth Charter were identified:

> The Earth Charter should be a product of a worldwide process of consultation and engagement involving a broad and representative cross section of people from all sectors and groups of society. The Earth Charter should advance a clear and timeless expression of the ethical and moral imperatives for achieving sustainability locally, nationally and globally.
>
> The Earth Charter should build on achievements of previous declarations and conventions. It should introduce or reemphasize ethical and moral imperatives and norms for individual, communal, national and inter-state behavior which are not adequately addressed or included in previous documents.[8]

The Earth Charter begins by saying:

"Earth is our home and home to all living beings. Earth itself is alive. We are part of an evolving universe."

Then comes the call for "fundamental economic, social, and cultural changes:"

> Principle 7. The current course of development is thus clearly unsustainable. Current problems cannot be solved by piecemeal measures. More of the same is not enough. Radical change from the current trajectory is not an option, but an absolute necessity. Fundamental economic, social, and cultural changes that address the root causes of poverty and environmental degradation are required and they are required now."

Then comes the call for zero population growth and zero economic growth; the needs of the world's poor will be met by "reducing material over-consumption by the rich minority:"

To enforce all this, there must be "global sovereignty" which must not be "subservient to the rules of state sovereignty, demands of the free market, or individual rights." The new international ruler must have "independence and power to facilitate agreement between all societal actors:"

> Principle 14 The idea of Global Sovereignty must be supported by a shift in values which recognize this Common Interest.
>
> IMPLEMENTATION 1. The creation of an international body for the sustainability of Human Life on the Earth. This body must have the independence and power to facilitate agreement between all societal actors to support the protection of the Biosphere as the Common

Interest of Humanity.[9]

With wide popular support they hope that the Earth Charter will be endorsed by the United Nations General Assembly in the year 2000. How ironic—please think about this—that the head of the Earth Charter initiative is the former head of the Soviet Union.

Mikhail S. Gorbachev, Chairman of the State of The World Forum, has said some interesting things in the past.

> "Those who hope that we shall move away from the socialist path will be greatly disappointed. Every part of our program of perestroika — and the program as a whole, for that matter — is fully based on the principle of more socialism and more democracy . . . . We will proceed toward better socialism rather than away from it. We are saying this honestly, without trying to fool our own people or the world. Any hopes that we will begin to build a different, non-socialist society and go over to the other camp are unrealistic and futile. We, the Soviet people, are for socialism. We want more socialism and therefore more democracy."[10]

In 1987 Gorbachev recalled the aim of the Bolshevik Revolution: "In October 1917 we parted with the Old World, rejecting it once and for all. We are moving toward a new world, the world of communism. We shall never turn off that road."

In a 1989 speech to the Soviet Congress, Gorbachev stated: "I am a communist, a convinced communist; for some that may be a fantasy, but for me, that is my main goal." As the last leader of the Soviet Union, this old line allegiance would make sense, though Gorbachev these days would probably call himself an international socialist.

James Garrison, who is under Chairman Gorbachev, serving as the President of the State of the World Forum, recently outlined the goals of the Forum in grandiose terms at their annual meeting:

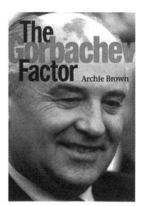

> We are living in a time of immense turbulence, challenge, and opportunity. Ancient institutions and systems of belief which have brought us to the present moment are being shattered by the force of change, compelled either to renew themselves or perish. This is so because what is arising around us is nothing less than the birth of the first global civilization. It is our generation and our time to which has fallen the great

task of its birthing and first definition.[11]

In another statement, Garrison makes it clear that it will be what he calls "creative minorities"—an elite—who will set the agenda for the New World Order that he envisions:

> The core mission of the State of the World Forum is to establish an enabling environment and to serve as a Secretariat for the gathering of leaders and citizens from around the world. . . That a group of thoughtful and motivated individuals would gather in this manner is not unusual; indeed, it replicates a very deeply human and historic response to crisis and change. Most of the twenty-four other civilizations which have appeared in the 6,000 years of our recorded history have largely been created by groups of so-called 'creative minorities' or 'sapential circles' — independent individuals who came together to articulate and take up challenges being ignored by declining and outdated concepts, organizations, and governments.[12]

At the opening speech for this 1996 World Forum, Mikhail Gorbachev called for "a global brain trust to focus on the present and future of our civilization":

> I would like to suggest that we consider the establishment of a kind of global brain trust to focus on the present and future of our civilization. . . . Of course, this idea of a brain trust can only succeed if endorsed and actively pursued by people who are widely respected as world leaders and global citizens.[13]

Mikhail Gorbachev set a five year time frame at the 1996 World Forum to redistribute the world's wealth, transfer all armaments to the United Nations peacekeeping Force, further empower the United Nations, initiate a global tax, implement the over population solution, and eliminate nationalism as well as national borders.

President Mikhail Gorbachev also addressed the Earth Charter Rio+5 Forum on March 18th, 1997. He spoke English with awkward erudition in the meter and cadence of his native Russian language (two clicks from Dr. Strangelove in his wheelchair):

> . . . To save humankind and all future generations, we must save the Earth.
>
> . . . We all have recently witnessed the crash of one of the largest experiments of our time—the communist model of bringing happiness to humankind As soon as we have managed to set ourselves free and open the way to the freedom of choice and democratic institutions for realization of those choices, there appeared new prophets

declaring that the only way out for now is "westernization of the world." I do not think that it is a wise decision. It is just a new attempt to dictate some artificial scheme which many countries would not accept. And what is to be expected in the world if someone tries again to impose their way of development using one's economic, technological and military domination? That is why we declare in the Earth Charter: the world is integrated unity, but it is also the integration of diversity; all of us are equal on the Earth, in the face of Nature in the face of each other, one nation in the face of the others.

Gorbachev got a standing ovation as the future of the earth was being scripted.

The New Inquisition

The new inquisition of earth protectors will tolerate no dissenting views. The inquisitors have already made up their minds where the guilt of civilization lies. They are simply rallying to gain momentum for their cause.

The current rallying cries parallel the earlier communists accusation that the *petite bourgeoisie* and the capitalists were guilty of greed. Since greed was considered endemic to capitalists, they were beyond rehabilitation. And since they could not be really reformed, they had to be purged. Communists did not feel greed, capitalists did — constantly.

When Stalin killed 60 million of his subjects, it was to purge society of the old capitalist paradigm that had corrupted them.

If pollution is evil enough in itself, a far vaster evil is to use this legitimate problem to barter a program of social change that would still not

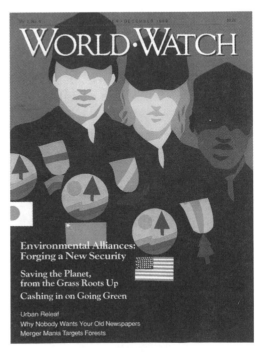

WORLD·WATCH

Environmental Alliances:
Forging a New Security

Saving the Planet,
from the Grass Roots Up

Cashing in on Going Green

Urban Releaf
Why Nobody Wants Your Old Newspapers
Merger Mania Targets Forests

solve the problem of pollution but
would have drastic consequences on
human lives, including population
purges! To call this system anything
other than demonic is to engage in
delusion.

What we must not do is what Esau
did, that is to trade in our birth rights
for some provision of healing the
planet under a planetary manage-
ment program in the New World
Order. It is a certain road to serfdom, and the few will still eat caviar and
drink champagne as the grey masses drift into deeper poverty and impo-
tence. If you want to see real pollution, go to India or the former Soviet
Union.

8
Entering the Mind

- A government psychologist has reviewed your personality tests screening deviant views. Since you have anti-social tendencies for hate crimes and homophobia you must undergo counseling until your views are brought into line with the recent norms set up by the American Psychological Association.

- You've just read the latest bestseller by a transpersonal psychologist. Not only have you learned that you can transcend your problems, but that the normal mode of consciousness that most people dwell in is only managing life in low gear. If you can transcend the normal mode and reach into super consciousness, you will have your own inner awakening.

The various psychologies are an obvious doorway into the mind. Few can probe as deeply into another person's mind as the therapist who, by definition, is allowed direct access to the mind of the patient. The therapist can even resort to hypnotism and mind altering drugs, if needed. It is a position of great access as well as influence. The therapist is by default a guru about reality and the self, an authority as well as a confidante, more intimate in some ways than a best friend or spouse. If that therapist's supreme authority, psychology, becomes increasingly co-opted, the therapist then becomes a powerful tool, a disciple maker, who can turn all those he touches. Therapists in the mass media have already done this.

Beyond the one-on-one patient therapist encounter, psychotherapeutic encounter groups that involve many people can influence people on a wider scale. Most encounter groups generate an incredible level of peer disclosure (and conformity), as each confesses intimate secrets before the group. They concur on worldview and reality, more often than not. Pioneered in the '60s at Big Sur's Esalen Institute, such techniques have reappeared in hundreds of other contexts including the public school, the military, the government, university, and the business world. This, too, shapes the mind, the public mind.

Psychology has become a cross platform discipline, a synthesizing tool reaching into other areas and disciplines from education to the corporation. Psychology can also legitimize and sanction new views of morality—homosexuality has been redefined at least three different times, from a depravity, to a pathology, to "an alternative lifestyle." Psychology can also sanction social views such as political correctness. It becomes the discipline that is invoked to sanction or *normalize* anything. It can also demonize what it considers outmoded, such as the belief in "sin."

If you wanted to change a culture from within, you might follow an agenda of gradualist penetration, crossing several generations of opinion shaping to arrive at a mass consensus. One would target and penetrate groups of people who were especially vulnerable in the initial process of gaining public consensus. To do this one would want to use such opinion shapers as family counselors and therapists, workplace training and seminars (job intimidation), and educators. Each has captive audiences over whom the power to influence is considerable. In today's full immersion world of technology, you can reach more and more minds with increasing speed and immediacy. A therapist can run an encounter group in a large auditorium. Or that same auditorium can be broadcast on public television and now millions can see the same thing. Or it can be required as part of a seminar series at a big corporation.

The "Evolution" of Psychology

Psychology has reinvented itself countless times since Freud started things off from an atheistic base at ground zero early in this century operating within the "Vienna Circle." Various competing schools have come up since then with their own view of the Self, the mind, and all that makes the whole person—starting with Freud's ego, super ego, and Id. They have also advanced competing theories for the causes of "pathology" and mental illness, again starting from such Freudian constructs as the Oedipus complex. Each psychological school has its own disciples, reminiscent of the ancient Greek Schools of Wisdom. These days various transpersonal, New Age and human potential schools have sprung up, with the Esalen Institute at Big Sur as today's Vienna School of New Age Psychology. The emphasis has shifted from making "normal" a "sick mind" to taking the "normal mind" to super-normal states of consciousness. It is no longer just "healing." That means that "normal" people are also future patients.

It is perfectly possible in the 1990s to go to a "therapist" who is willing to place you under hypnosis in order to take you through "age regression" so that you can then engage in "past life recall." Why? Because your problems today, according to these post-'60s psychological therapies, are rooted in things that happened in *previous lives*. So rather than trying to go back to early childhood, as Freudian psychoanalysis does, these new therapies take it one step farther, all the way back to "past lives."

Past life recall means a particular school of psychology accepts reincarnation and Karma as a foregone fact. Therapists and psychologists are still using the prestige of science as they wander into the spiritual realm which, by definition, is out of reach of science.

In today's perplexed age, bewildered people without roots are increasingly looking for an answer. And there is a wide range of psychological alternatives to choose from, starting with therapists on television. For those needing a quick moment of encouragement or self-esteem enhancement, it might be just a channel away.

Teletherapists

On television—the new therapeutic office of the air—convincing and charismatic authorities have begun to appear with powerful ideas. These salesmen of the mind seem to have all the answers, and millions look on and drink it in. The teachings of John Bradshaw or Anthony Robbins emphasize "freedom" and human potential in a feel-good, guilt-free atmosphere of approval and warmth. It is a powerful cocktail of the mind.

One of the most compelling teletherapists to appear has been John Bradshaw, who shows that you are just a victim and, therefore, not responsible—you can push the blame back to society. Some teletherapsts tell you that you can become anything you want, providing you undergo the process. Role models of people who have "made it" are then put on the air.

John Bradshaw has appeared on PBS specials before a national audience many times. Even surfing the dial you are bound to run into him. And his influence is enormous.

Bradshaw's lectures involve stunning self-disclosures amidst rapid-fire psychobabble—quick psychological fix-its that hang in a dense smog of seductive insights punctuated by esoteric psychological concepts that he has appropriated from various schools of psychology ranging from Jung to Eric Berne. He borrows at will, mixing schools of psychology with an intuitive use of the pallet as he creates his master work. Bradshaw has also dabbled extensively in New Age spirituality: "I was into shamanism, energy healing, spirit canoes, the whole trip" he acknowledged in 1991.[1]

Television audiences watch Bradshaw lecture large auditoriums filled with awestruck listeners who sit in reverent silence, mesmerized by his pronouncements. It has become a movement, a psychological creed, almost a faith. It is the creed of the wounded victim. Parents and the old order, with its Christian worldview, are made the perpetrators of the psychological horrors of our time. Deliverance for the wounded victim comes through discovering and freeing the "inner-child" who is trapped deep within by the traumatic wounds that have come from family and society. John Bradshaw has the key to deliverance.

Declaring ninety-six percent of Americans as coming from dysfunctional families, Bradshaw's workshops take participants on emotion-laden journeys within to encounter who they really are, their "inner child." First they have to deal with their "wounded inner child." Then they will encounter their "wonder child" deeper still and hiding behind the hurts and scars within. Like Eric Berne, founder of the once popular Transactional Analysis, Bradshaw has decided that all people are tripartite within: the pearl in the oyster is the wonder child. But finding him requires a journey, and journeys incur expenses.

To "embrace the darkness" of their past, Bradshaw's workshop audience is led through exercises that he has termed "collective grief rituals." According to one participant, (Mary Walton of the *Philadelphia Inquirer* Feb. 17, 1991), tears were not uncommon. Hurts and betrayals are summoned and relived. Other rituals are enacted, including meditating, clutching stuffed animals, and writing letters from the inner child to the parent about the abuse that took place or the needs that were never met. Then participants gather in small groups and each person in turn receives "infant affirmations" of unconditional love and acceptance from other members of the group, along with pats and hugs.

The workshop ends with a "homecoming" meditation in which Bradshaw guides the participants through a visualization of themselves as children leaving the abusive parenting of their fathers and mothers behind forever. "Leaving home means becoming your own parent," Bradshaw observes, "and becoming responsible for your own inner child. It means that you're not going to be a victim anymore. You're going to be a survivor moving toward empowerment. It's not that if you *leave* your family of origin you'll die, it's that if you *stay* you'll die."

Brooks Alexander adds insight into Bradshaw's belief about the inner-child.

> Bradshaw really exhibits his New Age connections when he defines the
> *object* of Recovery. "We are 'divine infants in exile,' a nation of E.T.s des-
> perate to come home" he says. That is classic gnosticism with a narcis-
> sistic New Age twist. It makes the majestic into the pathetic. Original
> gnosticism saw man as a spark of the divine, separated from its source
> but yearning to return. Bradshaw's neo-gnostic system turns that exiled
> spark into a frustrated infant whining about its separation.[2]

John Bradshaw sometimes hisses into the microphone with righteous rage. If I were to typify his voice at such moments, I would characterize it as carrying an angry bristling effeminacy, an almost overripe "male sensitivity," propelled by this haranguing anger. It is an anger from "deep inner wounds" that only true victims have earned the right to display on the hard slope of selfhood. Underneath all of it, however, Bradshaw has a mission.

Sometimes Bradshaw uncloaks rare admissions of belief that make him more resemble a New Age shaman than a psychologist when he says, "there is a massive evolution of consciousness moving toward '**deep democracy.**' This is occurring at all levels of social interaction." (*Current Biography* April, 1993) Such global-mystical statements parallel Marilyn Ferguson's *The Aquarian Conspiracy*. And as always, we are left to wonder what Bradshaw really means by his words.

John Bradshaw has become the voice crying in the wilderness that millions of Americans in our time have chosen to heed.

The full New Age spin on psychology is this: given that the self is God, then once it is unleashed, it can control reality, hence transform history. The more minds that can be "awakened," so that they become self-realized, the faster the transformational changes can occur. At some point there will be a critical mass when the collective minds that have been "awakened" will have the power to transform the world—in a paradigm shift. If this is done right, a utopian world will emerge. We will wish away the problems that have plagued the earth for millennia, from disease to poverty. Consciousness is the hidden messiah. Hence such terms as Harmonic Convergence, Paradigm Shift, and so on are used to describe this great awakening.

What if it is a lie?

Those who stop and question this, wondering if it doesn't sound like *The Emperor's New Clothes*, are perceived by hard core New Agers as among the resistance whose doubt is keeping the global event from happening. They must either be converted or rendered ineffectual so that their "negativity" does not interfere with the great plan. Some even quietly talk of a physical removal of these traditionalists.

Changes in Psychology

The field of psychotherapy has taken amazing turns, becoming its own maze, since it first started. During the course of this century, from Freud to Ken Wilber, it has covered the entire map of beliefs, from atheism to mysticism, from nihilism to existentialism. Over this same period, it has gathered under its umbrella over a hundred different schools of thought about the nature of man and the universe and the appropriate therapy required. It has tried to call itself a science, but how can it be? It is so complex as to defy verifiability. How can the unseen workings of the very consciousness of an individual ever be exposed and examined by any device for scientific verification? And how can any individual ever be subjected to scientifically valid lab experiments? We're still struggling to pinpoint the electron—is it a particle, or does it sometimes lapse into waves?

What scientist could ever create the identical individual and then grow him up in a thousand different environments, to test the effects of those different environments—each time perfectly monitoring them and controlling them?

Beyond that, which mortal scientist could ever live long enough to do this experiment? Likewise, how can the scientist even come to terms with all the environmental influences of a single day within a single environment? The problems of verifying the psyche through pure science are titanic, insurmountable—indeed, beyond the range of science. And that's the whole point.

In the end the gurus of human nature, the psychotherapists, are forced to generalize. They must play the role of wise pundits, and so they claim to be. But when they disagree, as when Carl Jung parted ways with Sigmund Freud, what court of wisdom is able to prove which one is right? It is no science at all; it is a battleground of different schools of belief. Inevitably, it comes down to a faith issue about the nature of human identity and ultimate reality. Is Freud's psychoanalysis right or is Jung's depth psychology right? What if they are both off base?

Sigmund Freud's psychoanalysis reflected his beliefs and opinions. Freud synthesized the reigning beliefs of his day—the popular conceptions of humanists on the vanguard of liberated thought—into a pseudoscience. Above all, Freud was an atheist. For him, quite simply, neither the universe nor psychoanalysis had a place for God. It was a closed issue.

In Freud's day scientific determinism was the order of the day. Popular wisdom claimed that we were all products of long, complex causal gateways confining the course of our existence to a choiceless determinism. Man was merely a byproduct of genetics and environment.

To Freud, the biblical God was an internalized surrogate father figure originally projected out into the world by a tribal people. Freud used Greek mythology to press this theme into respectability. As in the story of Oedipus Rex, Jehovah was seen as the jealous and feared father figure. The Judaism of Freud's background became the random saga of a tribal horde that imagined its God from its ancestral memories of wandering. It was the cosmic "no" to lust and assorted hedonisms in order for the tribe to survive and not dissipate into chaos and anarchy. But Freud wanted to liberate man from these taboos.

Freud was paving the way for public resentment over the fact that "religious" taboos, perhaps mere superstitions, kept them hemmed in and held them back from the "full experience of life." Freud explained that passions had to be released and explored, not repressed.

Freud offered sexual liberation to a world

still under the dictates of moral propri-
ety and biblical moral law. Moral customs still created pangs of conscience;
they still inhibited free expression. And
liberated intellectuals like Freud were
trying desperately to break down the
doors of sexual "repression" and find a
haven of free expression. Freud helped
provide the door to free sex, but
behind that door was the deeper
despair of determinism, of man's lack
of significance in a godless universe.

Woody Allen is a living example of
the psychoanalytic mindset. Sex and death are his obsessions. He looks into
the mirror to remind himself what will be erased from the universe when
he dies—himself. His angst keeps him frustrated, forever kept apart from
the illusory sensual moment. It is like watching a dog slobbering at a ham
sitting in a plate-glass window. The void becomes too close to escape into
the sensual dreamland.

By the sixties, people had had it "up to here" with Freud and the impasse
of scientific determinism. Now that they had finally acquired their freedom
from moral restraint, they were tired of the downside of Freudian deter-
ministic gloom. Freudian psychology was referred to as First Force psychology.

Then came behaviorism which utterly rejected the theories of Freud as
scientifically unfounded speculations and opinion. They were the "Second
Force" psychologists. Anything that could not be scientifically verified they
considered to be myth. Beginning with Fechner and Wilhelm Wundt and
going through Pavlov's stimulus-response experiments, the behaviorists
have logged thousands of lab hours testing simple things that can be tested.
Their most famous pioneer was B. F. Skinner of Harvard, inventor of the
Skinner box.

Skinner took determinism to its limits in his book *Beyond Freedom and
Dignity*. Skinner announced that basically man was a soulless animal who
had no free will, no guarantee of meaning or happiness. Therefore, man
had no basis to object when social engineers came on the scene to behavior
shape him to fit into a world that the intellectual elite planned to create.
War could be driven out of the human race in the lab. With the right probes
and enough current, the job could be done. (Skinner's daughter grew up

under Skinnerian behavioral conditioning and ended up in a mental institution not far from Harvard. She knew no love (for love does not exist),
merely positive and negative reinforcement.).

To the generation of the sixties, the Behaviorist mindset summed up the
grotesqueness of the humanistic experiment. They could not wait to enter
Freud, Skinner, and the rest into the museum of obsolete thought. So when
the Eysenck study was released at the University of London, there was a
furor. Eysenck's study simply showed that among neurotics divided 50/50,
those that underwent psychoanalysis had no better recovery rate than those
who just lived life and saved the massive therapy fees. The recovery was the
same, plus or minus .02 percent statistical error factor. *In other words, psychoanalysis did nothing.* Eysenck drove home the fact that psychoanalysis was
anything but scientifically proven. All it could do was hide behind its termi-
nology and verify itself by its own closed system of definitions of reality.
Freudian psychoanalysis became discredited among all but the most loyal
followers and/or those who had spent $20,000 in training to become high-
ly paid psychoanalysts.

The birth of "Third Force" humanistic psychology took place in the sixties, to restore an alternative dignity and value to men after the void created by Freud and the behaviorists. Humanistic psychologists like Abraham
Maslow and Carl Rogers speculated that there was meaning to life and that
there was a good deal of room for optimism in the universe. Humanistic
psychology declared that people were not the random collocations of mol-
ecules deterministically gathered into human biocomputers, but rather
were part of a larger spiritual dimension. "Feel-good" psychology made its
entrance. At the forefront of this was Carl Rogers, at one time president of
the American Psychological Association and winner of numerous awards
for his nondirective therapy.

This new psychology brought a sweet-sounding creed—that conscience
and guilt were like vestigial organs that no longer served a useful function.
The conscience was part of the primitive brain holding us back from full
self-expression, from freedom, creativity, and joy. In Rogerian client-cen-
tered therapy, the patient had all the answers within.

Humanistic psychology pointed to the idea that self-actualization could
be speeded up by exploring within and overcoming all one's inner fears and
areas of darkness by a total nonjudgmental self-acceptance. Then the
unfathomable depth of human potential could be tapped. It was upbeat and
optimistic. Change was never bad; it was always good. Rogers spoke of the
next evolutionary leap into the new man, but society would have to be rad-

ically changed first. A revolutionary agenda was needed for this to happen, a kind of psychological Marxism that repudiated institutions and traditions. By the mid sixties, Esalen at Big Sur had become a think tank for many of these famed psychologists: Fritz Perls, Rollo May, Abraham Maslow, Carl Rogers, and the rest. Their message was that it was a no-lose universe.

But as Barbara Ehrenreich observed, "If the human potential was intrinsically good, then there was no firm ground left from which to attack the deviant or nonconformist. All trajectories were possible as each unique and groping 'self' reached toward fulfillment."[3] It was a perfect creed for a culture of narcissism.

Ehrenreich observed: "Psychologists had always seen marriage as 'work;' the doctrine of growth transformed it into a navigation feat which would have challenged a ballistics expert." Self-interest could now be selfish and morally blind. Hedonism was okay, and feeling good was okay. Anything could be questioned, especially sacrosanct institutions. Freedom meant you could do almost anything. In short, "freedom" could turn into license without a conscience.

The creed of Third Force psychology mirrored the slogans of the sixties. Christopher Lasch's *The Culture of Narcissism* spells it out: non binding commitments, freedom from guilt or failure, personal fulfillment, the neurotic need for affection, reassurance, and gratification, as well as an inability to internalize clearly defined criteria of right and wrong.

Under these new rules, what you end up with are manipulators who are on the take. They can quickly assess how to use others to get what they want from them, then dump them as soon as they have used them. Loyalty is not their strong point. Communal experiments in the '60s become a free-for-all without reference points—from egalitarian tribes to cultish dictatorships. Communal anarchy pointed to a new barbarism further down the road.

"Fourth Force" psychology then arrived. The founders of humanistic psychology anticipated and then built the bridge to transpersonal psychology. Abraham Maslow, often at Esalen, traced a hierarchy of seven levels of need. When basic needs like food and shelter were taken care of, the higher needs—which were the spiritual ones—could then be addressed, leading to self-actualization. This was the key part of the bridge that led from the humanistic psychology of the sixties to the transpersonal psychology of the seventies and beyond.

Posturing as "experts," transpersonal psychologists had clearly left all pretense of science and entered the domain of faith. Maslow inaugurated transpersonal psychology by making popular the idea that human consciousness could be the link between man and the fundamental realities of the universe.

Carl Rogers crossed a different barrier. Prior to his wife's death, he tried spiritism. Today we would call it channeling. The spirit that addressed Carl Rogers spoke to him in the language of a non-directive therapist. It seemed the guru of unhooking the debilitating effect of the conscience was feeling a few pangs himself. He had an affair on the side and needed positive reinforcement (forgiveness, if you like) from his wife.

The spirit, claiming to be Ruth, his deceased wife, told Carl Rogers: "Enjoy, Carl, enjoy! Be free! Be free!" sounding like the permissive creed of Indian guru Rajneesh. When Carl Rogers wrote *A Way of Being*, he could say: "I now consider it possible that each of us is a continuing spiritual essence lasting over time, and occasionally incarnated in a human body" (p. 177). Psychology had just fused with the faith of its choice— Eastern mysticism. It would now be hard for this growing branch of psychology to be neutral to other faiths and traditions.

Transpersonal Psychology:
Bridge to the New Spirituality

Transpersonal psychology now includes studies of altered states of consciousness, mind-body healing, religious and mystical experience, spiritual growth teachings and practices, shamanism, meditation, pre- and perinatal experiences, studies of dying and near-death-experiences, as well as the various forms of experiential psychotherapy and psychospiritual transformation."

Transpersonal psychology, or "fourth force" psychology, has even branched into ecology. Recent book, *Toward a Transpersonal Ecology* by Warwick Fox (NY, State University of New York Press, August 1995), attempts to synthesize deep ecology and transpersonal psychology into a "new paradigm."

In the early '80s, large gatherings of transpersonal psychologists, representing the wave of the future, met in major cities across the United States. Harvard-trained psychologist Dr. William Kirk Kilpatrick attended the Fifth International Conference of Transpersonal Psychology. He left quite concerned.

In his book *The Emperor's New Clothes*, Dr. Kilpatrick wrote about the

conference in a brilliant essay entitled "The Brahmin in the Bahamas,'
Speaking of transpersonal psychologists, Kilpatrick described a group who
used the respectability of science to wear the ochre robes of the priesthood
of a new mystery religion.

At the Fifth International Conference of Transpersonal Psychology,
famed Indian guru Swami Muktananda, (whom I had met earlier in India),
graced the convention as the *guest of honor*. He was one of India's most
famous gurus, a "Shakti-pat" and *kriya* power yogi who claimed to be fully
self-actualized into God-consciousness. He had attained what Maslow the-
orized was at the highest mode of
consciousness—full enlightenment.
Muktananda was the living example,
the proof of cosmic consciousness,
that these Western psychologists
celebrated. Psychologists could
touch him and hear him
(Muktananda was also the former
guru of such New Age teachers as
Werner Erhard).

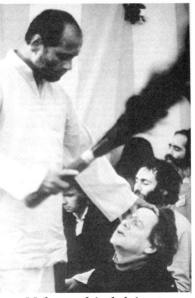

At the conference were cowbells
from India, pamphlets from a
Tibetan monastery, polarity charts
on the wall, mantra meditation
beads for sale, and so on. The theme
of the annual conference was "The
Nature of Reality." Reincarnation
was taken for granted. Past-life recall   **Muktananda's shakti-pat**
through regressive hypnosis was a hot
topic. One's problems could be explained by a radical new viewpoint: problems today stemmed from events in former lives. Twentieth-century psychologists were learning how to unearth this esoteric information from past
lives by regressive hypnosis.

Transpersonal psychologists were now a legitimate branch of the
American Psychological Association and by far their fastest-growing
branch. At their fifth annual conference you could attend such seminars as:
"Shamanic and Spiritist Modes of Healing," "The Tibetan Image of
Reality," "Ancient Indian Concepts of Sex and Love," "Siddha Meditation,"
"Living Tao," "Archetypal Stages of the Great Round," "Evolution of a
Yogi Trip to Awareness," "Kundalini Awakening and Spiritual Emergency,"

and "Aikido as a Spiritual Discipline."

William Kilpatrick was reading a book entitled *Profound Simplicity*. The psychologist who wrote the book had his following theories explored at the conference.

There are no accidents.
Events occur because we choose them to occur.
Every death is a suicide.
A rape "victim" is choosing to be raped.

In other words, social minorities are oppressed only if they allow themselves to be put in a position they call oppression.

One of the psychologists at the conference commented to Kilpatrick that *Profound Simplicity* was a great book. He, too, was in the business of past-life therapy. Kilpatrick was not so sure. He relates: "I asked if he thought there was anything of value in the Western tradition or in Christianity. 'Christianity,' he explained with an amused smile, 'makes people feel guilty; guilt is a crippling emotion.' The others at the table nodded assent, and the psychologist settled comfortably back in his chair. It was an open and shut case."[4]

To this enlightened crowd, reincarnation settled the problem of evil. By this new view, everyone gets what he deserves, what he wishes for. It's just that some people are not very good at wishing.

One psychologist observed to Kilpatrick: "You choose everything that happens to you, and you pretty much get what you deserve." He had learned this at an EST seminar. His wife, a social worker, then added that the same ideas were corroborated by the *Seth Journals* (Channeled by Jane Roberts).[5]

Kilpatrick, a Christian, was not impressed. He responded that this is the most guilt-provoking scheme he had ever heard. "You're telling a crippled girl, in effect, that she has no one to blame for her handicap but herself."[6] He might have also noted that she cannot even remember what she did in the first place—lifetimes back—to deserve such a condition. If you cannot remember what you did to deserve punishment, it is a wasted and cruel lesson. It is like punishing a dog a month after it chewed on the couch. It howls and cringes in ignorance. The dog's suffering is futile since it cannot connect what it did to deserve punishment, nor will it learn its intended lesson.

As one Indian critic of the East has observed, "Being a Hindu means never having to say you're sorry." It was a doctrine that left India's caste system unchanged for millennia in a land groaning under travail. Now India's philosophy had become the darling of Third and Fourth Force psychology. To quote "The Brahmin in the Bahamas" about the crippled girl, "She's only getting what she deserves."[7]

Freud, who had declared God irrelevant, was now as dead as a fossil to these transpersonal psychologists. Jung, Freud's rival, was now the favored figurehead of psychology. The search for the self had led the way to the overself, the *Atma/Paramatma* of Hinduism. Alan Watt's *The Supreme Identity* had anticipated this fusion.

There were now examples of psychologists who have become *holy men.* One of them is Ram Dass, the former Doctor Richard Alpert, Harvard psychologist, who had gone to India and found his guru and then renamed himself Ram Dass (Indeed, he visited me in South India when on tour with

Muktananda. At that time Ram Dass and I introduced our gurus to each another). He has been one of many change agents of our era—brilliant, seductive, convincing.

Transpersonal psychology has embraced the New Age views stated earlier in this chapter: *That if the self is God, then once it is unleashed, it can control real-ity. The more minds that awaken and tap*

Ram Dass & Tal Brooke in India

this reality, the faster the planetary change will occur. At a certain critical mass, the process will become a millennial explosion. A critical threshold of collective human minds that have been "awakened"—working in synchronicity—will attempt to transform the world in the twinkling of an eye. Consciousness is the hidden messiah, according to this view, while psychology has become as the science of consciousness and the mystery school of the new wisdom.

9

Wiring the Earth

technology has entered the town square of history that is already shaping the future as it digitally connects the world through a unique man-machine interface. This vast, formless machine has been wrapping itself around the earth like a "virtual glove" for the past 20 years—with satellites, cables and computers. Like the human nervous system, much of it lies underground, or hidden in the flesh of the earth.

Now and then inventions come along powerful enough to thrust history from one age to another. Such inventions have changed the world from the moment they entered the town square of history, towering above their own age. Such was the case with the Gutenburg press and the steam engine. And such is the case with digital technology spanning computers, satellites, cyberspace and many other areas.

With no doubt, this recent technology is a driving force of globalism, literally shrinking the earth with each fiber and impulse as it glues countries, communities and individuals together, making geographical distances of no effect. It is often invisible, yet it is huge. We are entering the digital age.

The potential for digital technology to alter the course of history could equal the Gutenburg printing press when it stormed the world in the early fifteenth century. At the time, this crude press opened an unprecedented information gateway into the heart of the Medieval world, thrusting history from the Dark Ages to the Renaissance. For centuries the vast cross-section of people had lived in the darkness of the Middle Ages. Serfs and artisans who were illiterate and ignorant suddenly had access to knowledge and information that was never before available. This single invention changed the social orders once dominant feudalism faded with the Renaissance.

"Cyberspace," coined by William Gibson in *Neuromancer*, a cyberpunk classic, is a computer generated landscape that characters enter by "jacking in"—and what they see when they get there is a three-dimensional representation of all the information stored in "every computer in the human system," great warehouses and skyscrapers of data.

Cyberspace is described as a place of "unthinkable complexity," with "lines of light ranged in the nonspace of the mind, clusters and constellations of data. Like city lights, receding." Gibson's description of cyberspace parallels deeper occult themes of cosmic storehouses of knowledge (from Edgar Cayce's psychic revelations of the source of his knowledge in the "Akashic Records," to tales of Atlantis with its massive libraries, to occult bestselling accounts such as *Saved By the Light* by Dannion Brinkley reporting "near death" journeys to cities of light with beings of light and immense libraries containing the knowledge of the universe.).

Lines of Light

But this is real live globalism in our living rooms and dens. Consider that someone in a shack on a tea estate in the Nilgiri Hills of Madras State, South India can access the same ocean of information as a university student in Stockholm, Sweden. They can wander into libraries and corporate databases. They can talk to millions and millions around the world. This alone would have put an Aristotle, a DaVinci, or a Newton on their ears to see this power in full operation.

In the Spring of 1995, I traveled from Berkeley to Cambridge University, England, over a period of several days. Yet I made the same trip by cyberspace and entered the same library in seconds. The cyberspace visit to Cambridge cost pennies and was instantaneous.

When I journeyed to Cambridge in the real world, I had to fly from San Francisco to Heathrow then ride on trains, subways and cars. I parked behind the Cam river on the back side of Trinity College and wandered around the perimeter of Clare College to the library. Books could be held and retrieved, but it took a lot of time and money. In the early days, I travelled by modem at 28,000 bytes per second. By the summer of 2000, I could travel by cable at 200 times that speed! And fiber optic hasn't even been tapped yet.

Virtual Reality

A far greater interactive, indeed tactile, universe is emerging through cyberspace's most complex and exalted doorway—**virtual reality**—which will allow full immersion into a computer generated alternate reality. What the mind imagines, becomes reality in this electronic universe.

Town meetings could take place in 3-D cyberspace with levitating participants from around the world meeting in some electronic designer universe with any kind of backdrop conceivable. Perhaps Mount Olympus placed on a summit in Bora Bora with a purple sky. Gathering from cities ranging from New Delhi to Bonn, participants could assemble in a vast virtual plane like Hindu gods gathering on some *Bardo* plane.

Only in its infancy, limited forms of virtual reality have just begun to appear in video arcades, movies, and virtual entertainment theaters. The technological wonder of virtual reality has appeared just in the nick of time

to enter the next millennium. This computer generated marvel promises to fully duplicate the real world to such an extent that the human mind and senses will not know the difference. Its effects will surpass movies of today to the same degree that digital cinerama surpasses the turn-of-the century silent screen with its halting motion and grainy film. If virtual reality can provide a breathtaking array of life-like experiences—with no limitation on how surreal or exotic—this same electronic genie might also penetrate the mind in unforeseen ways.

Once that door opens, we can never retreat to the era before the door opened. That is the nature of such historical doorways, as Milton illustrated in *Paradise Lost*. Yet this is an electronic genie that requires an engine and plenty of power to drive it. We have seen it evolve in our own lifetime from the vacuum tube model of the '40s, to the 1950s when Nobel laureate William Shockley at Stanford invented the transistor. After that came the silicon microchip, and things have continued to accelerate exponentially since then.

If a single Power Macintosh G4 computer has more power than a hundred thousand
Univac computers of the mid-1940s, what
happens if millions of these G4's are connected? George Gilder gives the following example:

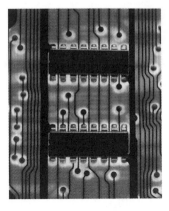

> The Emperor of China was totally infatuated
> with this new game of chess that had been
> invented for him. He was so grateful to the
> inventor that he came to him and said, "I'll
> give you anything you want in the kingdom
> as a tribute for this wonderful game you gave me."

> And the inventor said, "Well, I want one grain of rice. I want one grain of
> rice on the first square of the chess board, which has sixty- four squares,
> then I want two grains of rice on the second square. Four grains of rice
> on the third square, eight grains of rice on the fourth square and so on."

> In other words, this is an exponential process.

> And the Emperor happily granted this apparently modest request, and
> everything went fine for the first thirty-two squares. He could produce
> the several billion grains of rice fairly well on a quarter square mile of rice
> fields. But after the first thirty- two squares, things began to get interest-
> ing.

> There are two ways the story ends. One is, the Emperor went bankrupt
> because after sixty- four squares, this was several billion trillion grains of
> rice, which would take the entire surface of the earth, plus the oceans
> times two to produce. The other end of the story was that the inventor
> lost his head.

> . . . By 1993 there had been exactly thirty-two doublings of computer
> power since the first digital computers were invented in the early 1940s.[4]

The Darkening Future

George Orwell's literary classic *1984* introduced the concept of a two-way
television which looked back at the citizens. It was interactive and would
constantly monitor everything that happened in the private dwelling of each
and every citizen. Anyone whispering or conspiring, or who looked circum-
stantially guilty of "thought crimes," had only moments between the suspicious event "seen" by the TV and the arrival of State police in full force.

Orwell provided a perfect example of the dark side of techno-tyranny almost fifty years ago. And it is all lining up today more powerfully than what Orwell envisioned during his era of analog vacuum tubes.

Winston, the main character in *1984*, was utterly diminished by the two-way television overlooking his room. He was forced to duck around a slim section of wall out of its view to find his diary hidden behind a loose brick. Winston was permitted no solitude and had to scrounge for brief interludes of privacy. If he was out of view for more than a few seconds—one of his few remaining strands of liberty—the screen would bark at him. If this techno-eye of Big Brother was not satisfied with his response, he knew it could order storm troopers. It would begin with threats, such as when he refused to do his morning calisthenics. Winston was reduced to a number, a mere cog in the State machine. In the end, another monitoring device reported him to the central system, and he was sent to be brainwashed. Winston the individual was erased. There was no room for an independent mind in the collective State, which needed intrusive and interactive ways of monitoring its human fold behind every wall.

Such a device exists today. In fact, it resembles the two-way TV in *1984*. It is merely the Orwellian application that is lacking. For now, you can order pizza or tickets to a sporting event if you are in Europe. But there are ways, "for the good of the many," to bring in-house monitoring on a mass scale, for example, to keep intruders from breaking into your house. But then other crimes are "seen" as well. If the TV sees an "ecological" crime, such as pouring the pouring of solvent down a drain, in comes the State apparatus, not the police at first. Perhaps a fine is sent in the mail or debited from the offender's account. In time, more and more parameters of an individual's life come under observation—again, for the good of the collective.

Singapore has already embarked on that course. Today it could be described as a "benign techno-dictatorship." Singapore's proposed National Information Infrastructure (NII)—which aims to wire up every home by the year 2005 with optical fibers of almost unlimited carrying capacity—offers various attractive options from this new technology. Patients will be able to stay at home while linked to the hospital by a bedside terminal that monitors their progress and transmits the results. Dynamic road signs will automatically warn drivers of conditions ahead, and bus stops will display the expected arrival time of the next bus. The NII will also be used for watching sporting events around the world, for viewing the treasures of the Louvre or the Smithsonian Institution, for playing long-distance interactive computer games, or downloading video rentals.[6] Of course, it could be used to watch other things as well—its own citizens. The techno-eye can go both ways. And it has in Singapore.

In what the media call "another of Singapore's experiments in social engineering," taxis are soon to be monitored by satellite. Cablink, a company, will make sure that taxis work to maximum efficiency with minimum cruising time (If this works it can be extended to all automobiles, and why not?).

Already taxis are outfitted with alarms that go off when they exceed 50 miles per hour. Of real concern, however, is the thought that Singapore is trial-testing a system destined **Echelon Global Monitoring Network in England** for the industrial nations of the West during the promised era of the world order. Some social planners really do think that far ahead, as does Singapore's Oxford-educated leader.

Cyberspace right now is so "flexible" it can traverse from an "eye in the sky satellite" in space zooming down on someone lighting a cigarette on the Gobi desert, then showing this magnified life size, as though only feet away, on some large screen in Langley, Virginia (then printing their bio data on the screen), to offering heightened, unexplored, levels of entertainment and sensation. Jaron Lanier calls cyberspace the "LSD of the 1990s."

Recently, a company known as Digital Angel has manufactured an injectable microchip that can track any living thing that has it, man or beast,

via a network of global positioning satellites. Let's say that one day you get an innocent shot from the doctor, and little do you know that a new State mandate requires that the doctor include one of these miniature microchips in the serum. Whether you are in your car, walking a golf course, at your **Injectable microchip**

ATM, or crossing some border, your movements can be tracked within a range of a few feet.

Huxley's *Brave New World* portrayed a different type of techno-dictatorship than Orwell's. It was less austere and less blatantly cruel. It used the pleasure principle rather than punishment as the prime motivator of the docile masses. The citizens were manipulated through controlled economy and entertainment, "bread and circuses." If Singapore embodies the Orwellian approach as far as rules and punishment and disdain of the corrupting influence of the pleasure principle are concerned, the West could head, indeed is heading, in the Huxleyan direction, through permissiveness (a perverse redefinition of real freedom), pleasure, and guaranteed welfare.

Aldous Huxley described mass mind control in *Brave New World*. The public entered total immersion entertainment—"Talkie Feelies." Sitting vulnerable, they were socialized and did not even realize it. Huxley's technology is the same as what is now called Virtual Reality, the holy grail of cyberspace.

An Electronic Ganges

As Robert Wright of *Wired* Magazine observes of one cyber star: ". . . Barlow often cites Pierre Teilhard de Chardin, the Jesuit priest who envisioned the technological assembly of a planetary "noosphere," a global brain that would seal humanity's spiritual destiny: Point Omega. "Whether or not it represents Teilhard's vision," he has written, "it seems clear we are about some Great Work here—the physical wiring of collective human consciousness. The idea of connecting every mind to every other mind in full-duplex broadband is one which, for a hippy mystic like me, has clear theological implications."[7]

Cyberspace, by its very unitive structure, tends towards a kind of functional pantheism. Besides that, the reigning beliefs of cyberculture are postmodern, globalistic, and unitive. This electronic plane functions like a giant digital Ganges, unifying people, nations, thoughts, and concepts almost mystically.

India's great river is its living symbol of an ancient belief—Hindu, Pantheistic, Vedantist, Monist, Yogic and now New Age—that all things are

one and that all things return to the final source, the One, from which they
are said to come. The Ganges is India's natural symbol, its living metaphor,
of this process. For this ancient river is seen as the collector of lesser rivers
and tributaries, and the body into which all things flow and join. It becomes
in some ways the great repository of Indian civilization down the millennia.
Pantheism, by its very nature, finds unity at the lowest common denomina-
tor, at the base of existence. Unity, to the Eastern mystical mind, is the great
center of existence. But for those who see Hinduism up close (such as myself,
having once converted to it) this unity comes at a terrible price, for it is built
upon the oldest spiritual lie— that we shall be as God. The Ganges, upon
closer inspection, is able to unify, but only on a baser level.

To one pilgrim from the West, this unity at the bottom of the universe, is
also visually evident in the ebb and flow of the Ganges river, which he
describes with rare lucidity, echoing my exact impressions when I was spending weeks in Benares editing Avatar of Night for Vikas Publishing.

Molnar says of the timeless city of Benares (Varanasi):

> We reach the Ganges and take a boat ride. All the buildings we can see
> from the river are in various stages of dilapidation. The heat and the
> moisture have eaten into stone, brick, and plaster; everything is pock-
> marked, with that leprous aspect that overtakes even decently constructed
> buildings when, in tropical lands, nobody cares and everything decays.
>
> On the steps leading down to the river and on the stone landings are

masses of people. Pilgrims and locals doing their . . . well, what should one call it?—acts of private life. The dirty green river becomes bathroom, toilet, mouthwash, laundromat, drinking place for animal and man. Fully or half- immersed, people wash their hair, their underwear, rinse their mouths, and defecate, as the freely floating dung testifies. All this with the utmost matter of factness, without embarrassment. Our oarsman, sweating under the beating sun, leans over the side and slurps palmsful of water.

On this horrifying boat ride, I no longer know whether we are navigating the River Styx or gliding with Dante in a liquid hell. We come in sight of the funeral pyres. On the way to Benares we had passed trucks loaded with white wrapped bodies, corpses brought by families from distant villages. All day the pyres burn, and every three hours or so a white or red-clad, garlanded, cadaver is laid on top. There it burns for hours.

. . . What attracts and keeps them here is the degradation: of reason, of self esteem, of vital forces, of faith in God and man. Here they find innumerable gods and none at all; everybody may do his thing just like the monkeys and the cows, sinking slowly toward the Ganges or Nirvana. Intelligence and purposefulness dissolve on the trashheap, the body rots until it becomes one with the road, the grass, the dung. The great nothingness envelops all, and the ashes go into the river. —*Oh, Benares*, Thomas Molnar.

Cyberspace in some ways is a digital Ganges. It may create the appearance of unity, but only by centering around an expanse of darkness. Inevitably, a great part of its unity will come through the common ground among within the darkest regions of human manipulation, greed, ambition, and vanity—all in the lower depths of this electronic river. The digital incarnation of human godhood—still an illusion—will be achieved at the expense of the soul. This will be especially ironic if there is a ghost in the machine, a malevolent supernatural presence even older than the Ganges.

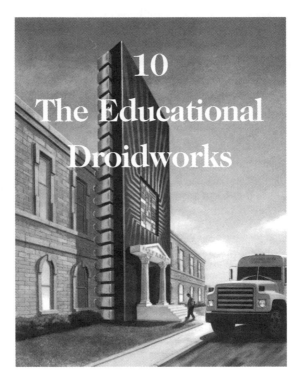

10
The Educational Droidworks

I t all starts very early in life for children in America—the assembly line of education—and is fast becoming a kind of droid works that manufactures future citizens. Opening the mind of a small child is almost as easy as stooping down and picking a ripe melon from a field. Bright eyed and trusting, these minds are there for the taking.

What is the crossover between learning and mind control? It depends on the degree you are fed truth or lies, whether your innate capacities are being expanded or contracted and whether your personality, your character, is being manipulated in the process. If education is used as a tool by an all powerful system, education will be subverted into a cookie cutter of the mind. Visionaries of totalitarianism early in this century, from Lenin to Gramsci (Clinton's ideological mentor), saw that the means to take over a nation could be achieved by slow indoctrination under the name of education. That is what has been happening. Consider the target.

The vulnerable young child sits in the schoolroom opening his eyes for the first time to a world that is totally strange and new. He is groping for the meaning to life, feeling the need to be rooted in something he can really trust. It is a desperate and primal need. He is a captive mind. Parental figures are automatic sources of trust in this quest for understanding. But most parents, at work all day and emotionally absent at night, have been taken out of the equation. Teachers, second in line among a child's trustworthy figures, can speak words of authority that sink deep into minds of these impressionable children. Their consciences can be sharpened or dulled. In just a few short years the worldview of these children will have formed—off by 180 degrees from what it was a century ago. If you stood two children side by side, separated by a century, you would wonder if they were from the same planet. What has caused this ferocious change?

Let's look at some recent examples of the classroom and see how education has "advanced" as these ripe melons are being picked. To illustrate education's "advancement" on February 25, 1998, the front page of the *San Francisco Chronicle* announced that after billions of dollars of funding and decades of programs, "In the most complete international study of schooling ever conducted, the U. S. high school seniors ranked near the bottom in math and science, reflecting what educators call a crisis in American education."[1] Even our advanced seniors were dead last in math, at #16 among the advanced nations, yet most "felt very good about themselves."

So what are they learning? Example: Eight-year-olds sit in class attentively after returning from a field trip to a cemetery. They must think about death. Now they are asked, "If your town was about to come under nuclear attack and there was only room for three members of your immediate family in the bomb shelter, which ones would you leave out and why?" A weighty decision for a formative mind. It is also one that delves into intimate family privacies as the kids explain why dad or mom should be left out to die in a nuclear attack. Deep feelings emerge. But that's okay. This course is based on the accumulated knowledge of decades of encounter sessions and T-groups at centers such as Esalen. The teacher's manual explains this fact with quiet authority. The teacher as therapist knows what to look for—that the kids will bond in the pain of disclosure and form a surrogate supra-family. They will learn that loyalty to "the group" is central in this new way of thinking. The teachers manual explains that "the Group is Alpha" while parents, authority figures, even a divine creator, "are not Alpha." One can only gather that "Alpha" will be important in a future world.

Nine-year-olds down the hall a grade above them face slightly more daunting questions in an exercise called "Who Shall Populate the Planet?"

The choices for populating the planet are a priest, a football player, a black minister, a micro- biologist, a preg- nant woman, and a teacher. Now they are told that only three will be allowed to live. Another life or death decision. One wonders who, to these  young minds, are the most expendable in making way for a new world.[2]

Succeeding generations of children emerge molded by a system that for all purposes is a State monopoly. By ten years of age, kids who would have been innocent in an earlier era, are jaded by comparison—they have heard extensively about homosexuality and lesbianism, they know about con- doms and AIDS. They also know they will be publicly excoriated if they "judge" these things. In 1992, William Kilpatrick wrote *Why Johnny Can't Tell Right from Wrong*, his sequel to *Why Johnny can't Read*. The results of a school system that is not allowing value judgments from a traditional moral perspective is seeing exploding rates of illegitimacy, abortion, vene- real disease (including AIDS), and violence.[3]

In his book *Schools without Failure*, Outcome Based Education's (OBE's) William Glasser wrote, "We have to let students know there are no right answers. . . ." OBE propagandist Theodore Sizer, in his {Five Lectures. . . on Moral Education says, "No longer can we list . . . objective moral 'truths' about the world and expect children to take them over intact."

Let's jump back a full century in time. In the *McGuffey's Reader* era of the 1800s, slovenliness, whispering in class, and lack of attention headed the list of high school delinquencies.

Now fast forward to the present, a hundred years later. The list of high school delinquencies in the 1990s include cocaine abuse in the school plus a host of other drugs, gang rape (bathrooms, empty classrooms, gyms), and killing or maiming teachers and fellow students.

McGuffey's era first grade classroom material was as innocent as snow. Compare that with first graders in hundreds of schools in Greater New York City who, by the late fall of 1992, were railroaded through an "anti-bias curriculum" that forced them to read books introducing them to the lifestyles of homosexuals and lesbians. Illustrated children's books resembling the old *Dick and Jane* series appeared with such titles as *Daddy's Roommate & Heather Has Two Mommies*. Daddy and his male lover roommate are portrayed smiling in bed together while little Johnny looks on in an "understanding" way.

These tender first graders cannot even read or do simple arithmetic, yet they are being forced to learn about things that are years ahead of their own sexual development. Incredibly, these young children are studying a form of behavior that their own nation declared a **criminal perversion** only a generation before.

Moral relativism has reaped a swift and bitter harvest—all within a few short years after our nation drove the last evidences of God from the classroom when the Supreme Court banned prayer. First graders cannot pray but they can read about perversion. It is the absolute opposite of the biblically based *McGuffey* era when kids could still blush and read about noble figures and heroes. Today's youth are being corrupted if not demonized.

Today's politically correct and multicultural views are forming the monolithic creed of our time—a creed that will brook no dissent. The oracular role of educators in most cases continues right through college. Even cynical and disinterested older students manage to absorb the latest approved worldview—political correctness has just arrived while evolution and "Big Bang" cosmogeny are old hat and have long been accepted as undisputed fact.

If the emergence of a *New World Order* requires a docile and passive public, there is no laboratory quite like the school room to invade the mind of a child whose views of reality are relentlessly shaped by the system. It continues from Kindergarten to twelfth grade. Strong individuals are weeded out and broken while peer-oriented leaders take the helm. All others—who have learned acceptance by peer-agreement and conformity—follow as members of a faceless conforming mass.

New Age leader John Dunphy made a telling observation in *The Humanist* magazine in its Jan./Feb. 1983 issue, in his award-winning essay entitled "A Religion for the New Age." Dunphy remarked:

> I am convinced that the battle for humankind's future must be waged and won in the public school classrooms by teachers who correctly per-

ceive their role as proselytizers of a new faith: a religion of humanity that recognizes and respects the spark of what theologians call the Divinity in every human being. These teachers must embody the same selfless dedication as the most rabid fundamentalist preachers.

The classroom must and will become an arena of conflict between the old and the new—the rotting corpse of Christianity, together with all its adjacent evils and misery, and the new faith. . . .

In *The Aquarian Conspiracy*, Marilyn Ferguson observed, "Even doctors, in their heyday as godlike paragons, have never wielded the authority of a single classroom teacher, who can purvey prizes, failure, love, humiliation and information to great numbers of relatively powerless, vulnerable young people."[4]

Ferguson's friend, Beverly Galyean, opened one of the earlier doorways for New Age penetration into the public school. Her program was called "Confluent Education." Galyean's beliefs were part of this classroom exercise:

Once we begin to see that we are all God, that we all have the attributes of God, then I think the whole purpose of human life is to reown the Godlikeness within us; the perfect love, the perfect wisdom, the perfect understanding, the perfect intelligence, and when we do that, we create back to that old, that essential oneness which is consciousness.[5]

Scores of children have been affected by Dr. Galyean's approach. Picture first graders being made to lie down on the floor of their classrooms while being told to relax and then visualize such "positive" things as the sun radiating within them. They picture the light of the sun filling their entire being. Then the teacher tells them: "You are inwardly perfect and contain all the wisdom of the universe within yourselves." First graders are introduced to spirit guides in the Galyean approach, although as she remarked at a plenary session at the conference entitled *Education in the '80s*, "Of course we don't call them that in the public schools. We call them imaginary guides."[6]

The Supreme Court bans prayer but has no particular interest in classroom "visualization" which is seen as a creative exercise of the imagination. Besides, positive affirmations such as, "You contain the wisdom of the universe," might elevate the pupil's self-esteem and relieve him of nagging fears that he might be an academic failure—even if he is. We did not arrive at this point in a simple swift *coup de academe*. There have been a series of steps, or waves, which have built on one another. Each wave has successively "softened up" the American psyche, and each in turn has prepared the way for the one to follow.

The First Wave

In the 1930s, the reality of influence in the schoolroom spurred John Dewey, the father of American progressive education, to write *My Pedagogic Creed*. In it, Dewey depicts public education as a massive behavior-shaping undertaking. Dewey knew that you could sway the beliefs of a whole generation in the classroom and thereby alter the course of a nation. While Roosevelt was introducing welfare programs, Dewey saw the public school system as an ideal platform to proselytize his radical socialistic views. Regardless of what the parents believed, it was only a matter of time before the successive generations took over. It was a quiet way to remake the culture.

Dewey

John Dewey was influenced by an insider group of intellectuals in England known as the Fabian Socialists. Dewey was an American ally of this clique. The Fabians had an agenda of gradualist global penetration by using education as a key tool of influence in this process.

Dewey, who remained close with Fabian leaders, had his own circle of academic disciples at Columbia University, especially Kilpatrick and Counts, who influenced textbooks and school curricula for decades. Through Dewey's influence, Harold Laski, right before becoming chairman of the British Fabian Society, lectured at Columbia Teacher's College for a semester in 1939, amidst John Dewey's best and brightest disciples.

What did all this mean for American public education? Columbia Teacher's College influenced other graduate schools and colleges of education. Before long, progressive education, the Dewey-designed tool for reshaping America, was a public school reality all across America.

Among the new views was a national self-criticism that spurned narrow patriotism for a broader globalism. At the same time traditional values, from parental authority to the validity of established religion, were to be questioned and ultimately dethroned.

Rather than equipping the child to handle the demanding academic and moral standards of the traditional order, with its *McGuffey Reader* and its implicit moral virtues, Dewey's progressive education considered behavior-shaping as its highest educational priority. "Socialization" was now defined as a type of learning at least equal to traditional learning. Now the old morals and ethics could be replaced by situational ethics or "values clarification." Reading, writing, and arithmetic took a back seat to experimental programs such as "sensitivity training." The virtues of hard work were replaced by permissive standards that would pass a failing child rather than harm his "self-esteem" by labeling him a "failure." Total equality was the new ideal; it would jealously guard against too much excellence in any child that might show others to be less endowed, thus implying that abilities were unevenly distributed.

Kirby Anderson of Probe Ministries states, "Today's students do not possess the basic information necessary to survive in our culture. They do not know the basic facts of history, government, or geography. A recent survey of 17 year olds revealed that a majority could not place the Civil War in the correct fifty year span, could not locate the state of New York on a map, and did not know what event brought the U. S. into World War II."

After decades of "advanced programs" concocted by "experts," the students of the 1990s would be shamed intellectually by their own predecessors from any previous decade in this century. They are functionally, culturally, and morally illiterate. The "experts" have spent more money per student than in any country in the world. We have students who cannot read the directions on the free condoms that they are given in school, but perhaps they can *"visualize"* non-fertility as they engage in "activities" sanctioned in sex education classes. Failing this, they can still resort to the next sex education option—abortion.

Two names keep appearing in this effort to change thoughts and feelings: Sidney Simon, the "expert" who introduced *values clarification,* and Lawrence Kohlberg, who introduced *moral reasoning.* Both programs annihilate traditional values. A handful of "experts," foist their views upon millions with impunity. They arrogantly become founts of wisdom—about the family, about sexuality, and about ultimate reality. In a sweep they can destroy the student's faith, beliefs, and moral system. Their ideas are omnipresent in today's classrooms—in stories, in class exercises, in discussions, from "who will live?" to "why can't Johnny and William get married?"

John Dewey's ideas did not just come out of a vacuum, but pursued the Fabian agenda of gradualist global penetration by using education as a tool of influence in this process.

Fabian Roots of the Educational Elite

The Bloomsbury Fabians of London were an elite intelligentsia of world socialists who envisioned an end to war and poverty by a united world order dedicated to the ideals of socialistic humanism. Their goal was to carefully plan a means to this end. Antonio Gramsci, the Italian Marxist, likewise taught that cultural penetration through the arts and education was a key means to changing society. Gramsci (President Clinton's ideological guru about whom he studied while at Oxford) fit more in the Fabian camp than Soviet style Marxists in planning for world change.

The Fabian Socialists formed within a year of the death of Karl Marx, who died in London. They were adherents of Marx and Darwin. Dewey was one of the

Antonio Gramsci

first of the elite in America to embrace their beliefs. He later signed *The Humanist Manifesto*. His meetings with key leaders of the British Fabian society allowed Dewey to incorporate their ideas of socialist penetration in their mutual educational agenda. The League for Industrial Democracy, of which Dewey was president in 1938-39, was one of America's cousins to the British Fabian Society.

Unlike Marxists, who advocated bloody revolution for world socialism, the Fabian Socialists of Britain advocated a more gradualist path to socialistic globalism. The plan of these early one-worlders was to use intellectual penetration, from the top of the pyramid down, into key areas of influence on society. Elite minds were to influence and change the social order. Their symbol was the slow-moving turtle which would pass the sleeping rabbit. Bertrand Russell referred to the Bloomsbury group as a mutual admiration society. But they penetrated one major field after another—literature, politics, education, science, and the media-and had some of the most renowned figures in the world.

English Fabians such as H.G. Wells, Rupert Brooke (one of my ancestral cousins), Aldous Huxley, George Bernard Shaw, G.M. Trevelyan, Lord Haldane, Arnold Toynbee, Sir Julian Huxley, Virginia Woolf, Arnold Bennett, Rebecca West, E.M. Forester, J.B. Priestly, and other similar

Beatrice and Sidney Webb

luminaries greatly influenced the public mind and the academy through literature, the theater, and the laboratory.

Oxford and Cambridge became central recruiting grounds. One recalls the Fabians at Cambridge University in the film *Chariots of Fire*, with their large banner next to the Gilbert and Sullivan Club. These days they don't need to hold their banners out; they are everywhere.

One of the most effective Fabians was famed Cambridge University economist John Maynard Keynes who turned Harvard on its ears when he came and charmed the students and faculty with his socialist economics. Keynes said that the state should guarantee welfare for all, that it should provide guaranteed employment

Keynes

through government programs, and that all of this could be financed by his revolutionary scheme.

How? By supreme Keynesian alchemy—the gold standard could be dropped for paper currency, then deficit spending through government loans would open up a money vault of endless supply. Indeed, it was a "New Deal," to use the Roosevelt expression—maybe too good a deal to be true.

Another Fabian to hit Harvard was Harold Laski, who with avowed socialist Lord Haldane, eventually started the London School of Economics. He later obtained an instructorship at Harvard in 1915 through invitation of Felix Frankfurter, Byrnes Professor of Law at the Harvard Law School. Frankfurter became Laski's closest friend. During the four years Harold Laski taught at Harvard, he edited the Harvard *Law Review*, inoculating the prestigious publication with socialist ideas. The Harvard Law School eventually adopted a socialist lean-

Laski

ing through its Fabian liaison. Justice Frankfurter of the U. S. Supreme Court, a member of the Harvard faculty, as well as his former pupil, Justice Louis Brandeis, also a Supreme Court judge, kept a line of communication going with their Fabian friends in England. This was important for the agenda of penetration.

Laski, for 25 years, remained an honored houseguest of Supreme Court Justice Frankfurter, especially when the latter was a member of Roosevelt's New Deal brain trust. By that era Harold Laski was chairman of the Fabian Society of Britain (from 1946 to 1948).

Employing Fabian gradualism, one of the most long-range and penetrating legal statements that Justice Frankfurter ever made was that *"through the use of due process, the justices could read their own economic and social views into the neutral language of the Constitution.*"[7] This statement has spelled out the very agenda adopted by lawyers in dismantling the U. S. Constitution. This Trojan horse rolled through the Fabian doorway right into the U.S. Supreme Court and has affected legal decisions across America.

Meanwhile, the far-ranging effects of the Bloomsbury group is seen in England today after its decades of socialist penetration. The Fabians started England's influential labor party and never looked back. Edwardian

Justice Frankfurter

England and the era of the aristocracy was to be no more. A more plebian England has replaced it, though it has used those from the intellectual aristocracy to bring this about. The glamour of the left remains a compelling mystery as it seduces bright and ambitious university youth, artists, and assorted aspiring intellectuals.

The New Age Wave

By the mid-1980s, New Age and occult thought was flooding the nation's classrooms including, how to do horoscopes, conduct seances, cast the witch's circle, use a Ouija board, meditate, and role-play such characters as warlocks and spiritists which appeared in required readings. Wiccans (witches) and Neo-pagans were invited on public school premises to speak about their alternate views (they do not use the word "religions"). Witches could now enter where ministers were forbidden to tread, a new milestone in America's "liberation."

Well-known New Age educator Jack Canfield—who is currently the author/editor of the 1990s *New York Times* bestselling "Mind-Body" books, *Chicken Soup for the Soul,*(NY: Health Communications, Inc. May, 1993), *Chicken Soup for the Christian Soul: 101 Stories to Open the Heart & Rekindle the Spirit* (August, 1997), *Chicken Soup for the Woman's Soul: 101 Stories to Open the Hearts & Rekindle the Spirits of Women* (October 1996)— wrote an article for *The New Age Journal,* (with Ann Klimek), entitled "Education in the New Age," which essentially spelled out the New Age agenda for penetrating and using the public school system across the United States. *The New Age Journal* stated, "They consult with schools, train teachers, and have co-authored numerous books such as, *The Inner Classroom: Teaching with Guided Fantasy*, and *Wholistic Education*." It was all happening with the invisible stealth of *Invasion of the Body Snatchers*.

A consortium of parents described it, "In the name of discovering their 'life purpose,' children are encouraged into trance-like states of mind where they communicate with 'guardian spirits.' The use of Yoga exercises and mind control techniques are other examples of the format of this program."[8]

Canfield admitted that "more and more teachers are exposing children to ways of contacting their inner wisdom and higher selves."[9]

Canfield, indeed, has devised a tactical manual on New Age incursion:

> Within the past five years we have also witnessed the birth of "transpersonal education," the acknowledgment of one's inner and spiritual dimensions, through working with such forms as dreams, meditation, guided imagery, biofeedback, centering, mandalas, and so forth. Now is the time to combine both of these focuses, for the New Age means integrating the soul and personality. . . . Holistic education . . . views the student as being engaged in an integral process of unfoldment under the direction of his/her higher self. This process is perceived as taking place in a universe that is also constantly evolving: each of us is seen as an important part of the larger planetary and universal evolution of consciousness.[10]

Intimacy games are described in which children get over inhibitions against touching one another. Then words are redefined. "Centering" becomes the more acceptable word for meditation. "Relaxation and centering exercises are a fundamental process for New Age education, because they provide a space for listening to the voice within."[11]

Canfield tosses out model questions for teachers:"What's this thing called The Force in Star Wars? How does Luke communicate with it? How does it help him?" The next question is, "Well, would you like to have this kind of experience?"[12] Canfield then addresses guided imagery:

> . . . We believe that guided imagery is a key to finding out what is in the consciousness of New Age children. . . . Children are so close to spirit if we only allow room for their process to emerge. . . Additional emphases in the transpersonal dimension are using nature as teacher, and aligning and communicating with the other kingdoms such as the elemental and devic realms (The term Devic is a Sanskrit word for the realm of the gods.). . . working with children's psychic capacities (such as seeing auras); working with astrological charts. . . . The souls that are presently incarnating seem to be very special.[13]

Canfield and Klimek's article, "Education in the New Age" ends with the admonition: "The only requirement is to provide a space and an environment where these beautiful young spirits can open up and allow their wisdom to be seen."[14] And that "space," that "environment," has been expanding through the 1980s and into the 1990s.

Gender Bending

In the late summer of 1997, the school board in Provincetown, Massachussetts, voted to begin educating preschoolers about homosexual lifestyles while hiring "sexual minorities." Local homosexual activist John Perry Ryan explained that the plan is to end the "dominance" of the perspective of the "white Europeans. . . who are also very heterosexual, very Christian, very male." [15]

The stated goal is to equip "students, teachers and the community at large with the tools needed to combat racism, sexism, ableism, classism, heterosexism and homophobia and all forms of oppression. . . ." [16]

The nation's public school teachers at the NEA (National Education Association) pass resolutions every year at the annual convention. In 1996, one of its resolutions stated, "Funds must be provided for programs to alleviate race, gender and sexual orientation discrimination and to eliminate portrayal of race, gender and sexual orientation stereotypes in the public schools." (Resolution A-13, 1996). At the NEA's 1996 convention, over one-third of the delegates sported "NEA - GLC" (Gay Lesbian Caucus) buttons.[17]

A decade earlier, in 1984, the U. S. Department of Education conducted hearings to gauge public opinion and propose regulations regarding the implementation of "The Protection of Pupil Rights Amendment" otherwise known as the Hatch Amendment. Testimonials revealed a new agenda was well under way in countless schools. One witness displayed a blue-print for our educational future, produced with support from the National Institute of Education. It was entitled *Future Studies in the Kindergarten Through Twelve Curriculum* by John D. Haas, and it recommended that teachers subtly introduce such subjects as fertility control, abortion, family planning, women's liberation, euthanasia, New Age consciousness, mysticism, new religions, changing older religions, guaranteed income, and so on. These issues had become hot stuff in many classrooms anyway. Haas wanted to expedite the process of preparing children for the new order. Gender bending kept coming up.

There was a time when Johnny was happy to be a boy and Susan was happy to be a girl. Now the kids, with the help of the experts, believe in the new myth of androgyny. A case in point is the Title IX-funded Sex Equity Program, or the Women's Educational Equity Act Program tested in five counties across the United States. The plan is to change the thinking patterns of America's children, starting with the youth in these five counties who have acted as guinea pigs for the greater national experiment. What happens in classrooms under this program?

The naked dolls experiment—On March 13, 1984, in Seattle, Washington, at the official proceedings before the U. S. Department of Education, one witness described the Sex Equity field experiment in Lincoln County, Oregon:

> One of the demonstrations was in a 1st grade room. The students each had two naked paper dolls, one male, the other female. They were asked to dress the dolls in work clothing to show that both genders could work at any job. The thing I found interesting was there were no dresses. All clothing was male oriented. Then the teacher had the students sit in a circle while she pulled out objects from a sack, like a pancake turner or a tape measure. She asked, "Who uses this, mom or dad?"
>
> If the student did not answer the way she had wanted, she would say, "Well, who else uses this?" Finally, one little boy raised his hand and said, "I don't care. Men ought to be doctors, and ladies nurses."
>
> The teacher then asked how many students agreed with the little boy. By the tone of her voice, they knew no one should raise a hand, so no one did. The little boy was so humiliated by the peer pressure and class manipulation by the teacher that he started to cry. This is classic of the type of discrimination, bias, stereotyping, and harassment that this program has included.
>
> As I reviewed different manuals that teachers were using in the schools . . . questions on family values, self analysis, opposite role-playing, unisex

ideas, discussion of family roles in students' homes, and sex-role values were discussed. One book said, "Students are no longer to be called helpers, or boys and girls, or students, but *workers*" (a part of the Socialist lexicon).

Another book showed only pictures of opposites to traditional roles, such as the father feeding baby, or mother holding a fire hose in her "fireperson" job. The children didn't realize they were being fed only one side of the picture. . . . Our school district received federal funds to teach "Sex Equity." . . . The teaching is firmly intact in the system after five years of funding. Teachers are required to attend sex equity workshops sponsored by Northwest Regional Laboratory in Portland, which received federal funds. They provide resource material and teachers.

I discovered there was no set curriculum. Teachers chose what to teach from several manuals. They were to integrate the teaching into the entire day's classes. Women were really exalted in all the material I viewed, while male minorities were almost ignored. The goal of the Sex Equity program was to eliminate traditional roles of male and female.

Clearly this is a cloaked and underhanded behavior-shaping program that uses the classroom as a laboratory under the cover of education. Dr. Benjamin Bloom, the father of mastery learning, in his recent book, *All Our Children Learning*, agrees that "The purpose of education is to change the thoughts, feelings, and actions of students."

The San Francisco Chronicle on March 16, 1988, in an article by Adrian Peracchio described an outrage in Britain: "It began last year with parents' howls of outrage at the publication by local municipal councils of *Jenny Lives with Eric and Martin*, a graphically illustrated pamphlet showing a cherubic little girl smiling at her father, naked in bed with his live-in gay lover."

The *Chronicle* then reported: "The pamphlet, printed with British government funds, attempted to prove that young children brought up by homosexual couples could adjust and thrive just as well as those reared in more traditional households."

The above book appeared in local school libraries alongside, *How to Be a Happy Homosexual*, and *The Children's Playbook of Sex*, two other publicly financed pamphlets in which homosexual themes were explicitly treated. Britain clearly leads America in the official promotion of "alternative lifestyles." But we may be catching up.

On January 21, 1992, CNN headline news had a short feature on the latest breakthroughs in the public school classroom. Elementary school children were nervously trying to elude the camera. They looked ashamed. They had just seen a movie that would easily qualify as pornography. The teacher proudly barked her disclaimers into the camera, "No, this is not sex ed, the kids are having their AIDS awareness heightened." These young kids had just seen a film of full-on genitalia with a condom being donned. What was illegal in the '50s in porno houses was now sanctioned in public elementary schools. And more is on the way.

Homosexual groups have been campaigning militantly to have "gay" sexuality graphically shown in this quest for "AIDS awareness." Perhaps in a few years, elementary school kids will see movies of sodomy. NAMBLA, the North American Man/Boy Love Association, also appeared on CNN angrily picketing a major network for legitimate recognition and the legalization of pedophilia. Speechless mothers were protesting in shock that this was actually happening. Homosexual groups are pushing hard for homosexual teachers quotas and "gay awareness."

The fevered rage that comes out of the closet and exposes the homosexual mindset and its agenda is shockingly portrayed in an essay by "gay revolutionary" Mark Swift and printed in the Feb. 15, '87 issue of *Gay Community News*. The following excerpts also appeared in the Congressional Record:[18]

> We shall sodomize your sons. . . We shall seduce them in your schools, in your dormitories, in your gymnasiums, in your locker rooms. . . in your youth groups. . . . Your sons shall become our minions and do our bidding. . . . They will come to crave and adore us. All laws banning homosexual activity will be revoked. Instead, legislation shall be passed which engenders love between men. Our writers and artists will make love between men fashionable. . . . We shall raise vast, private armies. . . to

defeat you. The family unit. . . will be abolished. Perfect boys will be conceived and grown in the genetic laboratory. . . . All churches who condemn us will be closed. Our only gods are handsome young men. All males who insist on remaining stupidly heterosexual will be tried in homosexual courts of justice and will become invisible men. Tremble, hetero-swine, when we appear before you without our masks.

The Last Wave Before World Order

The droidworks of the 1990s, the educational "environment," has continued to experiment with wild and audacious programs that push the envelope of radical change. Educators look closely to see which ones escape scrutiny and public outrage. These programs have been blanketing the nation since the late '80s with names like SOAR, QUEST, PAT, PAIDEIA, MEOLOGY, DECIDE, DARE, THE NEW MODEL ME. By the mid-1990s, OUTCOME BASED EDUCATION (OBE) and GOALS 2000 took over as the very latest, sleekest, and most high powered educational programs.

Hillary Rodham Clinton maintains, "It takes a village" to raise a child— from the name of her 1997 book—"village" in this instance refers to the state. At one point she writes, "We cannot move forward by looking to the past for easy solutions." "Extremists" who insist on clinging to the Founders' vision, according to Mrs. Clinton, "fail to provide a viable pathway from the cold war to the global village."[19] Keep in mind, the goal is the global village (New World Order).

The Nation's Alexander Cockburn, an English expatriate whose childhood acquaintances included members of the Fabian Society's social circle, comments, "Time and again, reading … *It Takes a Village*, I was reminded of [Fabian cofounder] Beatrice Webb," observes Cockburn. "There's the same imperious gleam, the same lust to improve the human condition until it conforms to the wretchedly constricted vision of freedom that gave us social-worker liberalism, otherwise known as therapeutic policing." [20]

Goals 2000 opens the way for an unprecedented level of social engineering along the line of Hilary Clinton's book (actually Simon and Schuster announced in April 1995 that Georgetown journalism professor Barbara Feinman would write the manuscript of the book based on audiotapes of interviews with Mrs. Clinton).

The Goals 2000: Educate America Act (P.L . 103-227) was signed into law on March 31, 1994, by Bill Clinton. United States Representative Henry Hyde (R-IL) wrote to his colleagues in Congress of the grave implications this program has for the country. "The plan for Goals 2000 was developed by Bill Clinton, Hillary Clinton, Ira Magaziner and Marc Tucker, president of the National Center on Education and the Economy [NCEE], prior to Clinton's election. It is a concept for dumbing-down our schools and changing the character of the nation through behavior modification. It is also an end run around individual state control of public schools, putting it under the federal government.

Congressman Mel Hancock (R-MO) outed this blatant plan, reversing a prior decision to support it. "After taking a closer look at Goals 2000, it is obvious. . . that the National Education Association, in cooperation with the socialistic segments of our government, are attempting to implement the Marxist theories of reeducating a society as part of a potential overthrow of our constitutional government—as advocated by Karl Marx and Joseph Stalin. Even though I originally voted for the bill, I am withdrawing my support and will do everything possible. . . to rescind Goals 2000."

Marxist theories?

Eugene Maxwell Boyce stated in his 1983 study, *The Coming Revolution in Education*: "In the communist ideology the function of universal education is clear and easily understood. Universal education fits neatly into the authoritarian state. Education is tied directly to jobs—control of the job being the critical control point in an authoritarian state."[21]

As one warning page, "The Winds," admonishes on the Internet, "The real object of Goals 2000 envisions the transformation of society as a whole. Jobs and career are tied into a womb to tomb progression. It is designed to lead into a world order where the global economy is managed at a central level. This is all leading to a world school system where standardized workers are harvested from the world labor pool. Goals 2000 is in the business of creating "products" who have no allegiance to Christian ethics, parents or country, but are simply being created to fuel the world economy."[22]

We can only conclude that the experts anticipate with great enthusiasm a racially and culturally amalgamated world. We gather it will be a tightly governed world with the capacity to observe its citizens quite closely, making privacy a luxury of the past. It will be a world with quota systems where "equality" is rigidly enforced. Knowledge and ability will be most rare indeed. More important in this future world will be one's attitude, the right kind of attitude, to repeat, a docile and passive acceptance.

Future citizens may some day be instructed by the planners to finally free themselves from the past. Perhaps it will be time for all the books of the past in all the vast libraries of the earth, "with racism, sexism and other thought crimes," to be tossed in the bonfire of history in a global book burning.

The United Nations might declare this future day of liberation "book liberation day" as bonfires light up the skys of the world. Obedient world servers here and there will struggle to read the words on the covers as they playfully toss the outdated works into the fire. A title or name will pass by. Those sounding out the titles and authors phonetically may feel the last traces of reading knowledge that is soon to be obsolete.

The classic novel **1984** is grabbed from a stack of books with the name George. . . . The second name sounds like "Oh Well." The name has a freeing sensation—"Oh Well." "George . . . Oh Well" whose book **1984** shows how out of date it is right on the cover. "Oh Well" is chanted around the bonfire as others see the outdated book eaten up by the flames. And America ends not with a bang, but a whimper, after decades of "education," which made straight the path for a New World Order while making simple and pliable the people, that they might become "world servants."

11

Dress Rehearsal for a New Age Christ

We have seen one front after another penetrated by the wheels of influence of the New World mentality: books, movies, television, psychology, education, the corporate world, political platforms, and so on. The rapid changing of the guard from the old world to the new has been remarkable. The march ahead has almost been unimpeded . . . almost. But there are a few obstacles left and they represent considerable barriers, in some cases fortresses. As we will see, the traditional family is one of them, traditional gender roles another. But the greatest barrier of all is the unyielding stand of genuine Christianity that cannot and will not accommodate itself just to have a kind of spiritual

An "appearance" of Maitreya

detente. It cannot be syncretized into the new temple that is being built by New World visionaries who want to show, as John Lennon stated in his last interview, that "Christ, Mohammed, Krishna, the Imam Mahdi, Maitreya are all equal and represent God equally in different ways. We don't say one is more important than the other." Lennon perfectly captured this emerging viewpoint when he said this—and so has Joseph Campbell on his much-televised "Bill Moyers Special" on mythology. But the unadulterated Christian faith will not yield to this multi-faith juggernaut. It stands exclusive and alone, and as such it is a supreme obstacle for the simple reason that the reigning view of the old order of Western civilization is Christian-based.

As an obstacle it must be remade into a new form or utterly destroyed. Either a New Age Christ must be created, lifted out of the confines of history, or the memory of this faith must somehow be expunged from the record books of history. It is a double-flanked approach, and it is going on: 1) Create a New Age Christ and 2) In a propaganda campaign, caricature the historical faith and Christians, making them supremely unpopular, irrelevant, and out-of-touch.

Something has to be done with Christ and Christianity. It's that simple. No matter what, this reality cannot be ignored. Christ is seen as either an impediment or a doorway. It is surprising how many groups have an obsessive preoccupation with Christ and with hammering him into place. It seems they feel a need to have his sanction, as though their consciences cannot rest until they have somehow included him into their beliefs.

But these same groups insist on taking Christ to the make-up artists and tampering with his attire. What they need is a broad-minded, nonjudgmental, cosmic Christ. Somehow he must be unearthed from history or rediscovered; a Christ who sanctions all paths as leading to God, who is not exclusive or judgmental, who, in fact teaches the ancient mystery religions of the divine within; that spark of divinity within all men waiting to be awakened.

This cosmic Christ is to be one facet of the capstone atop the massive pyramid now being built. It must be a Christ who will syncretize with Buddha, Krishna, the Imam Mahdi, and perhaps some future Jewish Messiah. This Christ will be seen as a type of the new man, a perfect master among other perfect masters, who is leading the way for the whole human race to enter into the secrets of enlightenment. He is an exemplar at the head of the pack.

But certain things need to be done to bring about this Cosmic Christ. Hidden writings must be discovered after having been buried for 2000 years, revealing a different Christ from the powerful figure in the New Testament. Channelers and psychics must communicate with this Cosmic Christ to the world-at-large and divulge his new teachings because the world is now "evolved enough to handle the deeper teachings." A few must encounter a being-of-light in near-death experiences who claims to be

Christ and who bears this universal creed of spiritual evolution.

There must also be new systems of interpretation for going into the New Testament and ferreting out this mystery-Christ. New meanings must be given to ancient phrases and words. For instance, when Christ told Nicodemus, "You must be born again," the new, hidden understanding is that He was speaking of reincarnation, and so on. But only certain "advanced" teachers—a closed union of mystics who will appear before the world, as they did during the ancient era of the Gnostics and mystery religions—will be able to interpret and reveal these hidden meanings.

The new teachers will announce, as some already have, that these higher teachings have been hidden and suppressed by the church—that they were quashed at the ancient councils, such as Nicea and Constantinople. The new teachers will claim that the church was engaged in a cover-up operation of obscuring the very "mystery-Christianity" which would have so perfectly fit like a piece to a puzzle to the other world religions, especially Buddhism and Hinduism, and that this suppressed "mystery-Christianity" would have helped to provide the groundwork for a universal faith based on the universal nature of God, the brotherhood of man, and the divine basis for all life. These teachers will show that, instead, the historic church has become a divisive obstacle that is not tolerant of all paths. It obstructs the smooth flow of this effort at world unity.

But now it is time for a universal creed. Planetary needs demand it. A universal, non-offensive creed will be a major element in providing so that the world might be one. It *must* be brought about, and *anything* divisive must be permanently quashed. Christ is to be rediscovered as the avatar, gnostic redeemer, incarnation of the godhead, and mystery figure who fits the pages of the world creeds. For historical accuracy, it must be observed that this mystery Christ is far from the Jesus who hurled accusations at the Sanhedrin, overturned the tables of the money changers, and bodily rose from the dead. The mystery *Christos* is light-years removed from Jesus Christ who was born in Bethlehem, healed lepers, spoke pointedly about sin and moral condemnation, fed thousands miraculously, and claimed to be the unique son  of God, without peer, who existed before time began, and who foretold his return to judge the world. The mystery-Christ is a different Christ altogether from the New Testament Christ, and he emerges from countless peripheral sources—except from the canon of the New Testament. From this sealed canon he cannot emerge, for the early manuscripts and autographs don't breathe a word about this other cosmic Christ.

This presents a problem which must be addressed. It must be dealt with from all sides in a pincer movement, logistically and strategically. It is a little like the problem of the Marxist who wishes to change the common understanding of the United States Constitution so that a gradualist skewing of word meaning can enable a socialistic interpretation of words whose intended meanings in the original were clearly different. He must deal with language manipulatively.

On one level, it is a problem of hermeneutics and exegesis. In the case of the Bible, if you can editorially cancel out certain words and phrases, or invent new contexts surrounding statements, you can skew the entire meaning of a major passage. Literal realities can be conveniently thrust into a symbolical context. Paul Tillich did this all the time. Then you can look for "Jungian" meanings behind ordinary events as these moments in history are doubted and now ascribed to being symbolic. Academic criticism provides this mode of attack. You begin by absolute doubt. You doubt the books and parchments; you doubt the writers and their motives. You throw it all away and defy the canon to prove itself to you first. Dates are doubted, methods of copying are doubted, and so on. And indeed here we have the German and continental schools of biblical criticism: redactive, historical, and form criticisms. Academic criticism turns out to be a most effective means of frontal assault on the historic Christian faith. It is one way to get Christ to the make-up artist and extract his prophetic and judgmental aspects that so grate against the modern tempo.

Today, divinity schools, graduate departments of religion, and seminaries have taken the cue from the academic posture of doubt and used this as a way to reshape Christ to fit current fashion with a tolerant, leftward-leaning, socially conscious, inclusive Christ. Once conformity-minded students take the cue that this is the only acceptable position among their fellow students and academic peers, it is a rare individual who will dare to step out of line. As someone has said, they have come up with an emasculated Christ.

This Christ of academia is such a conciliator that he loses ground at every strategy meeting in which he is discussed. These days he is a champion of the lesbian/gay caucus and radical feminists. He is even pro-sodomy as long as it is "responsible," "caring," and "safe" among "persons of alternate sexual preferences." This pallid invention of the academy is ready to fall right into line with the mystery-Christ of the New Age. It is a rare faculty member who will risk tenure to stand against this wave. Each faculty member—these doctors of knowledge—can grin knowingly as they add the emperor's new clothes to their already considerable collection of vestments and tassels. They can still walk in ponderous academic lines with furrowed brows, borrowing from their lineage of intellectual profundity, while passing on the mantle to those whom they choose. Individuals, especially brilliant "individualists," who differ with their agenda are instantly marked for opposition. By conformity in the academy, Christ has been remade in a few generations. This is a remarkable pincer movement, indeed, one of ponderous faces and furrowed brows, ambition, peer pressure, personal agendas in some and moral cowardice in others.

But there is an equally effective pincer movement composed of dizzyingly optimistic faces. These are the ones in touch with the cosmic Christ, and the messages that are coming in are compelling. Hundreds of thousands who attend New Age conferences and millions reading New Age books are feeling "confirmed" by these messages. Enter the cosmic Christ.

The Cosmic Christ

Though Edgar Cayce died in 1945, the books concerning this famous channeler still flood bookstores. They are top sellers among Bantam's New

Age paperback series. Cayce spent years going into trances in which he claimed to gain access to the hall of records of the cosmic mind—better known as the Akashic records. He had the look and bearing of a simple Bible Belt Christian. His demeanor of kindly innocence made him believable. For years all he did was diagnose physical illnesses in this trance state. Even if the subject were halfway across America, the impersonal "we" voice would almost always accurately diagnose the problem of a subject whom he had never met,

Edgar Cayce

giving the method of cure. One day a wealthy Jewish theosophist in the Midwest paid for his trance time, but then started asking the Akashic mind questions concerning the nature of ultimate reality. The startling revelations that came through confused and even frightened Edgar Cayce. When he woke out of a trance he never remembered anything, nor had he "met" the "voice" that worked through his body, using it as a medium. When this ground-breaking channeler heard what he had said in his first non medical reading, he was almost undone, for he was revealing a cosmos identical to that of the theosophists, mystics, and Hindus.

The loving personal God whom Edgar Cayce had read about in the Bible as a child turned out to be a "myth of the dualistic mind." What Cayce's channeling revealed was the impersonal godhead, like an infinite ocean of consciousness, without attributes, yet composed of and beyond all qualities and forms of being. The cosmos was made not *ex nihilo*—out of nothing—but out of God. The pantheistic system was, therefore, the true one after all.

Along with reincarnation came the inevitable law of karma, the Akashic records simply being the records of all prior events and past lives. Cayce began to give "life readings" of past lives. Presto! What came out were accounts of Atlantis, the occult civilization that blew itself up. Now we learn that these same "evolved" souls who had perished in Atlantis were streaming into rebirth on "the earth plane."

Atlantis conception

Though Cayce died in the forties, this would have been the sixties generation he was talking about. These same advanced souls had a mission: to restore to the earth the Atlantian spiritual secrets while taking civilization beyond Atlantis. Thus there would soon be a New Age with new powers unleashed. There would also be the return of the occult priesthood and adepts, oracles, psychics, astrologers, channelers, high mystics, and godmen who were here to change "the earth plane." (This revelation helped spur me to meet my spiritual destiny in India—at any price!)

Not just God, but the character of Christ changed as well. Christ was the perfect yogi, avatar/incarnation of the godhead, and god-man. He had already reincarnated on the earth a number of times to set up his messianic mission, perfecting himself even more each time. Melchizedek was but one embodiment in Christ's genealogy of past lives. In that sense he is a model for all men to follow in order to attain what is now called "Christ-consciousness." Strategically, the Akashic "voice" channeling through Cayce targeted the hidden years in Christ's life about which the Bible is silent. Now there was room to fill in the blanks.

With an elaborate explanation of astrological forces, the Akashic voice depicted the young "perfect master" traveling to Egypt to study at the temples of wisdom and beauty, where he learns certain psychic arts. Then the young Jesus goes on to India and Tibet to learn levitation and transmutation from certain Tibetan masters; while in India, he learns healing, weather control, telepathy, and ultimately reaches "at-one-ment" (the real meaning of atonement) with the cosmic overmind. From there, at about age 29, he returns to the Holy Land as the fully promised Messiah.

Perhaps what initially bothered Cayce most about this channeled revelation was the fact that the apostles left all these critical bits of history out of the New Testament. Cayce knew that the Bible does not mention so much as a hint about any of these mystical sojourns. None of the historians of antiquity ever saw the dimmest traces of any of this, nor from all the hundreds of letters from out of the era of the early church soon after the life of Christ was a word ever uttered about these trips to India. You would think someone would have gone along and written about it then. No, Cayce had to trust the invisible voice coming through him, and this took a certain leap of faith.

Thomas Sugrue, the major biographer of Edgar Cayce, in *There Is a River*, makes an observation about Cayce and all other channels of the cosmic Christ:

> The system of metaphysical thought which emerges from the readings of Edgar Cayce is a Christianized version of the mystery religions of ancient Egypt, Chaldea, Persia, India and Greece. It fits the figure of Christ into the tradition of one God for all people, and places Him in His proper place. . . . He is the capstone of the pyramid.[1]

But Edgar Cayce was by no means the first channeler to come up with revelations about the cosmic Christ. Another major source was Levi Dowling, a late nineteenth-century medical practitioner who traveled from town to town in the Midwest in a covered wagon. In the early hours of the morning he channeled and recorded through automatic writing the famed occult classic, *The Aquarian Gospel of Jesus the Christ*. Dowling records how he gave his body to a "higher force." Its purpose was to complete what the apostles had left out, updated for our coming "Aquarian Age." Dowling had already rejected the New Testament source. Dowling considered his chan-nelings to be higher scriptures and numbered them chapter and verse like the Bible. One could almost lament at this point: "oh, if only the scholars would bring their weighty redactive and critical methodology to bear on these channeled teachings from around the world, surely they bounce all over the map. What is a believer to do? Which channeled revelation do we trust?"

According to Dowling's revelations, Christ learned herbal arts in Benares, India. *The Aquarian Gospel* reveals in chapter 23, verses 2-4: "Benares of the Ganges was a city rich in culture and learning; here the two rabbonis tarried many days. And Jesus sought to learn the Hindu art of heal-ing, and became a pupil of Udraka, the greatest of Hindu healers. Udraka taught the uses of the waters, plants, and earths; of heat and cold; sunshine and shade; of light and dark."

We also learn that "Jesus was accepted as a pupil in the temple of Jagannath: and here learned the Vedas and Manic Laws" (21:19). Yet the reality is this: the only Scriptures Christ quotes from in the New Testament are from the Jewish Torah. Not a breath about the Vedas, but plenty from the prophets, psalms, David, and Moses. Not a reference to Udraka or the Jagannath temple with its thousands of Hindu gods.

Perhaps in a pantheistic mood, the Aquarian Christ reveals: "With much delight I speak to you concerning life—the brotherhood of life. The uni-versal God is one, yet he is more than one; all things are God; all things are one" (28:3,4).

At the feast of Persepolis honoring the Magician God, the Aquarian Christ has some good things to say at the invitation of the ruling magician: "Your purity in worship and in life is pleasing unto God; and to your mas-ter Zarathustra, praise is due" (39:5). When he goes on to Delphi, he has some great things to say about the oracle: "The Delphic age has been an age of glory and renown; the gods have spoken to the sons of men through ora-cles of wood, and gold, and precious stone. . . . The gods will speak to man by man. The living oracle now stands within these sacred groves; the Logos from on High has come" (45:8-10).

By the time Dowling's young master gets to Egypt, he is ready to go through the seven tests of mystical brotherhood to become a full master. In the chamber of the dead, he becomes a pupil of the Hierophant. Here he learns the mysteries of life and death and "the worlds beyond the circle of the sun." Faced with the body of a young boy whom he is to embalm, the cosmic Christ tells the boy's grief-stricken mother that "Death is a cruel word; your son can never die" (54:6,7). Indeed, these words can be found in the Bible, but are spoken by one other than Christ, to be sure: "Ye shall surely never die."

Today, we are 10,000 channels down the road from the days of Levi Dowling and Edgar Cayce and there have been a lot of history and words added to the cosmic Christ. It has been a most extensive and elaborate dress rehearsal. Currently, contemporary channels such as J. Z. Knight who channels Ramtha, "Jach" Pursel who channels Lazaris, and Elizabeth Claire Prophet, figurehead of the Summit Lighthouse, who channels multiple ascended masters, echo similar teachings to those of Cayce and Dowling. They have added sophisticated makeup to this cosmic Christ.

A Course in Miracles

Now, in the last twenty years, there has come a major new revelation to hit the stands, and it has created a New Age furor. It is *A Course in Miracles*, channeled through a Jewish atheist, indeed: a woman in the department of psychiatry at Columbia University who even as an atheist took down what the voice told her. *A Course in Miracles* is one of the most-sought-after sources of teaching among New Agers and even some churches. Here too is an event, a phenomenon, that should not entirely escape our scrutiny.

In short, Helen Schucman, Ph. D., who in the mid-sixties was an associate professor of medical psychology at Columbia University's College of Physicians and Surgeons, worked in a department riddled with strain, tensions, and academic competition. This job stress ate into her personal life, creating anxiety and pessimism as it did also with her boss, Dr. Thetford. Department and faculty meetings were like war zones as medical egos displayed themselves. The

Dr. Thetford & Dr. Schucman

two, often at-odds, made a joint commitment to straighten things out at almost any cost. One technique involved acknowledging and selectively seeing only the positive in the other person.[2]

Yet Helen Schucman, an avowed atheist, had always possessed a strange psychic ability that she had only peripherally acknowledged. Her "mental pictures," which she had been seeing in her mind for as long as she could remember, changed from black-and-white to color, then they started moving, motion-picture style, and invaded her dreams. In the summer of '65, the psychic process heightened. Schucman got a flash of herself as an Egyptian priestess. Then in a "vision" she discovered a large black book in a treasure chest. An inner voice began to accompany the moving psychic pictures. It told her that it was "her" book. Schucman told Dr. Bill Thetford that she might need to undergo a psychiatric examination herself, but that it might be pathological. Thetford was drawn to Edgar Cayce in looking for explanations. Cayce was a vital link, Thetford felt.[3] By September of '65, Helen had a premonition that something major was about to happen. The inner voice was appearing more and more.

Doctor Schucman finally phoned her boss, reporting that the inner voice would not leave her alone. He asked her what it was saying. "You're not going to believe me," she responded. Bill countered with "Try me." Helen announced, "It keeps saying, *This is a course in miracles. Please take notes. What am I going to do?*"[4] Dr. Bill Thetford encouraged her to take notes.

That night the voice came through loud and clear with the first words: *This is a course in miracles. It is a required course.* The atheistic scribe resisted but then followed her colleague's recommendation, skeptically doubting every word that came through. At first the inner dictation frightened her, but she went through with it anyway. This was in the fall of 1965. In seven years time, by 1973, the entire course was transcribed, resulting in a 622-page text and a 478-page workbook, as well as a short manual. Since then, the three-volume set has sold well over 500,000 copies. Years later her colleague, Dr. Thetford, described *A Course in Miracles* as "a spiritual document very closely related to the teachings of the non-dualistic Vedanta of the Hindu religion."[5] What was interesting about this was that the voice never divulged its identity. It stayed anonymous. Adherents of the course, however, have adopted Helen Schucman's hunch that the voice is really Jesus. It implies as much in the first pages of the course.

The emerging document produced by "the voice" was coherent and authoritative, but Schucman did not intellectually believe in its source. Should the dictation be broken at any point, when it was taken up again, hours or days later, it began exactly where it had broken off—like a computer modem, beginning again after a pause in protocol. A powerful intelligence was behind this event. Helen Schucman's biographer, Robert Skutch, observes with irony: "On the one hand, she resented the Voice, objected to taking down the material, was extremely fearful of the content and had to overcome great personal resistance, especially in the beginning stages, in order to continue. On the other hand, it never seriously occurred to her not to do it, even though she frequently was tremendously resentful of the often infuriating interference."[6] Skutch also observes: "Throughout the writing . . . the acute terror Helen felt at the beginning did gradually recede, but part of her mind simply never allowed her to get completely used to the idea of being a channel for the Voice."[7] It was only a matter of time before Helen Schucman surrendered herself to this unfolding revelation and became a believer.

When Dr. Schucman asked the voice why it was coming through her, it responded with the statement: "The world situation is worsening to an alarming degree. People all over the world are being called on to help, and are making their individual contributions as part of an overall prearranged plan. . . . Because of the acute emergency however, the usual slow, evolutionary process is being bypassed in what might best be described as a *'celestial speed-up.'* "[8] The coming changes were near, very near. World events meant that the crisis became a catalyst.

A Course in Miracles is not concerned with filling in the missing "bio" of Jesus. It is a spiritual teaching couched in Christian terms but giving them new cosmic meanings. As Dr. Thetford observed, it is essentially Vedanta. When Thetford gave the manuscript to Edgar Cayce's son, Hugh Lynn Cayce of the Association of Research and Enlightenment (A. R. E), Hugh Lynn became very encouraging. This was the same mystery-Christos that his father, the famous psychic, had channeled.

Soon the guiding powers brought some key figures connected with the New Age movement into the lives of the two New York psychologists, and proposals for publication were well under way. The inner voice of Robert Skutch's wife Judith directed her to Helen Schucman. It knew about her inner voice. Judith's inner voice ordered her to commit to publishing the work before finances were even available. Their foundation was already stretched to the limit in helping to fund ex-astronaut Edgar Mitchell's Institute of Noetic Sciences as well as Stanford Research Institute's breakthroughs in *remote viewing*.[9] When Judith Skutch first saw the manuscript she said to herself, "Finally . . . here's my map home."[10] In little time the Skutches published *A Course in Miracles*.

What new facets did it provide the cosmic Christ? None beyond a coherent, supernaturally based document that itself was seen as a miracle and proof of higher guidance. Ironically, not far away in New Jersey, Seth had been dictating similar revelations through Jane Roberts.

The course is totally positive and totally reassuring, the kind of thing a self-described "mousy, anxiety-ridden" New York professional woman such as Dr. Helen Schucman needed for reassurance. It is a revelation that uses the Hindu concept of *maya* to dispel the threat of evil. Evil is an illusion, the projection of the mind. With enough positive thinking, it will disappear. In fact, we can reshape reality because we have the godlike power to govern reality through expanded consciousness because all that is, is spirit, and spirit alone. We get into trouble when we vacillate between the two modes of consciousness: the old and the new. If evil is not real, neither is any misguided sense of sin. In fact, as *A Course in Miracles* states, sin is the illusion that separates us from our own innate divinity, our own godhood. We are extensions of the "thought of God." So our natural inheritance is a state of pure love. The Hindu word for such cosmic bliss is *ananda*. One of the course's exercises in consciousness is to replace all fear and other such negative emotions with love.

Christ is our exemplar, model, and elder brother. But we are his equal, being already perfect like him. *A Course in Miracles* even claims that we are more powerful than Christ. Our manufactured illusions of sinfulness have made the world a prison for Christ. Thus we are the ones with the power to free Christ by perceiving the world in the higher mode, that is, free of all evil. The course encourages a person to say, "God himself is incomplete without me,"[11] and, "There is no difference between your will and God's."[12]

Clearly, if *A Course in Miracles* is right, Jesus is the most misunderstood figure in history. History for 2000 years has had it wrong, the church never even got off on the right foot, and the long-promised *paraclete*—the Holy Spirit, which was to guide the church through history—has not even managed to get through to Christians about their misguided understandings. They have uniformly—all of them—believed a counterfeit gospel for 2000 years. Christ's messianic act of sacrifice on the cross—that central historical fact of Christianity—was wasted blood and pain. In fact, he never even needed to come to earth if all he needed was a good channel, for there was no real sin to atone for, and our separation from God was just an illusion all along.

Of course, if matter is only spirit in high theatrical dress, then real history doesn't matter. If we wish hard enough, all the evils of the world will just go away! Just wish and meditate and concentrate, as they do in India where physical reality is just an illusion, and the illusion will improve—right? As we can see from India, consciousness has indeed overcome the evils of the world, for there is no travail, no suffering, no poverty and disease in India—

right? Hindus have had three millennia to perform the grand experiment and reshape reality with their godlike feats of consciousness—behold. . . paradise on earth!

Yes, one must go to India and see how the millennial experiment has worked! Be amazed . . . and know that reality is merely an illusion of the mind. Walk through Calcutta and Old Delhi, as I used to, and perform the same feats of consciousness that I did. I reminded myself that it was only a test to take my mind off the reality of the perfection and bliss around me. Yes, the evils of the world were mere illusions that could be wished away. Prayer as mantra, and so on. Strangely, the harder I wished the more the evils didn't go away.

With such messages of hope coming from the cosmic Christ, one is tempted to quote the memorable words of Alfred E. Newman and say in all profundity, "What, me worry?" Or in the great words of Mr. Positive himself, Emille Coue, echo: "Each day in every way I get better and better and better." Now look in the mirror and say it again, "Each day . . ."

Indeed, as the true mystical believer will tell you the only real evil now is doubt, which prevents the miracle from happening. Something must be done with the doubters, for they are spoiling the harmony that the world is about to experience.

Who are the doubters? Among them are the orthodox Christians who do not recognize the new gospel coming from the cosmic Christ. They are still "hung up" over their carefully transmitted 2000-year-old canon that has survived the centuries intact. They claim it has already worked the miracle of grace upon their lives and does not need changing. They say they have encountered Christ personally, and when they read the New Testament, that it indeed describes the One whom they have encountered. Through the New Testament, they claim that they have encountered the true historical person of Jesus Christ, and that he in no way resembles this new cosmic Christ others are channeling.

Between these two faiths, the two paths, words, concepts, and traditions are at odds—irreconcilable odds. It is clear that something will have to give.

12

The Halls of Caricature

L ooming before me was a sight, a visage, too terrible to contemplate. It was a foreboding stone structure whose architecture was meant to be a universal human reminder of an event that blinds the mind in unspeakable paradox. The building depicted the essence of human evil, where in recreated images flowed the outrage and suffering of a race. This event, we were reminded, was only a stone's throw away in recent modern history, an event "we must never forget."

I was standing before the famed Jerusalem Holocaust memorial, the Yad Vashem—and multitudes of collective voices groaned through the rocks. Fittingly, it was a gray day in Jerusalem.

I was in Israel in the early spring of 1987, having just spent three weeks of exploration: I had witnessed wildflowers overnight turn the fields and hills of Galilee into radiant canopies. I had crossed the Sea of Galilee in silence as the sun burned away a strange gray mist and revealed stunning hills and mountains while the boat pulled into the port of Capernaum, its ancient synagogue standing as a reminder of an eternal moment. I had descended into the lush subtropical splendor of the River Jordan, traveled across the Negev, climbed Masada. Finally, I beheld the impressive sprawling Temple of Jerusalem from such vantage points as the souks of the Arab quarter to the Mount of Olives. I felt a deep disquiet about the one dark reminder that lay ahead. I couldn't just lose myself in blissful ignorance. A terrible essence of history had been captured and bottled up for all the world to see.

In the Holocaust memorial, I felt anguish and horror, as though caught in the middle of a Francis Bacon painting, as I walked down aisle after aisle. From picture to picture, and in collected fragments, oozed the terrible memories of Dachau, Bergen-Belsen, Auschwitz, Buchenwald and other concentration camps. People with sensitive, intelligent faces stared out of pictures in pained bewilderment.

The Jews were a people whose
ancient heritage perhaps made them a
little different, but who were nevertheless the progenitors of countless historical giants from Einstein to Tolstoy,
from Karl Marx to Sigmund Freud.
Whatever culture they entered, they
seemed to excel. As I moved silently

through the museum, I studied face after face, and I was haunted. There was
Anne Frank in her pretty loneliness, a poet here, a violinist there. I felt it in
my pores—a tragic, haunting melody. Here was a people who had wandered through an eternal diaspora as though searching for their soul, adapting here, adapting there—from high German culture to the ghettos of
Warsaw. It was just a stone's throw away . . . a mere 40 years ago in modern
history when it all happened.

Then we entered the halls of caricature. It was an object lesson about the
dreaded reality of "anti-Semitism." Faded newspaper illustrations and car-
toons and other captioned drawings lined the walls of a long exhibit. It represented the public opinion machinery of Germany where images of Jews
were portrayed. The media, literature, newspapers, and textbooks wove a
uniform theme, skewing Jewish faces into grotesque caricatures. The worst
racial characteristics were exaggerated into deformed, treacherous, conspiratorial, hate-filled, and arrogant faces.

In the halls of caricature, illustrated children's books depicted Jews as
aliens who had infiltrated German culture, with no intention of fitting in,
but whose secret intention was to take over and dispossess the German people of their culture. Wealthy merchandisers, whose eyes were on acquiring
and controlling wider domains, stared out from hidden vantage points. In
other drawings, wealthy Jewish lenders ejected honest and hard-working
Germans from their homes should they be late in their mortgage payments.
One picture series that I stared at for a long time, from some book or another, pictured a large, rotund, evil-eyed, bearded Jewish man with a hook nose
and thick glasses following and then exposing himself to ("flashing") a helpless and innocent nine-year-old girl. He then abducted and raped her, getting rid of the evidence by murdering her and hiding her body. Quotes from
Hitler's *Mein Kampf* put the blame for prostitution and immorality in
Germany squarely on the shoulders of Jewish conspirators who wanted to
wreck the moral fiber of the German people. Jews were depicted as an evil

race full of hidden depravities. One was made to wince from the weight of the message.

The Museum implied that when these images had gained permission from German society to emerge, they foreshadowed the coming persecution. They were a tool for blaming the collective ills of the German people onto a convenient scapegoat—in this case, a people who were "different."

The end result of this propaganda campaign of hate could be seen in further exhibits down the hall: black-and-white photographs of bone-thin bodies lying in heaps, like bundled wheat, waiting to be bulldozed into quarry-sized pits. In descriptions and illustrations, wave after wave of people were lined against walls and machine-gunned, while in the background chimneys belched the black smoke of their cremated bodies. Massive ovens were depicted burning the evidence. These were scenes out of Hieronymous Bosch—grotesque, amazing, mind boggling.

I could not help but wonder about the naïve arrogance of liberals who unilaterally affirm human goodness in the face of history, liberals who scorn those who have pinpointed the reality of human evil. They thrust open the doors of blind permissiveness without a moment's thought about consequences. The only freedoms these liberals would deny are those of disagreeing religious groups—the new bad guys. Ironically, if I can be quite pointed, one of the amazing things is that a multitude of these liberal and permissive voices are Jewish!

It is not a new pattern. When the ancient prophets of Israel reminded the people of their folly and how it would summon the reality of evil and cause dire consequences, they scorned the warning. Such is the response of "enlightened" people of today who say, "Surely *that* cannot be real. We are enlightened, civilized folk, and we will not entertain such things." Tangible evil implies a side to reality that people do not want to know. Few wish to face the implications of what it means if this is a part of reality. It is easier to remake the universe, to just think evil away. I had been a past master of this myself. I should know.

Unfortunately, history could repeat itself. In another form the same evils of 50 years ago could return. The collective machinery of civilization could yet again arbitrarily turn against some group, conveniently scapegoating them. Is the human race really less capable of evil than it was 60 years ago? Have we "evolved" so much in a generation or two as to have changed our fundamental human nature? Is that what the daily headlines show us, that we have changed as a race? Is that what we have concluded after viewing recent history from the pogroms of Russia where more than 60 million resisters were purged (many times the number murdered in the Holocaust) to recent Los Angeles gang slayings, cocaine wars, terrorism, and so on? In reality we must ask whether a campaign of image and innuendo could start up again, directed against those who don't go along with the consensus. Recent history resounds with a loud "yes." Depending upon the consensus, there are "in" groups and "out" groups. The consensus can easily change, as it has numerous times.

Nowadays in America, appropriately due to this recent "embarrassment" of history known as the Holocaust, we live in a time of pin-drop sensitivity to any discussion concerning Jews or Jewishness. This is such a taboo subject that any statement suggesting less than full-hearted support for Jews is instantly seized upon as being potentially anti-Semitic. The Jewish people live in an era of grace. They are above reproach—no ill dare be imputed to them. Reminders of their victimization are so great that never again will anything conspiratorial be imputed against them—not after Germany and World War II. The wrong public innuendo with any Jewish references gets the full ire of the media, the ACLU, civil rights lawyers, the ADL, the Israeli Lobby in Washington, as well as a host of other groups. Yet Jews are honest about their own human vulnerabilities and perhaps feel uneasy about "too much grace," for again it may mean being singled out as "different."

But if they are experiencing a time of grace now, as are other "minorities" such as homosexuals, blacks, Latinos, women (if you can call them a minority), and so on, it seems to be open season on other groups who are now being made culpable for society's ills. Latitude offered one group does not stretch over to another, because they may not have experienced the same victimization and oppression level. That seems to be the criterion of special privilege: a history of past oppression—namely, oppression by someone else! Those who are viewed as previous oppressors are often candidates for becoming the newly oppressed. The grand cycle continues!

Increasingly, there are mounting attacks on Christians and Christian character—it is open season. This condition is like the creed in George Orwell's *Animal Farm* that says, "All are equal, but some are more equal than others." Strangely enough, it is a standard that we see applied selectively, as though some deserve special favor over others. People forget that this very condition might have helped bring about earlier instances of dislike between groups. Perhaps we are dealing with a sad fact of human nature.

Without a doubt, if I were Jewish and had relatives who witnessed the Holocaust, then when I detected any social currents mounting up that could start some of the same dreaded old prejudices, I would try to anticipate and head them off. I would protest, voice my views, use the media, and so on. I would try to lobby with all the political clout I could. That sort of well-warranted hypersensitivity is only normal. One learns to smell out potential trouble. That would also explain the perceived threat of Christian "right-wing" fundamentalist politics to Jewish groups who see embodied in them the possibility of a new fascism or oppression. So potential adversaries are demonized ahead of time.

So here is the result: More and more Christians are now on the receiving end of images and innuendo in the academy and the media. If "minority members" such as Professor Allan Dershowitz of the Harvard Law School, or Arthur Miller, another Harvard law professor, are on Ted Koppel's *Nightline*, they are acutely sensitive to any number of civil rights, such as the rights of gays or the rights of vendors like Larry Flynt to peddle all manner of pornography.

PROFESSOR ALAN DERSHOWITZ
ATTORNEY

But with the same breath, they cannot resist caricaturing some public Christian figure through innuendo. It might come as a quick, offhanded reference, but there it is, as they use the full force of the academic and intellectual mystique of their office—they are, after all, Harvard law professors. They get equally emotional about other perceived threats, so there is almost a self-righteous outrage as these professors of law address feminist issues, abortion rights, gay rights, and public school prayer and why it should be banned. The audience tacitly absorbs what is acceptable, what is "in," dazzled by their brilliance, articulation and ability to frame thoughts and opinions much more adroitly than the public mind can switch gears.

Indeed, Dershowitz and Miller are on the forefront of fashioning what is acceptable legal opinion, thus shaping the future of the nation. With some, I imagine, this is almost a messianic task. Perhaps their vision is a safe "secular" state that is fully pluralistic, even "rabidly" pluralistic, if I might speak in irony. In ways I can identify with them supremely.

Thus Christians are now on the receiving end of wide scapegoating. Another fact is that some of them deserve it, and that complicates the problem. There have been men representing Christianity in the media before the world who have been less than exemplary in every domain. They have caricatured the Christian faith. The backlash will be a rising mood of public contempt on several fronts. To repeat an earlier observation, are we dealing with an arbitrary class of privilege where one minority is immune at the perpetual expense of another group, now defined as "bad," its back against the wall? With Christians, it is clearly heading in that direction.

Misdirection is a dishonest way of dealing with the problem of evil. Often the actual bad guy points the finger. Parents can do this when they project their own evils on a child, disfiguring him for life. They take attention off themselves at the child's expense (this is the one redeeming insight in Scott Peck's *People of The Lie.*—that it is the most evil people who cannot tolerate any thought of their own imperfections so choose instead to project them on others.)

The doctrines of political correctness and multiculturalism have decided who is to blame for the evils of society using dishonest misdirection, group think, as they decide who is culpable. But what if they are projecting to avoid being under the spotlight?

Anti-sex Leagues

Feminist doctrine portrays women as having been "oppressed victims" from millennia of male rule and patriarchy. As victims they can do no wrong. They are above reproach. They are gentle victims of male barbarism, and obviously society's ills are from men's misgoverning of the affairs of the world. Today's evils thus are proof that men failed and are not cut out for the task. Implicit in this is that women would have done a far better job. They would have created utopia if given the chance. The new myth is this: Women's superior "caringness," "nurturingness," and "feminine intuition and attunement to earth rhythms" would never have allowed war or other forms of oppression.

So who is the source of history's evils? "Male chauvinist pigs" (See—they are free to name-call!), especially as embodied in masculine males. The safer, more tolerable men are the more feminized or effete males. They will go along with the feminist program, unlike the old-fashioned John Wayne types who are dangerous and will never change. Indeed, as a major Ivy League seminary deducted in a required theology class, the cause of societal evil can be boiled down to the patriarchal system, especially as seen with white men who are "chronic oppressors." The assistant professor of theology was one of the more non-threatening effete males who disdained classic male traits and could be seen championing so many of today's gentler causes. He, too, had his own non threatening and gentle way about him as he minced harmlessly across campus—everybody's friend, especially to irate women who were forever vigilant for signs of threatening male traits. One gets the feeling that if these hyper-feminist women got control of the police, army, air force, and government, they would imprison any male whose attitude they found offensive. If it were possible outside of fantasy, they would imprison the founders of the nation, the framers of the Constitution, and 200 years of soldiers who have defended America's freedom. All but "safe" androgynous males would be put out of society's view. Enter the new ideal: feminist matriarchal culture.

Who in the name of the new fair-mindedness is being singled out? White males. Not just that, but white conservative Christian males. Show any number of groups a picture of strong traditional male, and he is hated. They jeer and scorn. He represents the strong, traditional, old-fashioned male who believes in God, country, and family with the man at the head of the family. Are we seeing shades of the new Holocaust memorial? I can see the halls of caricature: news photos of white males being shot and imprisoned; school books portraying drunk, irresponsible white male fathers leering at their young daughters and ready to molest them; white males abusing their wives repeatedly, etc. Creeping images are almost getting to this point, anyway.

The Christian academy has taken up the women's agenda. Yale started once as a divinity school, so did Harvard, and so did Princeton. These three schools have shaped the denominational church in America. Virtually every week, these schools host women's consciousness-raising events. It is their own tireless round of reminders of their own oppression. There are talks and films about wife abuse, films and seminars on domestic violence, films and seminars on fathers and stepfathers molesting their daughters. The family is a collapsing and inappropriate institution that must change or be abolished. There are seminars and planning sessions on totally egalitarian marriages. It should be a world of emasculated men submitting to assertive women. In such a world the gay caucus can announce homosexuality as the new alternative. It will be a golden age of lesbianism and homosexuality and perhaps the banning of such evils as marriage. God forbid that we ever see an era like "Little House on the Prairie" again!

There is a new ideal of androgyny. Self-described "minorities" (gay-lesbian task forces, etc.) have propounded this new ideal as the merging of male and female into one in which sexual differences would be minimized.

Men would glory in their effeminacy, and women would become pseudo-males. So many butch women have defaced what little genuine femininity they might have had, a British journalist described them as blockish or chunky, waddling in potato-sack dresses or trousers, with octagonal glasses and butch haircuts. To him nothing uglier or more unattractive to a normal man was conceivable. The allies of these women have become the whispering, effeminate males who are either attracted to other men or who have

become ashamed of maleness and who have conceded defeat to the feminist and lesbian causes. Undoubtedly, androgyny in the future will further increase the split and alienation between the sexes. It is quite a campaign of recruitment and social change.

Times have changed. In the sixties I went to Franco Zeffirelli's movie *Romeo and Juliet*. I left with tears flowing down my face as I rode my motorcycle out into the Virginia countryside.

I was always struck by my own longing for the beauty of the truly feminine, that allure that feminine women and unspoilt women possess. When I fell in love in those days, I really fell in love. Girls from Hollins and Sweetbriar colleges with their pretty dresses and long hair would

show up for dances at the University of Virginia and the attraction I felt was like a huge magnet. Girls in that era treasured the mystique of their femininity. I long to see such women again but fear they have

gone with the wind—an evidence of the terrible changes of our time.

Let me engage in overstatement: instead of lithe and feminine Olivia Hussey at 19 playing Juliet with her vulnerable eyes and beautiful face, we have "Ms. Betsy Gombler" waddling across the screen announcing her non-negotiables to Romeo in that fascinating voice that some of them have (an imitation of the male voice just reaching puberty—not yet deep, but trying hard). Call it

Romeo and Ms. Gombler, today's adjustment to an old story. Perhaps George Orwell was indeed a prophet of all these things with his "anti-sex league."

With no opposites, there is no attraction—at least this is true between the sexes. When feminist linguists adjust all the great works of literature to their satisfaction, maybe they can insert into Shakespeare's great work of genius their own inclusive language as well as the new women's ideal, Juliet replaced by the androgynous person perhaps known as "Person 1" in the play. It is ugly beyond belief.

On April 17, 1988, *The San Francisco Chronicle* reprinted a recent news story from *The New York Times* by Timothy Egan that highlights a significant national issue: the changing roles of women and the role of university campuses in this change. The article reported: "When Pete Schaub could not get into a crowded business course at the University of Washington one quarter, he signed up for an introductory class in women's studies, thinking he might learn something about feminism. What he learned was that when he repeatedly challenged course assumptions in class, he soon became the focus of the class itself. . . . Schaub said [about the class instructors], 'They ardently boast of lesbianism and deliver shallow sermons on socialism while making hate-breeding statements about men.' " He was dismissed by the two women instructors.

Schaub described his experience in this women's study class: "But from the first day on, they started in about how all men are wife-beaters and child molesters and how the traditional American family, with a mom and a dad, doesn't work. . . . They classified everything I had to say as racist or sexist. Where's the freedom of inquiry?" A picture of a handsome, muscular blond athlete accompanied the article. Schaub, 20 years ago, would have been pursued by another generation of women in another way. He looks like an all-American football star at six-foot-one and 220 pounds. But he said that his size and business major made him the target of "everything that's wrong with men." Perhaps if he had been an effete ally and blended in, Schaub would have been tolerated. There are women's courses like this at every university in America, almost without exception. Invariably, only women attend them, and invariably, they start to change.

Meanwhile, there is a new trend. Some men are flying to Asia to get mates to whom they are attracted—feminine women who want to be wives. They have grown weary of the shrill alternatives, often combative and unattractive. As many men have observed: who wants to marry someone with even shorter hair in trying to look like him, disdains femininity, waddles and resembles a potato.

A backlash of male hostility could easily happen once all natural attraction and protectiveness has gone. Things could get ugly. Then the State's remedy for dealing with this polarization could come.

The legal machinery of "the State" might define the confines of male and female roles and what is acceptable. The State would be "forced" to monitor individual lives even more closely. There may even be legally enforceable code numbers for gender-related behavior, creating a gray conformity—premonitions again of Orwell's "anti-sex league." Many feminists would love to provoke some form of legal intervention upon men, where men's maleness would be curtailed. This trend is already happening as wife-abuse cases gain public airing. A case is quietly being built. There might come a genetic and cultural solution to manliness—a kind of chemical inhibition to maleness.

From Grievance to Caricature

In their attempt to be freed from God, traditional roles and subjection to men, feminists are destined to enter an alternate form of bondage and tyranny. The fruit of this "liberation" is bound to emerge in all of its ugliness. Reports from the lesbian underground show that there are even more battered women coming out from under abusive lesbian relationships than heterosexual ones. Their attempt to have an egalitarian culture and escape hierarchy, invariably causes new hierarchies emerge.

Mistreatment between men and women seems to be happening more as families fare worse and role models disintegrate. One age old cause for this is simple human depravity. There is no question that abuse is wrong, but increasingly, such instances are being used for propaganda with radical ends in view.

Imagine you are a young college girl going to the campus women's center run by older women. Most universities have them. There are no men's centers. Women's solidarity is in view. Looking for guidance or companionship, the young freshman sees something else. The center shows an endless round of films and seminars on domestic violence and wife abuse, then films on fathers molesting daughters. Suddenly all men will seem almost biologically predetermined to rape and abuse women. Marrying one of them would be like marrying a wild animal.

If the young college girl in question is truly hurting inside, perhaps from a remote or alcoholic parent, then she is even more vulnerable. But rather than being helped, in the long run, she will become more alienated and angry.

After this "consciousness-raising" process at the women's center, the average college girl will harbor such animosity that her chances of a workable marriage are further lessened. If the man is less than perfect, it is almost doomed—especially if he has anger of his own.

The woman is now trigger-sensitive about male abuses and on the lookout for infractions. Rather than exhibiting trust, the relationship will be based on acute suspicion. The resolve, loyalty, and commitment that held together marriages of earlier eras have virtually evaporated from modern relationships, while polarizing alienation fares ever more intense in a self-fulfilling prophecy.

Women's centers do not show films and seminars about men as victims of women, such as men who are married for their money or manipulated for selfish ends, or where alluring women set one man up after another "for the kill." They do not show cases where a man's intimate vulnerability is betrayed, when he has opened up his heart to a woman he has trusted who then turns this against him to undermine and destroy him. To think that women cannot abuse men is pure blindness. No one gets out of this unscathed.

When women's groups recite the long litany of male inadequacies and abuses, the reality of such things cannot be repudiated, merely the editorial slant and solution they offer. Often the major women's voices are anti-male and anti-family. Often they come from the lesbian viewpoint. Their solution is a feminist-controlled world, or lesbian marriages, or marriages with "changed" men. But this begs another deeper issue. Are women less sinful than men, or are their dark sides merely expressed differently, as many ex-lesbians have admitted? A woman may not necessarily be physically violent with another woman (though this is increasing dramatically), but she can be coercive, manipulative, treacherous, and jealous. She can oppress her fellow sisters as much or more than the most abusive of men. To use all the propaganda of feminist "consciousness-raising" to jettison the heterosexual family relationship, especially the traditional family, is to enter a greater unknown where the evils of abuse are by no means eliminated.

People know intuitively that there is a deep good to a loving, whole family. Latchkey kids and kids in homes torn by strife and divorce hunger for the ideal of the harmonious, integrated family as they look longingly at "Little House on the Prairie," "Father Knows Best," and "The Cosby Show." They see in a workable hierarchy a chance for love to operate. Dad is truly attracted to and protective of Mom; she wants to please him and is fulfilled. They get along, and they love their kids. They are not at war, but have joined in commitment to an ideal of love, mutual need, and clear understanding that their created differences are to be treasured!

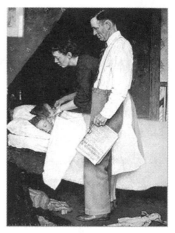

The family is very much a part of the old world order, as are traditional roles of men and women whose differences are seen as being intentionally created by God. Different roles between the sexes are also seen as God-ordained. This is critical in the case of the family. A healthy Christian community will not be able to breathe in the kind of atmosphere the feminist/minority agenda has in mind, and that is part of the darker purpose.

The Christian Holocaust Memorial

Perhaps someday the entranceway to the Christian Holocaust memorial will chronicle "The Media, The Christian Money Hucksters, and The Televangelists." We will be painfully reminded of the fact that the public for decades was treated to an escalating spectacle, a rampaging burlesque that left a bad taste in everybody's mouth, especially among nonbelievers who obviously showed more discernment than the more simpleminded believers who "will believe in anything if they believe in this."

As we saw with the Jewish Holocaust memorial, we will see the propaganda machinery of the collective at work. The movie industry will have spent years portraying Christians as either bland, characterless wimps or wild-eyed fanatics, small-minded bigots, and madmen who hear God's voice in their heads. There will be those cameo westerns—suddenly it is "the Christians," wild-eyed, prejudiced hate-mongers ready to lynch and kill anyone who is not like them. In another film, the Christians are superstitious rednecks, quoting King James Scripture in a drawl and seeing some prophecy come true in the full moon. More often than not, they will oppress women and minorities. In the next film we have a serial killer with a dayglow cross on the wall of his trailer next to his weapon collection. He hears voices on who to kill next.

If it is a father-and-daughter movie theme, he is cold, distant, suspicious, and unloving as his inflexible and puritanical beliefs try to pin down her youthful soul which is crushed by his bigoted fanaticism. When the two have an argument about her social life, he slaps her and calls her a whore. If her boyfriend shows up, he glares at him, shotgun in hand, while standing in the door in bib overalls held up by suspenders. Evening meals are oppressive events as the father mutters some archaic prayer of grace, while the other family members bow their heads in hushed fear. You can sense it: *Don't trigger him off; he might start executing God's judgment.* He is not loving, sympathetic, and understanding, embodying the true graces of the New Testament, but he is severe and accusatory. He represents the Christian man. If Hollywood had spent this much effort portraying Jews and Jewish families in this light, the outrage and litigation would be beyond belief. The Anti Defamation League would have such films shut down on opening night.

At the same time, in the Christian Holocaust museum we would see how the national media went out of its way to bias public opinion. News programs would go out of their way to pinpoint embarrassing, deviant, and cultish fundamentalist incidents of any and all variety. Nothing would ever be shown in a positive light. A miniseries on Christian parents would portray them praying to God to heal their son who has diabetes. Naturally, God is never reachable and the parents finally withhold the insulin needle "in faith" while the boy dies. The picture portrays the tension between primitive superstition and a modern world. Ironically, two channels up the dial there might be a "positive" program about channelers and crystals and their healing effects, but that is unbiased and open-minded. Documentaries on Jesus, such as Peter Jennings special report in the Spring of 2000, would skewer the panel of experts to unilaterally invalidate the Christian faith as an outmoded superstition. Try to do that with Judaism and the network would be shut down overnight, the staff given their walking papers.

Movies and the media, in the hands of the few, become irresistible propaganda tools over the minds of the many—the simple masses—and can create likes and dislikes by turning an image or innuendo.

Meanwhile, the world will have been treated to hundreds of thousands of television hours of self appointed "Christians" who gloried in their own mediocrity or, in the world's eyes, boasted about their inferiority in everything as though it were a virtue. The public audience would see self-appointed representatives of Christianity on television who made a mockery of their so-

called religion by their vulgarity; flippancy; and lack of awe, dignity, and integrity. When the personal lives of these media stars became revealed through inevitable scandal—and this has happened just about every time—the Christian faith became even more burlesqued in the public eye. Viewers saw lifestyles no more worthy of merit than a scene out of "Dynasty." In the end this made Christianity a laughingstock of the world. One is reminded of the old aphorism, "With friends like that, who needs enemies!"

The non-Christian observes to the Christian, "If you have been so undiscerning and naïve as to believe in that ranting idiot on TV—a used-car salesman in polyester—then this Jesus of yours must be equally doubted. By default, that Savior you believe in is no better than the vulgar idiot manipulating money out of you on the TV. You have shown blind judgment about the TV preacher, so why should I consider the one you have never even seen—this Jesus of yours! Neither you nor your Savior is to be taken seriously." It is perfect guilt by association. And many more are being alienated from Christianity than converted by the televangelists, above all, the best and brightest of society who have all been closed out from the gospel for life.

The money hawkers have done their job well. They have not attracted the world to Christ; they have made him a point of supreme derision. Not only that, but they have given Christians a bad name. The noble sacrifices of 10,000 pious missionaries on the field are plowed under the rubble of a single garish mansion. The one-time Jim-and-Tammy Bakker mansion (before their divorce and his ministry scandal) with its $2000 air-conditioned doghouse and gold faucets in Hee-Haw city, auctioned off by escalating lewdness, invalidates over 10,000 missionary huts in jungles and villages. The world remembers the ridiculous and tasteless

spending binges of the Bakkers, as they drew the world's eye to themselves. God in the Old Testament warned the Jews that his name would become scorned and jeered at by the unbelieving pagan world because of their own bad examples. The "Christians" are no better.

Christians have become so simpleminded these days as to be blown around by circus sideshow doctrines that they then inflict on the world. The world looks on as mass rallies claim prosperity. They think God will give them mansions and pink Cadillacs with rhinestones if they pray with enough fervency. There they are on TV: gobbling away, hands outstretched, eyes closed, and asking God for goodies. They are assured that if they believe enough, they can have anything. The non-Christian skeptic looks on as

these simpletons confirm his suspicion about their powers of judgment. Here are people who cannot connect the fact that the very Christ they proclaim to follow told his followers that if He had been persecuted, so would they; if He had no place to lay his head, nor would they; if He had suffered hardship, so would they. They were told again and again that they would have their own crosses to bare—crosses, not Cadillacs. To the world these people are junk-food Christians.

The world turns on the TV set and looks on incredulously. On one channel we have Oral Roberts in his prayer tower telling "the faithful" that if they don't send in ten million dollars in the next few months God will take him home. Oral is crying on TV. The next shot is the faithful in tears. God's going to give Oral the death sentence if they don't cough up the cash. God is bankrupt is one implication. The other is that he is not too loving with his so-called servants; he kills them punitively for things over which they have no control. It is blackmail, extortion, and a lie. The world knows it, and these people look like the fools that they truly are—right on national TV. A genius could not invent a more devastating scenario. It is a scandal for Christ, who never asked for money but made a point of warning of the dangers of the role of money. Paul the apostle never asked for money for himself—that is why he made tents. He did not forbid Christians to let their needs be known to other Christians, but this was to be done in private, in the family—not in a nationwide theater-in-the-round.

Paul warned the Ephesian elders at Miletus to look out for signs revealing false brethren, wolves in sheep's clothing—signs such as we see in empire building and private lust binges of these media evangelists. If God has not sanctioned such ministries as we see embodied in these televangelists, who has? The blind and ignorant people who will believe anything?

Those who don't believe?

An atheistic banker, hostile to Christianity, might do well to fund some outrageous and bogus ministers to represent and cari- cature before the world the faith he hated. He would not bankroll hero figures; he would bankroll anti- heroes—vulgar, manipulative, crude, uneducated men without any social graces or dignity. He would bankroll the Jim Bakkers, Robert Tiltons, Ernest Angleys, and practically every other televangelist you see on TV— men in polyester leisure suits with phony mouth move-  ments, unnatural and affected voices, who beg for money in the name of Christ. He would bankroll losers, not winners.

This principle should be obvious in the world of corporate accounts where Wall Street advertisers go for the cream of the crop of the beautiful people—poised, healthy, articulate, radiantly good-looking people—to rep- resent their products. Winners, not losers.

A billionaire who despised Christianity would never bankroll someone like Eric Lidell—the faithful, humble, intelligent track star from the University of Edinburgh who became a Scottish missionary and Olympic champion; the man whose life story was so stunningly portrayed in the academy-award-winning film *Chariots of Fire*. He would not bankroll a good-looking, self-sacrificing, principled believer, a man of character and humility who had a Cambridge University education, to represent the faith.

No, he would get someone half a grade lower than a dishonest hog farmer to auction away Christ like a farm animal. He would bankroll peo- ple with inferior minds, inferior dress, inferior faith, who would stand before all the world as the clowns of Christ, laughable in the world's eyes. They would suffer persecution, but not because of their nobility of charac- ter or faithfulness to the gospel—but for the opposite reason. They would justify themselves with the Scripture that "God has chosen the weak to shame the wise," and then manipulate their followers with this, forgetting that God also chose Paul, Apollos, and Augustine—some of the greatest minds in the ancient world.

Final Epitah

Perhaps the Christian Holocaust memorial will show that the "Christian masses" were in no way sobered by how easily they had been duped by their own appalling lack of discernment in scandal after scandal. Many instead would renounced the Christian faith en mass. They would blame God or the con artists, but never themselves for poor judgment, poor taste, or their own shoddy knowledge of the true historical faith. The final straw would be when God refused to answer their prayers of positive confession for houses and expensive cars or lives free of suffering. And when they expected to be "raptured" up into the sky the moment things got tough, and it didn't happen, they abandoned ship.

The Christian Holocaust Memorial will show that when public opinion turned against these so-called "Christians," when they were singled out by a hostile society at large, most of them denied that they ever really believed. They had neither the guts nor the character to stand up. They had gotten aboard the train because it looked so inviting: the good life here and now for any and all. Being pragmatists, when dial-a-prayer did not work, they readily turned to something else.

The secular media mockers—lying in wait to finally pounce on these idiotic Christians—would find universal sanction from the public. Interviewers like Jerry Springer and Sally Jessie Raphael would ask endless embarrassing questions to the trailer park crowd, outing the ignorance, the out of fashion views. Some Howard Stern of the future would go ballistic. It would be high season on the Christian caricatures, a grand chess move of cultural marginalization of the once dominant Faith, the one America was founded upon. By then, other minorities will have totally dominated the culture without a whimper of protest—a brilliant "castling" move.

Howard Stern

The remnant of sincere Christians would then retreat into the shadows, silenced and wondering how their heritage had gotten away from them so quickly. Perhaps with yellow crosses sewn into their jackets, they will wonder how in one single generation, the very Faith that fueled wholesome families, a once bold and bountiful nation, would plummet to the depths of debasement, making them the new pariahs.

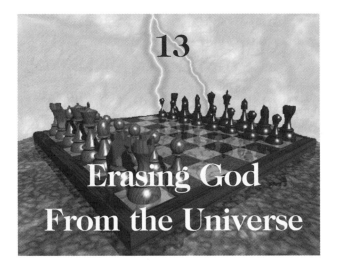

13

Erasing God
From the Universe

S ome of the most powerful minds in history have, wittingly and
unwittingly, been caught in a chess game that for centuries has
squeezed them slowly into a checkmate. Erasing God from the
universe didn't suddenly, all magically happen; it has been centuries in the
making, starting out as a confident spree to arrive at philosophical certainty about what the mind could know. It ended up with the players not certain that they could even know their own names. One can imagine what it
would be like to play chess with an immortal being whose IQ is half a million, who has been around for millennia (like Satan). The best human players would be trapped in no time, perhaps wondering what their own names
were!

Philosophy, over the centuries, has taken away man's certainty as to what
can be truly known, or what the nature of reality is. The rest of the human
race has waited nervously like onlookers in a vast stadium looking down at
the ongoing game, believing their whole fate hangs with every chess move.
The onlookers are powerless, knowing they are not clever enough themselves to figure out the next move, but are captives in a deadly serious
game—captives, that is, as long as they submit their fates to the outcome.

So far, philosophy is still searching for a clever rejoinder to the vast questions it has encountered in its search. Philosophy itself has been "waiting
for Godot." It has become a player in the theater of the absurd.

Not only has there been a long-term chess game that the philosophers have been playing over the centuries, but each individual philosopher (or team player) has been tempted by lesser games and wagers that are quickly settled.

We find that some of the old sidewalk tricks have worked on some of history's greatest minds. The game looks easy for the confident intellectual at first glance. An ordinary street sleight-of-hand artist has a pea and three cups. He quickly switches them around. Famed British empiricist David Hume points to cup number three to reveal the pea. The pavement artist grins as he lifts the cup—behold, the pea is not there. It is under cup number two. Now con-

David Hume

sider the weight of David Hume's decision about where the pea is if all of civilization hangs on his decision. It would go from a lighthearted challenge to a distended moment of unspeakable horror. If Hume's mind fails to detect its location, all of history feels the consequences. This is not too far from what has been going on between the human race and the participants in the philosophical inquiry as philosophers have been gambling with the truth, from petty wagers to long-term chess games.

Thoughts written on the philosopher's table in one century can rule another century. Karl Marx's *Communist Manifesto* was written in the last century. Today—a century later—its philosophical view of reality affects the lives of two billion people. Russia, China, and other Marxist nations would not exist in the form they do today if Karl Marx had never existed and if no one had ever thought of communism.

Indeed, it has been ideas all along which have dethroned one age and thrust up another, altering the course of civilization. Far from being an innocuous ivory-tower pastime, the realm of ideas and beliefs has changed civilizations in the most concrete ways. Marx borrowed from Hegel and Feuerbach, and so on. Meanwhile, most of the citizens of a given age have often been unable to articulate the forces that mold their lives—the ideas that lie behind the spirit of the age—but these ideas stir their thoughts all the same. Those that shape history have chosen to believe the supreme wisdom of the philosophers' stone. From political leaders, intellectuals holding the seats of learning, and artists and novelists, the newest ideas begin to pervade society—and the influence spreads.

The Crisis

Our spiritual crisis in the West has its roots in the Age of Reason, that seventeenth-century period out of which emerged the rationalists and the empiricists. In the 1600s and 1700s, strains of humanistic, man-centered thought came together and flourished, producing a widespread change in assumptions about reality.

The Age of Reason started with the assumption that the mind of man was an all-sufficient, autonomous agent for comprehensively understanding human nature and reality. Incredibly, it was no more than a small roomful of men who brought in the Age of Reason. This minority asserted that human intelligence could comprehend man and the world with adequacy. This was quite a heady assumption given the limited experience of man with his small allotment of time and space. It is an ambitious project to try to logically disassemble and account for the cosmos. Such a task requires an overview that is more than humanly derived, but the challenge of the game created a heady confidence.

A group of thinkers known as the Continental Rationalists, composed of Descartes, Leibniz, and Spinoza, assumed on faith the mind's ability to function correctly, independent of any external guidelines for thought and independent of God's revelations about his creation. The mind could build a sound, unshakable system of thought, they felt, by deductive reasoning from simple premises, reinforced by truths retained from the biblical worldview from which they could borrow for the sake of convenience. These biblical absolutes, after all, ensured ultimate meaning behind their endeavor. Leibniz and Descartes were theists. They did not want to dethrone God, after all; they merely wanted to secure his knowledge within the bounds of pure reason. So they placed all the biblical absolutes within the mind as "innate ideas" so they would be unassailably safe in a category where no other chess pieces could "check" them with skepticism—or so it seemed.

Descartes began building his rational philosophy from a single seemingly unassailable truth: *Cogito, ergo sum* ("I think, therefore, I am"). This was the single fact upon which no doubt could be shed. Having established man as the ultimate fact in the universe, and the only unshakable fact, he proceeded to "prove" God's existence as well as the existence of the external world. God and the created universe were being rendered dependent upon man for authentic existence.

Then another group of philosophers known as the British Empiricists took things a step further toward modernism. This group, composed of Locke, Berkeley, and Hume, denied the existence of the "innate ideas" held by the rationalists. All that man can know, they proposed, must originate in experience. All "abstract ideas" such as God or truth must derive from some sense impression in order to be noetically valid.

Of the three philosophers, only David Hume explored the implications of a pure empiricism with unremitting vigor. All that man can legitimately know from experience, Hume concluded, is a succession of sensations. Therefore, since things like God, one's personal identity, and the events of life are not immediate sense impressions like pain or color or size, we cannot know that they exist (because of this observation by Hume, the philosophical category of metaphysics was effectively abandoned). Man experiences only a succession of events which habit and memory lead him to connect together into various unifying experiences. Our experience has no necessary connections with the future; therefore, no reliable knowledge is possible.

What Hume was, in fact, saying was that just because the sun has risen every day for thousands of years gives us no warrant to predict it will come up again. Hume had just declared the death sentence on what philosophers call causality—the very foundation upon which modern science is founded. Connections between things and events perceived by sense impressions could no longer be made. You can imagine how this notion shrank the field of acceptable knowledge. The world reeled from this proclamation of David Hume. It was just one more faulty chess move.

The result of Hume's analysis left man without possibility of significant knowledge, without self, in a world without substance or structure. The scientific community of the 1700s was thrown into an uproar because, granted Hume's initial premises (which they did not dispute), they could find no flaws in his thinking. For Hume, knowledge became only possible in the most limited sense. Yet for Hume the practical demands of daily life still had to be assumed. You still had to *assume* that the sun would come up, that water would flow out of the faucet, and so on.

William Barrett in *Irrational Man* captures Hume's absurd dilemma when Hume "in a moment of acute skepticism, felt panicky in the solitude of his study and had to go out and join his friends in the billiard room in order to be reassured that the external world was really there."[1]

When Hume finished his empirical analysis, the very possibility of true scientific knowledge was in question. Immanuel Kant, shaken by Hume, sought to extract thinking from the impasse into which it had worked itself, and his solution laid the groundwork for thought in the nineteenth century. Kant worked the chess pieces into a tighter situation, even closer to a final entrapment.

Kant's revolutionary move was this: In order to rescue science and philosophy from skepticism while at the same time preserving humanistic assumptions, Kant removed the form and structure of reality from their precarious place in a problematic external world and established them within the mind of man. The patterns that science studies, the dynamic orderliness of nature which rewards the efforts of science, are not the result of habit and custom as David Hume had proposed. Instead, Kant now argued, this order originates in the mind of the observer. This subjective ordering process is the condition for perception itself. Kant called this "The Transcendental Unity of Apperception" (TUA). All of a sudden the mind contained the creative power which produces what we know as "reality." This had vast new implications that would send philosophy reeling in a whole new direction, paving the way for Hegel and his concept of the evolution of history—with beingness mystically growing in the universe—and for the Romantics, who would delight in this breakthrough.

Suddenly, Kant's move threw open the door for a system of knowledge independent of God. Beyond that, it opened the way for mysticism, monism, and the pursuit of the occult. The nature of the mind, Kant argued, is to order the indeterminate stuff of sensation so that it can be perceived or known. This ordering takes place before the experience is possible. Therefore time, space, and causality are not "out there" in a real world; they are extended from the subject's mind for the act of perception. Science is successful in its generalizations about the normal relations between objects of experience because these relations between objects of experience are established *a priori* by what Kant called the forms and categories of human understanding which allow objective experience to occur. What reality is, what "things in themselves" are, cannot, therefore, be known. What we "know" is made possible not by God, not by the mind's penetration of a real world, but by the mind's projections of what we can know upon an essentially unknowable world. Kant placed God, the soul, moral freedom, and the like in the realm of the unknowable "things in themselves." This conceptual framework became known as phenomenalism, a foundation stone within the German school of idealism.

Needless to say, these "breakthroughs" spilled over from the philosophy departments into the departments of theology in Tubingen, Leiden, Berlin and the other German universities, paving the way for the nineteenth-century German higher criticisms of Julius Wellhausen, Harnack, Ritschl, and many others. The theological left-hand turns within these schools of theology had an immediate impact upon other centers of learning outside of Germany, as well as upon the entire German Lutheran church, putting all the traditionally accepted tenets of the Christian faith into total upheaval. By the early twentieth century, it would be a totally toothless church, incapable of voicing moral comment as the National Socialist platform rose to power, bringing in Hitler. A few individuals like Bonhoeffer were rare exceptions within the church and the academy. By then such opposition as his represented little more than a twig trying to hold back the waters of a broken dam.

Kant's thoughts in Germany soon hit the international intellectual community. Samuel Coleridge, the nineteenth-century English poet, could now say that we half create, half receive the world, so that what man fabricates in perception cannot be separated from what is really there. Man knows only experience, not "things in themselves." Walt Whitman, an American poet and a contemporary of Coleridge, elaborated on this by saying that man is like a spider who spins the world that he knows out of himself. The world as we know it, according to Kant, was merely a construct of our minds. The chess board had narrowed even more in the West.

But now there was a terrible problem that the original quest of Descartes and Leibniz could not have foreseen a century before Kant. If one reasons earnestly about religious questions from Kant's philosophic position, one can only arrive at an agonizing agnosticism because God has been structurally removed from any relationship to existence—He has been erased from the cosmos. Even if God does exist, in the Kantian system, mankind cannot know Him.

Proceeding from such Kantian assumptions, faith can never be more than a blind, desperate leap into the unknown. Faith can never be biblical faith rooted on the evidence that what is out there is real. In biblical epistemology you don't need to keep proving to yourself the reality of the external universe. It is a given that it is created by God, therefore, real, and therefore, has a purpose. Not so with Kant.

So what did the world lose when modernism disposed of biblical epistemology? A priceless treasure.

In the biblical worldview, the significance of individual life was guaranteed. Time and history were intelligible and real. The fact that the universe exists was explained in a way that allowed for sustained, intelligent inquiry because the vast patterned structures and dynamic energies of the universe were seen as an outgrowth of God's wise and sovereign purpose. Form and structure were real and not Kantian projections from the mind of man; rather, they were inherent in the reality of a knowable world. When Isaac Newton wrote *Principia Mathematica* in 1687 at Trinity College, Cambridge, he rested on an intellectual assurance that the cosmos was trustworthy, and that his deep Christian beliefs were in no disharmony at all with the scientific task. Newton could be assured that Christianity links the world of the rational to the spiritual. It shows the harmony and continuity of all knowledge. There were physical laws such as gravity, and there were moral laws, each affecting different domains of God's creation.

But as the knowledge of God became suppressed through philosophy, these given and obvious truths became philosophically problematic. A hundred years after Isaac Newton, David Hume's *Dialogues Concerning Natural Religion* would be released posthumously in 1778 almost at the same time Kant released his *Critique of Pure Reason* in 1781. By the time Immanuel Kant took his final bow on the world stage, the chess game was at a point where nobody was able to stop it.

Kant's influence on the modern world was immense, and it is no exaggeration to say that he dominated the nineteenth century. Some scholars argue that the nineteenth and twentieth centuries are footnotes to Emmanuel Kant.

Kant laid the groundwork for an artistic and intellectual response known as the Romantic movement, which swept the Western world. The Romantics, too, would open some terrible new doors, the implications of which they would not fully realize until it was too late.

14
Letting Mr. Gumby Control the Universe

The Romantics were a group of influential avant-garde thinkers, poets, and artists of the nineteenth century who strongly felt the diminished portion of reality that philosophy left them. They were given a reductionism coming from the eighteenth century that left no room for metaphysics. The hard, natural determinism and unfeeling, soulless universe they inherited offered them an impoverished vision of life.

Frederick Hegel

The Romantics did not question the humanistic and naturalistic assumptions of the Enlightenment. They merely sought to reverse the tendency toward impersonality by asserting the value of private experience over and above what was mere scientific fact. Hume had shrunken the universe with his unyielding skepticism. Mystery was gone. Now Kant was giving the Romantics new room to breathe. They loved Kant's idea about the mind creating reality. Hegel's influence after Kant marked the era of a new optimism, but this solipsism had not only an up side, it had a downside as well.

By the time Nietzsche entered the philosopher's chair, he took Kant a step farther and held "mere scientific fact"—indeed, the scientific undertaking itself—in complete contempt. Nietzsche was the one to rub the implications of what had happened over the past centuries into the faces of his contemporaries. He bemoaned the desolating universe that he and his contemporaries had inherited from his predecessors.

It was Nietzsche who declared "God is dead!" Then he proceeded to show the dire implications of what this meant. However, the Romantics still had not yet caught on. They had not yet detected the inevitable despair and nihilism that lay down the road for them, rendering meaningless every Romantic undertaking to celebrate life. They continued glorying in the hopes and pleasures of private experience, but this required tunnel vision.

The Romantics no longer needed to worry about a sovereign, transcendent, and moral God looking over their shoulders. They gloried in their initial freedom, their autonomy. Now they could go on a binge and taste all of life's little delicacies. The English Romantics from Coleridge to Carlyle were swept up in this celebratory frenzy. Soon it spread from them to America, where it was seized upon by the New England transcendentalists: Thoreau, Emerson, and Whitman. Thoreau was to assert in *Walden* that "The universe constantly and obediently answers our conceptions. . . . Let us spend our lives in conceiving them." Man can create the universe he so desires simply by revolutionizing his thinking, Thoreau observed, marking the early beginnings of "consciousness-raising."

Mysticism attached itself to the Romantic quest. To penetrate the secret world of "things in themselves" required an occult approach. Many adopted the attitude that since by definition the rational, causal structure of the world is an aspect of man's consciousness, the rational faculties were merely an obstacle to true knowledge. Penetration to the true essence of things required deep intuition, mystical mind states, or some meditative epiphany. Ecstatic self-absorption into a mystical oneness with or through nature— most obvious in Wordsworth, Shelley, and Whitman—had become an almost conventional form of religious experience.

Nature began to be regarded as somehow divine. It was a tabloid for the sacred experience. Pantheism crept in. By the time the first translations of Hindu and Buddhist texts were made in the nineteenth century, they had an immediate influence on Western minds. Walt Whitman applauded these new mystical breakthroughs in his celebrated poem "Song of Myself." Whitman announced to the world: "Divine am I inside and out, and I make holy whatever I touch or am touched from."

Whitman's fellow transcendentalist, Thoreau, celebrated the occult potential in man with the help of the recently translated Vedantist Hindu texts, saying, "I have read a Hindoo book." Then he reveals the new teaching: "So the Soul, from the circumstances in which it is placed, mistakes its own character, until the truth is revealed to it by some holy teacher, and then it knows itself to be Brahma (God)."[1] This was pure pantheism.

The Romantic movement clung to pantheism as a result of Kant's thought, and with that came the effort to lay aside traditional conceptions of God and of good and evil. These categories were seen as limitations upon human consciousness and its quest for unlimited experiences. Besides, "sin" was never a popular word among artists, intellectuals, and the avant-garde. Blake, the English mystic poet, with lucid foresight called this project on which he was embarked the marriage of reason and hell.

Later on in the nineteenth century, the very terms "good and evil" were made irrelevant by persistent reductive analyses of experience. The most famous and influential of these came through the Englishman Walter Pater in his critical work *The Renaissance*. Pater sought to isolate value judgment from experience. He extracted the teeth from moral judgment by saying that "not the fruit of experience, but experience itself, is the end." He said that we should quicken ourselves by intensifying our experience. "To burn always with this hard, gem-like flame, to maintain this ecstasy, is success in life."[2]

Moral questions are irrelevant to Pater who says, "The theory or idea or system which requires of us the sacrifice of any part of this experience has no real claims upon us."[3] Truth of any sort has no reference here and no normative effect. Truth is not true but useful, as long as it serves our interests. Man's own experience is the god for whom all is sacrificed.

Soon D. H. Lawrence and a host of other Romantics became champions of the pursuit of novel experiences and new pleasures, with no reference to morality. There was now a radical freedom to explore what used to be called "evil." Hosts of Romantics entered the forbidden and the occult, experimenting with opium, hashish, and other drugs as they broke through one morality barrier after another. Strangely, there are always some inevitable connections between serious pursuit of the pleasure principle and the occult.

The nose dive into nihilism would not come until some of these Romantics put down their opium pipes and, with the help of philosophers such as Nietzsche who had far more intellectual insight and penetration than they, would realize the implications of the sort of universe with which they were left. There was a downside to living in a "godless universe." A child running away from home may feel an initial elation with the first temporary burst of freedom. The day is spent exploring and doing the forbidden, but by nightfall a terrible fear and loneliness takes over—there is no meal for the empty stomach, or nice warm bed and parents to tuck him in. Perhaps for the first time he becomes aware of freezing rain,

Nietzsche

cold alleys, and threatening strangers on the street. It's a whole new world.

The Closing of the American Mind, by former Yale professor, Alan Bloom, addresses in broad scale what has been going on culturally in America, revealing something very telling:

> There is now an entirely new language of good and evil, originating in an attempt to get "beyond good and evil" and preventing us from talking with any conviction about good and evil anymore. Even those who deplore our current moral condition do so in the very language that exemplifies that condition. The new language is that of value relativism, and it constitutes a change on our view of things moral and political as great as the one that took place when Christianity replaced Greek and Roman paganism. A new language always reflects a new point of view, and the gradual unconscious popularization of new words, or of old words used in new ways, is a sure sign of a profound change in people's articulation of the world.[4]

Those who rushed headlong into the experiential quest, like Faust, by disposing of the categories of "good and evil" as arbitrary and no longer binding, landed in a far darker universe than the universe created and sustained by an infinite, loving, and transcendent God.

It was a universe in which anybody could sit at the controls, like a Palisades Park bumper-car ride. Indeed, Mr. Gumby could control the universe. Suddenly the romantic joyride was entering the house of horrors, as such twentieth-century intellectuals as Camus and Celine contended with angst and despair. Sartre could claim that "man is a meaningless passion." Having God dethroned and replaced with some mediocrity is a grim idea indeed to an intellectual who still prizes excellence, to a mind still aware of individual differences and hierarchy. Now God's throne was up for grabs, like a lottery. As Nietzsche said, supermen were needed to replace God. Looking over your standard candidates from Nietzsche's perspective, it was slim pickings indeed. There were a lot of toothless peasants out there, grinning idiots who would take the world for a madman's roller-coaster ride; incompetents who couldn't even take a left-hand turn from an intersection into a parking lot without taking the side off someone's car.

But Nietzsche's supermen, wherever they might be, inevitably would look ridiculous in the role of pretenders to the throne of God. So vast are the differences between the size of the task and the participants. It vastly dwarfs, say, a man pitting the strength of his left arm against a nuclear aircraft carrier in a pushing contest. It enters the full incongruity of the absurd, and true to form, it was the absurd which became a literary genre of the nihilists and the existentialists.

There are insurmountable problems with the great philosophical quest to understand all of reality while declaring whether or not God exists, when the players in the game are merely men, merely mortals. If there is a purpose behind the cosmos, it is too vast for us to discover or comprehend by our own efforts. As we attempt this task from our own little square mile of land, limited by our mortality—a few sparse years—it seems like an ant trying to comprehend the rich complexity of a Beethoven symphony, or walking over the mathematical equations in celestial mechanics. Yet the ant analogy doesn't approach the gulf of capacity between men and this philosophical quest, which only God is capable of performing. It would require a mind greater than the cosmos to reveal its true purpose to us. An intelligence of any less magnitude would not be equipped to provide an ultimate answer. Without revelation, we are hopelessly blind. There is no other way around this dilemma.

Yet in the Age of Reason men dismissed God's self revelation as an unacceptable source of knowledge. Its statements about the nature of ultimate reality were thrown out. The transcendental, supernatural basis for existence was rejected. If, by rationalist criterion, God could not speak satisfactorily through revelation, the only alternative was for man to turn his faith toward himself as the final arbiter of existence and truth. If man could not have access to God on his own terms—either by his reason or direct sense perceptions—then God could be considered unknowable, if not nonexistent. This was quite a heady assumption for finite man to make, and he made it at a tremendous cost, as postmodern philosophers have articulated.

The field of knowledge did not grow; it shrank almost to nothing. As the Age of Reason made pronouncements about the validity or invalidity of various approaches to knowledge, the arena of philosophic inquiry shifted from ontology—the study of the nature of being and reality—to epistemology—the theory of knowledge. Thinking down-shifted from the study of God to the study of the human mind and its capacities and limitations in apprehending reality. Kant posed the question, "What can the mind know, how does it know, and how does it know that it knows?" Then the field narrowed down even more as we entered the twentieth century, and such Logical Positivists as Alfred North Whitehead and Bertrand Russell reduced the known further. By the time Ludwig Wittgenstein of Cambridge University published his *Tractatus Logico-Philosophicus* in 1922, philosophy was virtually forced to limit itself to the field of philology—

word definitions. Can language even be trusted?—So asked Wittgenstein.

Diogenes Allen of Princeton, a professor of philosophy under whom I studied, commented on how the *Tractatus* of Wittgenstein radically narrowed what could be discussed in language:

> This very much restricted what we can say meaningfully. Not only are the concerns of metaphysics and theology unstatable, but so too are the concerns of ethics and aesthetics. Wittgenstein, however, was misunderstood by the logical Positivists, who saw him as an ally. For Wittgenstein himself actually believed that there was more than could be said, and he believed that what could not be said was far more important than what could be said.[5]

For a long time, philosophy students loved quoting Wittgenstein's famous comment, "What cannot be said clearly must be passed over in silence." After that, in most philosophy departments there was either silence or loud wrangling.

To see it in overview: since the age of the scholastics, during the era of Aquinas, philosophy has gone all the way from the grand horizons of theology to ontology to the ant-sized considerations of philology. Human hopes and dreams have trailed along—so have its rebellions. Civilization has been compelled to go along for the ride.

In the meantime God has been removed from the dominion seat and replaced by the average generic citizen. Mr. Gumby and anyone else walking into the video room these days can grab the dominion seat. It's really like standing next to one of those life-sized cardboard photographs of a celebrity or two in order to appear in the picture, and presto! There you are next to several faces normally seen in the pages of *People* magazine—just you, David Bowie, the Dalai Lama, and Ronald McDonald leaning in with a wide grin.

Humanism becomes inevitably confronted with the despair of its own ill-fated project. Continental intellectuals like Sartre and Camus saw this long before their grinning American neighbors across the Atlantic. If reality cannot be grasped in any meaningful sense, then what's the use? they asked. It is really no exaggeration at all to say that punk attire like purple Mohawks and rock subculture, with its heroin needles and "agro," are inevitable fallout from despair. What else can you expect in a society that has lost its moorings?

The academy on the American side of the Atlantic, of course, inevitably did start to ask the same despairing questions. Gunther Stent, a molecular biologist at the University of California at Berkeley, in his book *The Coming of the Golden Age: A View of the End of Progress* states that science is already on the decline because young students entering the sciences are no longer convinced that true knowledge is possible. Speaking as a secular observer, Stent feels that since God has been dethroned, there are no longer any clear-cut standards or values; and so, feeling that correct discriminations are no longer possible with regard to human aspirations and behavior, the pleasure principle becomes the highest value in men's lives.[6]

Today, almost 20 years after Stent wrote this, the University of California at Berkeley campus continues to pursue the pleasure principle even more fully than in the sixties. The preferred highs are designer drugs like ecstasy, where you skip truth quests in favor of pleasure—that they can count on. Unlike their sixties predecessors who still believed in something enough to search for it and make sacrifices for this search, the postmodern youth want money and status. While the remnant hippies from the sixties still sit on Telegraph Avenue as relics of a failed experiment. Insanity and poverty are their inheritance.

Older Americans have yet to face up to the despair faced by Europeans. Many are riding on a wave of the borrowed optimism of former eras. We are dealing with unbacked paper money in the realm of ideas. As teen alcoholism and suicide should illustrate, American youth are encountering whole new levels of meaninglessness and alienation. Today's perverse and defiant despair makes the rebellions of the Romantics seem naïve in comparison.

Jumping off the Chessboard

Rejecting the revelation of God, the postmodern citizen has no standard, no basis of truth to make moral and spiritual discriminations. Tolerance has become the only way of dealing with conflicting, even contradictory worldviews. Each belief is viewed as being equally valid. Truth becomes a matter of private opinion.

More people are gearing their lives by truly unprovable things. Syndicated astrology columns appear daily in practically every newspaper in the country. A growing din of spiritual voices fills the air, and every brand of teacher is available—from Neale Donald Walsch telling us his inner voice is really God to Van Pragh talking to an audience's dead relatives. It is spiritual pluralism with no guidelines.

Once people have been seduced into abandoning reason, you can no longer reach them through reason. The concrete result is the New Age physicist, like Berkeley's Fritjof Capra, who consults the ancient Chinese I-Ching, where wooden sticks are cast as lots. Capra can then stroll up to the Lawrence Berkeley lab to resume some experiment in quantum physics. It is truly a picture out of C. S. Lewis' prophetic novel *That Hideous Strength*, where a postmodern agnostic science synthesizes with the occult—a strange grafting indeed. Former enemies of belief are now allies.

This is the irony. Philosophy has come full circle. Rather than establish the knowledge of God, it has erased Him from the universe and replaced God with a range of things—from nothing or the void, to Mr. Gumby, the latest guru, and anyone else whose name emerges in the daily raffle.

The West has regressed and reentered the forbidden land of occult practices which enlightenment rationalism once promised to abolish forever. Modern man has leaped from the checkmated position of rationalist despair to the extra-rational free-fall of blind faith. Without any spiritual guidelines, man is now truly vulnerable in a wholly new way.

He has returned to an inner-directed religious subjectivism—from New Age shamanism to Satan worship. The equation begins to look more and more like some diabolical *tour de force*. It keeps suggesting that the opponent on the other side of the chess table, whom the philosophers have been playing over the centuries, may well be Mephistopheles after all. Revelation could have told them that all along, if only they had listened!

15

Bridges to the
New Consciousness

As the twentieth century began, a small group heralded a new consciousness. One freedom they sought was freedom from any moral restraint. They had the "right," after all, to do as they pleased as long as they did not hurt anyone, and the right to live without the constant fear of being stigmatized by the present social order (this has become the banner of Wicca today). They wanted to be liberated from the Christian restraining force of morals and beliefs that had been a pillar to the West. They hungered for a changing of the guard.

The idea of "sin" was something repugnant to mystics and free thinking libertines. They wanted it buried forever. Leaders of the new consciousness resented having to cross moral boundaries secretly. Madame Blavatsky, the founder of Theosophy, who touted her freedoms, ate hashish and had countless affairs of all kinds. Such brashness would be nothing by today's standards, but in the late 1800s, it stood out.

One way the new beliefs spread in the early days was through what we now call "consciousness-raising events." They were like energized particles colliding in increasing numbers prior to a chain reaction. The 1960s was that final chain reaction where the critical threshold was finally passed.

Uniting with the East

One key early event, which took place in Chicago in 1893, was the World Parliament of Religions, attracting 140,000 people. The speakers included Buddhist monks, theosophists, Shintoists, a token number of Christian

modernists in search of a new ecumenism, plus several highly persuasive mystics. It was the mystics who stole the hearts of the audience.

The most articulate and brilliant of these speakers was Swami Vivekananda, an impassioned Bengali who was the premier disciple of Ramakrishna Paramahansa, who had recently died in India in 1887. Even today, the radiant face of Ramakrishna appears on Indian postage stamps, for he occupies a position of renown as great as that of Gandhi. He is considered one of India's greatest enlightened godmen.

At the time of the World Parliament of Religions, the spiritual force of Ramakrishna was lighting up India like lightning flashing across a night sky. The ancient gods of India were having a revival through their instrument. Ramakrishna's 12 top disciples were spreading his life story and teachings all over the land. With Vivekananda, the premier disciple, this revival of Indian mysticism was now reaching the West.

Vivekananda was an inspired orator whose pleas for unity became irresistible to the thousands attending the World Parliament of Religions. Anyone who condemned the spiritual treasures of this noble figure from the East was simply exhibiting those "narrow-minded biases" typical of Western "Christian" culture. One can almost hear the accusations of "cultural chauvinism." Take note: Here began the early traces of today's common cultural/anthropological argument which defines different religions as being universal spiritual truths filtered through variant grids of culture and tradition. Spiritual truths could now be seen as wearing the clothing of a given culture's language and imagery. So what the world needed were religious pundits acting as transcultural interpreters of religion. "Open-mindedness" became a key word.

Vivekananda had been a law student when he became enraptured with his guru. Now he was a swami in an ochre robe. His command of rhetoric, apparent nobility, and virtue of character won his case time and again. His key admonition was: "All roads lead to God."

Vivekananda's guru, Ramakrishna, was the syncretist's saint. He had studied the scriptures of each of the major world religions, verifying each of them by claiming to reach "samadhi," or enlightenment, with each path. Whether it was by "merging" with Christ, Buddha, or Krishna, Ramakrishna claimed he was taken to the same godhead. Each world faith took him back to the pantheistic One of the Vedantic godhead. Westerners loved this imagery—God as the ocean of being and infinite bliss, the static eternal, the oversoul ("paramatma"), and so on. When I became a Ramakrishna follower, the same imagery was seductively powerful—powerful enough to get me to go all the way to Calcutta.

Vivekananda, like his master, used the following illustration: The faiths of the world are like five blind men trying to describe an elephant. One describes the trunk, another grasps a leg, another the ear, and so on. They all seem to contradict each other until their reports are unified into a whole—then one sees the whole elephant. Vivekananda was not shy in stating that the most complete description of the whole shape of spiritual reality lay in India's ancient storehouse of revelations given by its "seers," "rishis," "mahatmas," "avadhuts," and "avatars." India was portrayed to the World Parliament of Religions as a land on fire with spiritual truth. India's role among the materially wealthy nations was to enlighten them with its spiritual wealth.

The cardinal Vedantic truths are that the soul is eternal and divine and part of the godhead. It keeps evolving through reincarnation after reincarnation until it rejoins the impersonal godhead. Life is merely an illusion, sucking us all in with its sensualist pleasures and pains that deny the underlying unity of all existence. The dualisms of sweet and sour, light and dark, and good and evil, are two sides of ultimate unitive reality, like light coming out of a prism and breaking into colors. All reality is composed of consciousness. Existence, therefore, is the "dream" of the godhead. It is Vishnu lying on the thousand-petalled lotus forming the phenomenal universe out of his undifferentiated being. Only when the droplets of consciousness merge back into the primal ocean will this illusion of separateness end. A godman such as Ramakrishna claims to be none other than this—one who has sojourned the grand circle from eternity to eternity. When he speaks, he claims it is the voice of the eternal coming through a human frame. Exquisite indeed.

Mysticism had the ability to use deep longings within people to capture their allegiance. Ramakrishna won people's hearts by his apparent selflessness, sensitivity, and tenderness. What an overwhelming ace card to refute any attack of deception on his character—he seemed primevally innocent and sweet. Indeed, he oozed with love for his young disciples, transmitting the voltage of his possessing force to their foreheads with a single touch of *shakti-pat*. Therefore, when teachers such as Ramakrishna seemed to embody such goodness, they were above reproach. The power of this sentimental goodness cannot be underestimated.

What drove me to India initially was the lure of Ramakrishna combined with a number of mystical experiences. The power of this hook of sentimentalized Vedanta must not be underestimated.

Western Adepts of The East

Another group of players on the world stage at the turn of the century were the early figures of the Theosophical Society. The most notorious of these was the founder of the Theosophical Society, Madame Blavatsky, a strange Russian noblewoman who had been into the occult from her childhood. The headquarters for this society, which started in 1875, was in New York. But within a few years, Blavatsky moved it to Madras, India. She died two years before the World Parliament of Religions, choosing as her successor Annie Besant, a member of the British Fabian Society, the top of the pyramid of Britain's left-wing intelligentsia. Besant was a suffragette, most likely a lesbian, as well as a former member of Parliament.

Another member of this occult triad was Alice Bailey, whose writings as much as any have directed the course of the New Age movement. She later branched off from the theosophists, forming the Arcane School, taking with her the Lucifer Publishing Company of the theosophists which she renamed the Lucis Trust. The main remnant of her organization is now headquartered at United Nations Plaza.

These turn of the century occultists pieced together a body of beliefs that look like a constitutional charter for the entire New Age movement. Where did they get these ideas? From Indian mysticism and from their own spirit guides! Before the term "channeler" was ever popularized, replacing the older term of "medium," they were channeling down "higher" revelations from the "masters."

James Webb in *The Occult Underground* states that the early theosophists felt themselves "specially chosen to bear the light to the newly evolving global society."[1] The hierarchy who had "chosen" the theosophists claimed to be superhuman Tibetan spirit masters whose disembodied presence was in the Himalayas. They were setting up the world for "global evolution" and "the appearance of a messiah." One plan was that "Lord Maitreya" was to possess the body of Jiddu Krishnamurti. Webb comments that the latter's body "was to become the vehicle of the 'Lord Maitreya,' the coming 'World Teacher' of the New Age . . . preaching the Theosophical message of love, brotherhood, and the unity of all religions."[2]

Krishnamurti renounced this role in 1929 and became a guru in his own right. Krishnamurti also claimed to lose all memories prior to 1929. A little before then, Alice Bailey split away from the theosophists, and a disappointed Annie Besant died in 1933. Who was this Lord Maitreya? The "Master who had inhabited the body of Jesus in ancient Palestine, and who would take possession of the body of Krishnamurti in the same fashion."[3] Bailey again predicted Maitreya's return to establish a one world order and that this cosmic messiah was above all religions and all faiths. Bailey, like the others, got her revelations from forces outside of herself, namely, from "the masters." Today Benjamin Creme is the latest prophet of Maitreya.

Blavatsky spoke about her master in a letter: "All I can say is that someone positively inspires me—more than this, someone enters me. It is not I who talk and write: it is something within me . . . that thinks and writes for me. . . . I have become a sort of storehouse for somebody else's knowledge. . . . Someone comes and envelops me as a misty cloud and all at once pushes me out of myself and then I am not 'I' anymore . . . but someone else."[4]

In the *Mahatma Letters*, which are purported writings from the masters to Colonel Olcott, a theosophist leader, one master referred to Madame Blavatsky as "it, and the brother inside it." Olcott stated that no one knew the real Blavatsky since she was possessed and they "just dealt with an artificially animated body."[5] With Blavatsky, this began at an early age. Indeed, the "masters" that channeled through Blavatsky, Bailey, and Besant formulated an intricate and far-reaching occult revelation.

Early Creed for the New Spirituality

This Eastern occult revelation stated that man's problem is that he has fallen from his previous status as part of the divine godhead into material existence and that he has been deceived into doubting his oneness with the godhead. Only the hidden truths can set him free. Sin is nothing but ignorance. The theory of evolution, now applied to spiritual existence, was used to show that beings evolved as they reincarnated. The Hindus, of course, thought of this centuries before theosophists used Charles Darwin. Resembling gods, the ascended masters, en route to the godhead themselves, could extend a hand down to help those beneath them on the ladder of spiritual evolution. The hierarchy was there to help man's evolution. And who was Jesus Christ? Again he is redefined into a New Age cosmic Christ and another member of the hierarchy.

Jesus was simply an occult adept, one of many masters, who the "Christ consciousness" possessed. His teachings needed to be rescued from Christianity. Extra canonical sources were needed, from early Gnostic heresies to revelations from the masters. The culprit hiding the esoteric truth was Christianity itself. Blavatsky's *Isis Unveiled* is one long 800-page attack on Christianity, anticipating today's now-familiar posture of moral outrage at any biblical or moral judgmentalism (which itself is judgmentalism against Christianity). The council of Nicea was attacked for supposedly throwing out reincarnation along with other secret teachings. Christianity seemed to be nothing but a cover-up campaign lasting 2000 years. And its great adversary—Lucifer—was really man's greatest ally.

Lucifer as Hero and Savior

Blavatsky launched a stinging attack on the God of the Bible calling him "capricious and unjust,"[6] "a tribal God and no more."[7] Blavatsky then reveals that the biblical account is reversed, that Satan is the victim of Jehovah. She says:

Theosophical Emblem

> The appellation Satan, in Hebrew Satan, and Adversary . . . belongs by right to the first and cruelest "Adversary" of all other Gods—Jehovah; not to the serpent which spoke only words of sympathy and wisdom.[8]

Blavatsky declares:

> Once the key to Genesis is in our hands, the scientific and symbolical Kabbala unveils the secret. The Great Serpent of the Garden of Eden and the "Lord God" are identical.[9]

Satan, indeed, is viewed as the savior of mankind, freeing men from ignorance and death. He becomes the creator of divinized man. Blavatsky says:

> Satan, the Serpent of Genesis, is the real creator and benefactor, the Father of Spiritual mankind. For it is he . . . who opened the eyes of the automaton (Adam) created by Jehovah, as alleged. And he who was the first to whisper, "in the day ye eat thereof, ye shall be as Elohim, knowing good and evil," can only be regarded in the light of a savior. An adversary to Jehovah . . . he still remains in Esoteric Truth the ever loving messenger . . . who conferred on us spiritual instead of physical immortality.[10]

Lucifer becomes the greatest initiator. Churches that oppose this savior "are fighting against divine truth, when repudiating and slandering the Dragon of Esoteric Divine Wisdom."[11]

Albert Pike

It is only a small step from this to Alice Bailey's talk about a "Luciferic Initiation of Mankind." The road was well-paved. Nor was Bailey the only one to say this.

A hundred years ago General Albert Pike, the top Masonic leader of the Scottish Rite of Freemasonry in Charleston, South Carolina, anticipated a global Luciferic initiation in his letter to Mazzini in Italy.

Blavatsky calls Christ "the first born brother of

Satan." Christ, too, becomes a great initiator who brings in the hidden light. "Atonement" is now seen as "at-one-ment" with the divine inner self. It reverses the fall of divinity into the realm of matter. Blavatsky and her masters hate the biblical view of the Fall and speak of this with considerable emotion:

> Finally, it has created the god-slandering dogma of Hell and eternal perdition; it has spread a thick film between higher intuitions of man and divine verities; and, the most pernicious result of all, it has made people remain ignorant of the fact there were no fiends, no dark demons in the universe before man's own appearance on this, and probably other earths.[12]

How do they view the Second Coming of Christ? Theosophists precede New Age beliefs by more than half a century: "The coming of Christ means the reawakening of the Christ-spirit in mankind or in as many as are able to receive it. . . . For man, essentially divine, having wandered away from the knowledge of his own divinity, has to regain it."[13] The Second Coming of Christ is now reinterpreted by theosophists as the descent of a massive "Christ consciousness" upon the inhabitants of the earth. It becomes a global transformation through consciousness-raising as the human race reclaims its lost divinity. To most New Agers, this best explains the Second Coming. In reality, their scenario provides for what the Bible calls the Great Lie, on a massive level. In that light it is a vehicle for the delusion of the human race. Even the blessed hope becomes disfigured by occult spell-weaving. To those who reject the truth, who are hostile to it, it is an attractive alternative to Christ's visible return.

"Lord Maitreya" on April 25, 1982, was announced in newspapers around the world in a full-page ad predicting his return as the global messiah. It proclaimed at one point: "What is the Plan? It includes the installation of a new world government and new world religion under Maitreya." Benjamin Creme, who placed these paid ads, claims to be Maitreya's channeler. Creme is the founder of the Tara Association. So far there has been no worldwide appearance, only secret ones, and the blame invariably falls on the lack of spiritual consciousness in the world.

Making Early Contact

Both Annie Besant and Alice Bailey, like Blavatsky, claimed to be channels for a number of ascended masters including "The Tibetan," or Djwhal Khul.

Alice Bailey knew she had been marked for a task. There is no greater way to increase feelings of self-worth than to feel that you have been chosen for a major cosmic task. She might have secretly gloated that she was now light-years ahead of her better-looking sister.

The same entity entered Alice Bailey's life in seven-year intervals. It was not until 1915, when she was 35, that she finally discovered that this turbaned visitor was "Master Kutchumi."[14] In 1915, in Lucknow, India, Bailey was close to a mental breakdown from overwork and mental exhaustion. Then Master Kutchumi appeared:

> Suddenly a broad shaft of brilliant light struck my room and the voice of the Master who had come to me when I was fifteen spoke to me. . . . He told me not to be unduly troubled; that I had been under observation and was doing what He wanted me to do. He told me that things were planned and that the life work which He had earlier outlined to me would start, but in a way which I would not recognize.[15]

In 1919, two things happened to Alice Bailey. She met her first husband, Foster Bailey, an officer in the Theosophical Society, and she met her highest Tibetan master, known as "The Tibetan," or Djwhal Khul. The Tibetan, according to Bailey, was be the true author of her many books. It was her moment to enter the world stage. How could she say no?

Little did Alice Bailey know at the time that the organization which she and her husband would eventually found would be in United Nations Plaza in New York City by the 1980s and that "The Plan" dictated to her by "The Tibetan" would be something held up by world leaders of the New Age movement as the most comprehensive overview of the New Age agenda. Bailey had taken her dictations from Djwhal Khul word for word.

Bailey admitted, "After all, the books are His, not mine, and basically the responsibility is His. He does not permit me to make mistakes and watches over the final draft with great care."[16] It is hard to resist the notion that because of the great logistical and strategic effort focused on Bailey, Blavatsky, and Besant by the masters, something dealing with world events was critical to their agenda. The masters had a vested interest in the destiny of the human race apparent in their concentrated efforts.

For almost 30 years, Alice Bailey became the mouthpiece of "The Tibetan," producing 19 books in the process. Probably the most powerful revelation, the one containing "The Plan," was *The Externalization of the Hierarchy*. All of these revelations went from "The Tibetan," to Alice Bailey, to the world-at-large. But what if "The Tibetan" is not who he claims to be?

It's a ploy as old as the Trojan horse of the ancient world. The Greek army did not have the power to batter down the huge stone wall and gates of Troy, so they presented the Trojans with a "gift" that was wheeled inside the heavily fortressed gates. Inside of this colossal carved horse hid an army waiting to spring out at night and slay the slumbering inhabitants of the kingdom. It worked, and the Greeks destroyed Troy without losing a single man or battering down the gate.

The FBI will sift every nuance of detail concerning the private lives of public officials of national importance, such as a member of the cabinet or a Supreme Court justice. Supreme Court nominee Robert Bork got knocked out of contention over opinions in articles he had written for law journals years earlier.

During the era of the Old Testament, a prophet was ruthlessly scrutinized. But "The Tibetan" and similar entities have been accepted by millions of people who don't even question their credentials or their origin. They stake their eternal souls on some voice wired to the other end of the universe. It is a strange double standard: the same people who rattle off minor points about the Bible that they think will dispose of its validity and hence its authority will offer their souls to some channeled revelation or godman without hesitation. Their focused skepticism is selective and self-serving. It's as if they have already made up their minds. Herein lies a deep mystery—it is the mystery of the human heart. The Bible makes a powerful point—those who have a love of the Truth will find God. It may take years, as it did me in India, but those driven by a love of the truth will find it in the end.

America passed through the rainbow bridge as many decided what sort of "truth" they wanted. What a handful had experienced at the turn of the century would blanket an entire generation of the sixties who reveled in the delicious newness of the promise of unlimited horizons.

16

The Reality of Evil

Goethe's *Faust* proposed a seductive means of consciousness-expansion—by unlimited experience, both good and evil. The Indian Tantrics long taught that one must go beyond good and evil. Then, and only then, can each transcend the false duality of good and evil and merge with the One. The Indian guru Rajneesh explored this Tantric teaching by saying that if one exhausted the experiences of pure evil, then one can truly know good and truly become God. His ashram in Poona, which I saw in its heyday, pushed things to the limit. Experience was the key to personal expansion. For liberated Westerners this was truly an inviting doorway because it meant unlimited pleasure with no accountability. Of course there were casualties all over the place which I reported in *Riders of The Cosmic Circuit*, including people being killed.

There was a time in the Western civilized world when nobody would have believed the level of immorality—indeed, evil—that society has unleashed in our time. Humanism appeared and declared good and evil to be relative, but unlike the Tantrics, unlike Faust, unlike the New Age movement, it did not really believe in or understand the supernatural. What humanism did was blur distinctions of good and evil. It said the old traditional understandings no longer applied. Once humanism performed that task, a new supernaturalism could appear. It was a doorway of permission.

In today's entertainment the audience gets dull to heightening thrills, then in turn wants to see more. It keeps feeding like a fire. Young children become more jaded than middle-aged adults of several generations back through this corruptive voyeurism of films that take them to forbidden areas.

Movies are a very powerful index of this blurring process. Films have changed drastically. Particular films have stood out as major trendsetters of public thought. In that sense, they are tools of propaganda and behavior modification. Some films are landmarks of conscience-searing—they push the mind to new boundaries, sometimes morally, sometimes conceptually. What would have been terribly bizarre or shocking at one time can quickly enter the realm of the ordinary. Increasingly, movies have abolished distinctions between good and evil. They have offered to millions what only a handful of Romantics like Marquis de Sade explored in the last century.

We become more experienced in knowing evil, not in knowing good. It doesn't work the other way around. It is like most compromises: One side usually gives more than the other.

How much have films really  changed? There is an experiment that would be very revealing were it possible: for instance, sending a few movies back in a time machine to New York's old Ziegfeld Theater of the 1930s to see how the audience might react to several powerhouse conscience-searers of our era, and then interviewing the audience to see if things have really changed that much. Tell them that it is an experiment in intracultural appreciation, from the future to the past. Tell them our "cognoscente" have appreciated some of their old black-and-white movies, things like *Petrified Forest* with Leslie Howard, and films with Lombard, Barrymore, Mary Pickford, and Douglas Fairbanks all playing noble souls whose virtue, integrity, and humanity always manage to stand them in good stead against the dark forces. When they fall in love, it is believable. Men are still men and women are women. Their words are deep and sincere, their eyes searching and vul-

nerable as they speak to one another with  endearing respect. Nary a crudity passes their lips. Such are the old celluloid heroes who still believed in good and evil in those days.

Now, in our experiment at New York's old Ziegfeld Theater, have the house packed from stem to stern with the good old folk of the 1930s, the solid citizens.

Maybe include a representative sample of rural folk from all over—from the Midwestern Iowa corn belt to citizens from quiet towns in New England and the deep South. Then do a triple-header: imagine their gasps as beak-face appears in *Clockwork Orange* with a bowler hat, mascara high-lighting a single eye, at one point, a false genital strapped to his nose and holding a cane, acting out Gene Kelly "just singin' in the rain" while dancing on somebody's face. By now they will need to be strapped in their seats. Then imagine Bob Guccione's *Caligula* with the Roman emperor, played by Malcolm McDowell, once again, ranting in an effete, androgynous, blood-drenched orgy, with scenes of bestiality, sodomy, and dismemberment. Then end it up with Clive Barker's *Hellraiser*, where none of the characters are either remotely likable or human, everyone plotting against everyone else in vulgar stupidity-black humor at its most sardonic.

Finally, conclude the gala occasion with a rock history appreciation concert. From Mick Jagger and the Rolling Stones Dancing with the Devil to David Bowie as

Ziggie Stardust, Billy Idol singing "Whiplash Smile" in leather and chains, while standing in the middle of a penta-gram and sneering

at the audience. Then KISS, Motley Crue, Nine Inch Nails and finally Marilyn Manson—the androgenous composite of Charles Manson and Marilyn Monroe—singing "Antichrist Superstar" while tearing up a Bible and spitting on his adorers.

Most probably the outraged audience would
literally tear down the movie house and repent
that they could ever be the ancestors of such a
future world only 60 years down the road. They
would wonder in stunned horror how we got so
evil. How did beliefs so disintegrate? How did
our relative innocence so completely go down
the tube? They would probably suspect they had
just seen some collective Antichrist.

Then, while they were all raging or beating
their breasts in despair, they could be shown the
television gospel message to meet such horrific
needs. Have Jimmy Swaggart or Smopper Bob
the Evangelist slide across the stage in a metallic
polyester leisure suit while putting on the barnyard growl, shaking with
sweat, and howling into the mike—guttural slang as gravelly and cacopho-
nous as a chicken yard during an earthquake, morphemes and phonemes
coming out at ten per second in a drawl as thick as molasses and with as
much content as an idiot without novocaine in a dentist's chair.

Malcolm Muggeridge, Britain's one-time liberal, intellectual media
commentator and writer who became a Christian convert later in life, suc-
cinctly pinpointed the self-destructive tendencies at work within our time.
Muggeridge observed:

> It is difficult to resist the conclusion that there is a death wish at work at
> the heart of our civilization whereby our banks promote the inflation
> which will ruin them, our educationalists seem to create the moral and
> intellectual chaos which will nullify their professional purposes, our
> physicians invent new and more terrible diseases to replace those they
> have abolished, our moralists cut away the roots of all morality, and our
> theologians dismantle the structure of belief they exist to expound and
> promote.[1]

The answer for why the liberated West is in a process of self-destruction
is coherently explained by the biblical view. Its clear teaching is this: sin and
evil will take down individual lives as well as entire civilizations. The
process and the answer serve to become, in the end, a kind of validation of
the Bible and biblical truths which emphasize that good and evil are real.
From Sodom of antiquity to Los Angeles today, a Pandora's box is opened
when evil is allowed free reign. When the language of value relativism

replaces clear statements about good and evil, it becomes that much harder to back out of the trap. Good is mocked at and people become trapped. As people lose their God—guaranteed dignity and their value in the eyes of others—then literally anything becomes possible with them.

To our 1930s film audience in the old Ziegfield Theater, certain basic givens of life seemed unshakable to that more innocent generation: the preciousness and dignity of human life, the goodness of the family, the fact that men and women were truly different and unique. Pregnancy and birth were still precious then. Abortion was still seen as an inhuman act, the killing of a human life. They had not learned Weber's language of value relativism.

The astronomical level of abortions today would have been beyond their wildest nightmares. Abortions have become matters of cold decision on the level of buying a kitchen appliance and condoned by the strident, moralistic-sounding slogans of the women's movement demanding their rights. That someone would have to die in order *not* to "oppress them" or disturb their comfort zone would defy imagination of the old order.

Groups line the mall of Capitol Hill to protest their "rights," to champion their freedoms—to abort fetuses, to perform sodomy—things that were barely mentioned above a whisper during the old Ziegfield era. Now with countless numbers dying of AIDS, they demand that antisodomy laws across the nation "limiting freedom" be repealed. With one foot in the grave, they still want to engage in sodomy.

This crusading coalition will lead you to believe that they are "caring" and "nurturing" and oppressed victims as they murder infants, commit anal intercourse, or engage in lesbian acts. Imagine our audience at the Ziegfield Theater seeing a news special on some of these mass rallies, then with hidden glimpses of the camera seeing the acting out of what is being spoken of with such noble language. They would be assaulted. If only we could see it from their perspective, but it is too late.

The Communist and Nazi atrocities showed us something: people hide the horror by removing the evidence. Occasionally by accident, someone will be overwhelmed by the spectacle of seeing a mountain of dead infants stuffed in a trash incinerator, but this is a rarity. On the evening news of

May 20, 1985, there was an embarrassing story about the discovery of thousands and thousands of dead fetuses in California. A growing mob of protesters waited to hear if the court would rule the babies as human or as products, and whether they would be buried or cremated. Collagen from such flesh is used in certain cosmetics. Those who encountered the rotting flesh were struck with the reality of abortion as opposed to tame descriptions of it by the spin artists.

Peter Adam, an associate professor of pediatrics at Case Western Reserve University, within only six months of the *Roe v. Wade* decision, joined some of his medical associates conducting experiments on 12 babies: "These men took the tiny babies and cut off their heads—decapitated the babies and cannulated the internal carotid arteries (that is, a tube was placed in the main artery feeding the brain). They kept the diminutive heads alive, much as the Russians kept the dogs' heads alive in the 1950s. Take note of Dr. Adam's retort to criticism: 'Once society's declared the fetus dead, and abrogated its rights, I don't see any ethical problem. . . . Whose rights are we going to protect, once we've decided fetuses won't live?' "[2]

Walker Percy dwells on an alarming pattern, that has only become worse since he wrote about it in his brilliant book *Lost in the Cosmos*:

> The suicide rate among persons under twenty-five has risen dramatically in the last twenty years. . . . The incidence of drug use in teenagers and pre-teens has increased an estimated 3000 percent in the last thirty years. On a recent talk show on "tough love," it was claimed that about one-third of all teenagers were depressed. Of the one third, as many as 75 percent were on drugs.[3]

Walker Percy continues to shine light on another sacred institution— marriage:

> Of all sexual encounters on soap operas, only six percent occur between husband and wife. In some cities of the United States, which now has the highest divorce rate in the world, the incidence of divorce now approaches 60 percent of married couples. A recent survey showed that the frequency of sexual intercourse in married couples declined 90 percent after three years of marriage.[4]

Walker Percy reveals the worldview behind these strings of statistics. It is a relativism of values, that there are no absolute truths, thus making all moralities impotent in the end. They have no teeth—they are not able to make any real judgments or say "no" to evil with any authority.

In Germany in the late 1930s the state became open to killing undesirables. This could be justified if men have no intrinsic value—then it

becomes okay to kill the mentally handicapped and others who would biologically pollute the species. It makes sense for the state to abort babies that
might be inferior, whose parents have low IQs. If the state decides that a
certain group is detrimental to it, then racial genocide becomes the solution. At that point, Weberian value relativism had sunk its teeth into the
German mind, and all things became possible.

One frightening artifact that the news media has unearthed in the last
decade is the reality of satanic crimes.

The San Francisco Chronicle, one of the most prestigious papers in the
United States, had the following bold headline on Thursday, November 5,
1987: "SATANISM LINKED TO SCORES OF U.S. CHILD ABUSE
CASES." Edward Lempinen's article stretched to a third of the back page.
The front-page section summarizes this frightening reality:

> Children as young as 2 and 3 years old
> have come forward with harrowing tales
> of drinking blood, animal sacrifices and
> sexual abuse as part of the rituals, accord-
> ing to law enforcement investigators,
> child abuse experts and parents.

The article discussed the latest horror
involving 58 children who attended the
U.S. Army Presidio Child Development
Center in the San Francisco area. Temple
of Set founder Michael Acquino was under
investigation for Satanic ritual molestations
of a number of Presidio children. I debated
him on Seattle TV and found him pro-
foundly repulsive. On the ABC Town Meeting, Acquino was trying to do
damage control regarding the recent media reports connecting Satanists to
pedophilia, especially targeting him and his Temple of Set.

Ted Koppel, the popular moderator of *Nightline*, said something quite
profound when he was speaking at Duke University in the fall of 1987.
Koppel left the standard posture of so-called objective impartiality that the
media is supposed to embody and spoke from his heart. He portrayed the
bankruptcy of the permissive liberal approach to morality, saying: "We have
actually convinced ourselves that slogans will save us. Shoot up if you must,
but use a clean needle. Enjoy sex whenever and with whomever you wish,
but wear a condom. No! The answer is no. Not because it isn't cool or
smart or because you might end up in jail or dying in an AIDS ward, but

no because it is wrong. . . . In its purest form, truth is not a polite tap on the shoulder. It is a howling reproach. What Moses brought down from Mount Sinai were not the Ten Suggestions."

A doctrine of meaninglessness has real consequences. Our latest example is the novel/film *Less Than Zero*, where life meant less than zero. This problem has grown acute in the twentieth century, stretching from the Dadaists of Berlin in the early twenties, to the existentialists in Parisian cafes on the banks of the Seine coolly planning suicide in the thirties and forties, to the multicolored punk rockers in London and Merseyside slashing and kicking one another as they dance, to the Los Angeles school kids O.D.'ing on cocaine. They are the products, the unwilling participants, of a world in which they found themselves. Their lives are the echoes of thinkers such as Ibsen, Ionesco, Beckett, Camus, Sartre, Kafka, and Henry Miller, plus a host of nameless humanists and social engineers of every hue conceivable.

The price of present-day denials of biblical truth is different from what it was in the past. Once, people could bury themselves in the myth of human decency and respectability. Complacency masked over any deep sense of spiritual need. Most still retained their traditional rules of decent conduct. The invasion of the demonic was completely unforeseen. Now it is sitting on our doorstep. Imagine an old Model-T ride from the Colonnade Club of the 1920s right into a satanic mass where an abducted child is being sacrificed to Satan—a child whose face might well appear on some Safeway milk carton.

We have gone way beyond moralistic posturing for the sake of appearing decent. There is little pretense of innocence, especially in the youth. The writings of Henry Miller 25 years ago typify America's first awakening into continental nihilism and despair:

> It may be that we are doomed, that there is no hope for us, any of us, but if that is so then let us set up a last agonizing, blood-curdling howl, a screech of defiance, a war-whoop! Away with lamentation! Away with elegies and dirges! Away with biographies and histories, and libraries and museums! Let the dead eat the dead. Let us living ones dance about

the rim of the crater, a last expiring dance. But a dance! . . . A fatuous, suicidal wish that is constipated by words and paralyzed by thought.[7]

Soren Kierkegaard, the philosopher of the nineteenth century, foresaw the basis of our nihilistic crisis a century ago:

> If there were no eternal consciousness in a man, if at the foundation of all there lay only a wildly seething power which writhing with obscure passions produced everything that is great and everything that is insignificant, if a bottomless void never satiated lay hidden beneath all— what would life be but despair?[8]

Kierkegaard himself saw the route out of this terrifying despair within the pages of the gospels. He saw Christ as providing the only hope in the world.

When belief in the reality of good and evil really ceases, you are left with a world that either has a sense of hopelessness and meaninglessness, and people exist in a state of despair, defiant hedonism, or else, a new kind of mysticism enters their midst. When either of these happen, the doorway for the pursuit of evil will open up and almost anything can happen. Humanism is only a halfway point. There is another specter further down the road. The fictional letter home below perhaps illustrates this point. It was penned by my close friend George Byron Koch to make a point.

A Letter from the Future

Dear Mom,   22 January 2023

Gosh, can you believe it's 2023 already? I'm still writing "22" on nearly everything. Seems like just yesterday I was sitting in first grade celebrating the century change!

I know we haven't chatted since Christmas. Sorry. Anyway, I have a few things to tell you and I really didn't want to call and talk face to face.

Ted's had a promotion, and I should be up for a hefty raise this year if I keep putting in those crazy hours. You know how I work at it. Yes, we're still really struggling with the bills. You were right about over-buying on the house, but it IS nice.

Timmy's been "okay" at kindergarten although he's still not happy about going. But then he wasn't happy about daycare either, so what can you do?

He's become a real problem, mom. He's a good kid, but quite honestly he's an unfair burden at this time in our lives. Ted and I have talked this through and through and finally made a choice. Plenty of other families have made it and are much better off.

I don't expect you to "understand," but you need to be sensitive to our circumstances. I can't afford years of parenting with Timothy and have any sort of career, much less any time with my husband. Do you know how long its been since we just went out together?

Our pastor is supportive and says hard decisions sometimes are necessary. The family is a "system" and the demands of one member shouldn't be allowed to ruin the whole. He told us to be prayerful, consider ALL the factors, and do what is right to make the family work. He says that even though he probably wouldn't do it himself, the decision really is ours. He referred us to a children's clinic near here, so at least that part's easy.

I'm not an uncaring mother. I do feel sorry for the little guy. I think he overheard Ted and me talking about "it" the other night. I turned around and saw him standing on the bottom step in his pj's with the little bear you gave him under his arm and his eyes sort of welling up. The way he looked at me just about broke my heart. But I honestly believe this is better for Timothy too. It's not fair to force him to live in a family where there isn't enough money or room.

Please don't give me the kind of grief grandma gave you over your abortions. It's the same thing, you know. Anyway, they say the termination procedure is painless.

I guess it's just as well you haven't seen that much of him. Love to dad.—Jane

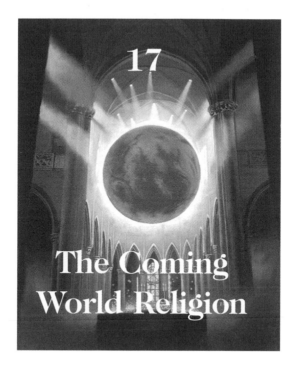

The Coming
World Religion

The Planetary Mass at San Francisco's immense Grace Cathedral heralded great events due to intersect history. This sacrament, the Planetary Mass, was seen as a pinpoint of light that would help catalyze the earth's ignition of consciousness. Similar devotionals would fuse to form a spiritual sunburst, inaugurating a new spiritual era. Many looked with expectancy towards this threshold at the edge of the new millennium towards the coming world religion.

The high priestly celebrant and innovator of the Planetary Mass was Matthew Fox, the renegade New Age Catholic priest who had been silenced and recently excommunicated by the Church of Rome. Now it was time for main line Protestantism, open-minded and liberal, to welcome the heretical Catholic priest into its ranks with open arms.

On the other side of America, New York City's Cathedral of Saint John the Divine —another massive historical monument to a once robust and orthodox Protestantism—had been having similar global celebrations.

Since the 1960s, New York's oldest and grandest Episcopal Cathedral had grown new innards that obscured its once uncluttered and expansive sanctuary of stain glass windows and unobstructed pillars. Now exhibition hall style add-ons, which were included in the name of "holism," vivisected the great cathedral like a New Age Fair. There were sectors of the Cathedral that resembled a New York subway—with mystical graffiti and posters— all creating a sense of confusion and chaos. It is what happens when anomalies are grafted to beautifully ornate architectural harmonies. At the base of magisterial columns were sectors dedicated to various special interest platforms—feminists and devotees of the goddess, environmental groups, Gaians (who saw the earth as divine), areas for "gay-lesbian-bisexual" issues, and areas for Native Americans, Eastern mystics, New Age leaders, and gurus.

Grace Cathedral and the Cathedral of Saint John the Divine had been widened by constant doctrinal road work, from their once narrow path into a spiritual superhighway containing enough lanes to hold all the world's religions. The multitudes could commune regardless of belief as long as they were not part of the narrow way of orthodox New Testament belief. The Cathedrals were preparing the way for the Cosmic Millennium. And exclusive Christianity was not invited to the altar.

In another part of New York City, not far from Cathedral of Saint John the Divine, the United Nations building loomed in the air of Manhattan like a vast secular cathedral.

From the UN General Assembly, the World Court, World Bank, World Health Organization, to its own UN forces and flag, the UN had everything in miniature to develop into a full fledged world government—a United Nations with teeth—if the nation states would concede their sovereignty. Until then it was just a symbol and vehicle for world goodwill. Yet, even if the UN acted as midwife for another form of world rule, it would have still served its purpose. Global unity was the quantum evolutionary leap of civilization that Teilhard de Chardin foresaw and wrote about with expectation, even coming by the end of this century.

The United Nations had its own spiritual sanctuary, a meditation room. It was constructed as a hologram depicting, by its very design, the unity of the major religions of the world. Not a pretty sight, to be sure, but a utilitarian statement of sleek functionality. It was under the watchful eye of Sri Chinmoy, who also served as the chaplain of the United Nations. He guided and spoke to thousands. This UN chaplain was not a Christian—the once reigning faith of the host nation where his cathedral skyscraper stood—but

UN Chaplain Chinmoy

an Indian Yogi whose face resembled a death mask, eyes half-closed, staring into the cosmic void. And indeed, no one could be more fitting as high priest of the UN than this Indian guru, who claimed to be in a state of perpetual Cosmic Consciousness while embodying the Divinity of Man. In this *brave new world*, Man was the final measure of Truth. It would be a dream come true for mystics who had prepared the way.

Meanwhile, in the aging cathedrals of Christendom, cosmic sacraments such as the Planetary Mass were seen as gateways through which all the world's faiths could converge. They were the Western gesture towards syncretism—spiritual disarmament—involving a total abandonment of history, tradition, and religious sovereignty. It was a capitulation for the sake of peace, world peace — but willingly, with eyes open, and running to the invading army to lay down its weapons and possessions at the feet of these gateways.

The challenge was to harmonize the holy books of the earth into one unitary voice while brushing aside the diverse faiths and fundamentalisms of the Old World Order. Disarmament was necessary. And this took visionaries who could see far and wide. To repeat, they had to be dizzyingly optimistic about mankind and world government and very trusting about the whole process.

The participants who filled the two largest and oldest Episcopal Cathedrals in New York and San Francisco, beheld a new Faith rising from out of the earth. It came in time to meet a world at the geopolitical cross-roads of the long heralded New World Order. It would be a time when nation states entered the dusty back shelves of world history as a new world was born. Most of its prophets felt that this could only come about by an evolutionary leap in consciousness. There was a whole vocabulary for this transition—*planetary convergence, omega point, paradigm shift, transformation, the coming of the Cosmic Christ, New Age*. And true believers could be spotted from out of the multitude by their infectious, manic, perhaps nirvanic, opti-mism, as they sped gleefully towards the millennium without a fear or a doubt in the world.

Teilhard de Chardin (1881-1955) is almost without question the leading candidate in the West for *spiritual* father of the rising spiritual and political globalism now taking the world by storm. He formulated the dominant conceptual framework in the West for a planetary religion and social order.

In the early part of this century, Teilhard outlined and predicted a coming "convergence of religions" (his own term) to rise in tandem with political globalism. Each force would accelerate the other. It is a vision that has fired the imaginations of a wide swath of people now in leadership positions (including even those who have misunderstood or modified Teilhard's views).

Teilhard described himself as a mystic and evo-lutionary scientist. What he fully expected was an evolutionary leap in consciousness to come upon the human race, possibly at the year 2000. He felt that the spiritual and political unification of the earth was the next great leap to come and that it was vital for the survival of mankind. He often said, "The Age of nations has passed. Now, unless we wish to perish we must shake off our old prejudices and build the earth. . . Life cannot henceforth advance on our planet (and nothing will prevent its advancing—not even its inner servitudes) except by breaking down the par-titions which still divide human activity and entrusting itself unhesitatingly to faith in the future."[1] Naturally, he saw the United Nations as a key ves-sel for this process.

Teilhard's diary contained something even more radical. He mentions

the transformation of the Hindu god Shiva by Christ. And here he is virtu-
ally in the camp of Vedanta. Teilhard resolves good and evil by merging
them, like all polar opposites, into the godhead. Though he calls it
'Christifying.' Teilhard scholar Ursula King found this reference to Shiva in
Teilhard's diary. She quotes him in her book, *Towards a New Mysticism:
Teilhard de Chardin and Eastern Religions*, with her own comments:

> Among the many tentative suggestions in his diary, one of the most puz-
> zling and least expected is the reference to the Indian god Shiva and to
> "Christ-Omega/Shiva" in 1948. After referring to the overpowering
> forces of the cosmos which can neither be tamed nor appeased, he says
> that '. . . It is not enough to refuse or ridicule Shiva: for he exists. What
> is necessary, is to christify him. Christ would not be complete if he did
> not integrate Shiva (as a component), whilst transforming him.'[2]

Ursula King found among Teilhard's cryptic diary notes and letters that
God had to be altered:

> It was especially the image of God which Teilhard saw in need of urgent
> redefinition. Modern man has not yet found the God he can adore, a
> God commensurate to the newly discovered dimensions of the universe.
> In 1950, he noted in his diary: "God is not dead—, but HE
> CHANGES." In a letter to a friend, he referred to "the transformation.
> . . of the 'God of the Gospel' into the 'God of Evolution.' . . .[3]

And so we get to the center of Teilhard de Chardin's greatest act of theological defacement—his redefinition of the very nature and being of God
to suit his cosmic summa theologica. He is also paving the way for the
undiscerning or indifferent masses in a post-Christian world. He exchanges
the true Christ for a "Universal Christ," and all but a minority of people
these days would even know the difference. It is a perfect set-up for the
globalistic spirit of the age and its planetary transformation, now being proclaimed as a soon-to-come revival. Barbara Marx Hubbard has termed it
"Planetary Pentecost."

Global strategists outside the faith will see the unification of the planet
as far more important—from their perspective—than the tiresome separatist whining by a minority of "true believers" stuck in theological minuti-
ae. And they will eventually take a hard line. To them, the ends will justify
the means, even if it means drastic solutions.

The United Religions

Theosophist Alice Bailey expected the New Religion, which she called
the "Church Universal," to emerge by the close of the twentieth century[4]

– in other words, now. Bailey says that "Only those will remain as guides and leaders of the human spirit who speak from living experience, and who know no creedal barriers; they will recognize the onward march of revelation and the new emerging truths. These truths will be founded on the ancient realities but will be adapted to modern need and will manifest progressively the revelation of the divine nature and quality."[5]

Bailey believed that the New Religion would work closely with the UN: "Thus the expressed aims and efforts of the United Nations will be eventually brought to fruition and a new church of God, gathered out of all religions and spiritual groups, will unitedly bring to an end the great heresy of separateness."[6] Bailey said that in the New Religion, there will be two levels of religious practice – one for the masses and one for the adepts of the New Age, those who "know the potency of formulas, mantrams and invocations and who work consciously."[7] Robert Muller has gone further, proposing to deify the UN: "At the beginning the UN was only a hope. Today it is a political reality. Tomorrow it will be the world's religion."[8] Robert Muller favors using the European Union as the basis for "World Union," unless the UN is "rapidly transformed" into "an effective world political union."[9]

The United Religions Initiative (URI), which intends to become "a permanent assembly, with the stature and visibility of the United Nations"[10] encompassing all "religions, spiritual expressions, and indigenous traditions,"[11] is advancing steadily. The 1995 interfaith service that launched the URI, took place at San Francisco's Grace Cathedral. During the ceremony "holy water from the Ganges, the Amazon, the Red Sea, the River Jordan, and other sacred streams" was mixed in a single "bowl of unity" on the altar of Grace Cathedral.[12] Bishop Swing made the meaning of the ritual clear as he intoned to the thousands on hand: "As these sacred waters find confluence here … may the city that chartered the nations of the world bring together the religions of the world."[13] In his book *The Coming United Religions*, Bishop Swing says, "The time comes, though, when common language and a common purpose for all religions and spiritual

URI flag of symbols

movements must be discerned and agreed upon. Merely respecting and understanding other religions is not enough."[14]

Episcopal Bishop Swing, the founder of the URI, told the 1997 URI summit conference: "If you have come here because a spirit of colossal energy is being born in the loins of earth, then come here and be a midwife. Assist, in awe, at the birth of new hope."[15] In a sermon given while attending the 1999 Parliament of World Religions, Bishop Swing said, "What a time to wait on God … for the coming new light among religions, spiritual expressions, and indigenous traditions."[16]

Bishop Swing

Bishop Swing condemns Christian evangelism, which he calls "proselytizing." Swing says that "proselytizing, condemning, murdering, or dominating" will "not be tolerated in the United Religions zone" – the whole world. URI leaders say "proselytizing" is the work of "fundamentalists," and URI board member Paul Chafee said in 1997 that "We can't afford fundamentalists in a world this small."[17]

The New York-based Lucis Trust, which spreads the teachings of American theosophist Alice Bailey, praised the URI in two 1999 issues of its newsletter World Goodwill, citing it as part of a "global shift in consciousness" that will usher in "an era in which the glory of the One will be free to shine forth in all human actions."[18]

Neale Donald Walsch is a member of the URI steering committee. Walsch's channeled source ("god") favors communism and world government. Walsch's god says that highly evolved beings—smart extraterrestrials—practice pure communism: "They share everything. With everyone. … All the natural resources of their world, of their environment, are divided equally, and distributed to everyone."[19] Nations must disappear. Instead, there should be a world government,[20] backed up with a World Court and a world "peacekeeping force."[21] Each nation would have two representatives in the Congress of Nations, and "representation in direct proportion to a nation's population" in the People's Assembly.[22] Under this plan, the U.S. would have as many votes in the Congress of Nations as the Sudan, where Christians are sold into slavery or executed. The U.S. would have about one-fourth as many votes in the People's Assembly as the People's Republic of China, which persecutes Christians and enforces a one-child policy on families. Would anyone care to guess how long our

Constitutional protections of freedom of religion and freedom of speech would survive?

Some Rights are More Equal than others

Atheist Madelyn Murray O'Hair in 1963, won a landmark Supreme Court decision barring religious practices—specifically Christian prayer—from all public schools. The atheistic viewpoint of the O'Hair family, including that of her son (whom I met years later after he became a Christian, and rejected all that his mother stood for), was being violated due to the fact that public schools allowed and practiced Christian prayers. Christians ever since have been literally prohibited by the state to practice their religion in America's public schools. The rights of a fraction of one percent, O'Hair, shut down those of the overwhelming majority.

The O'Hair decision is a legal precedent for the secular State: The religious practices of some are not to infringe upon the religious rights and freedoms of others. This can have far-reaching permutations.

If an average public school in America were suddenly to engulf the nation in size and in operations, all voluntary Bible studies and prayer, revivals and church meetings, and all manner of religious activities would have to be prohibited and frozen for the good of all. Those who wished to engage in such practices would have to sneak across the border—that is, if America were run along the lines of *one of its very own public schools*. This is an interesting thought.

To a future world-at-large that is without even the memory of a United States Constitution or Bill of Rights, such limitations as we put on those in our public schools might seem quite reasonable in a globalist-pluralist world.

And the deconstruction of America's Christian heritage has steam rolled ahead. Courtesy of the ACLU and others, numerous displays of Christian symbols that since the inception of this country were displayed openly in public have been banned, and cities across the country have been forced to take down crosses, street names, and nativity scenes.

The students of Harvard listened to the alarming words of Aleksander Solzhenitsyn when he spoke at their commencement. He was still a radical chic *cause de celebre*. On the eighth of June, 1978, they gathered in curious anticipation, perhaps hoping to be flattered or entertained. But in his address, *A World Split Apart*, Solzhenitsyn told the Harvard audience that they were soft and had no idea what their hard won liberties were worth and that "a decline in courage may be the most striking feature that an outside observer notices in the West today." Of course he had spent decades in the Soviet's worst Gulags where he endured things that these kids could not imagine.

The words of warning of this great Russian author went right over their heads. Many still touted chic leftist lapel buttons because they had learned the language of role-modeling for "intellectuals" who protest only the most vogue causes and in fact, can be identified as intellectuals by sporting all the right causes and paraphernalia. The liberal mystique allows some to posture themselves up to intellectual status—cheap imaging that the truly gifted usually see through at a glance.

Alger Hiss, who helped formulate the United Nations charter in San Francisco in 1948, with the help of his Communist bloc comrades (he was convicted as a traitor), based the charter document on the Soviet charter.

The United Nations' line of reasoning is that it is a religious right of every follower of a given religion not to be aggressively proselytized by those of another religion. In the name of the religious rights of one person, the rights of the adherent of another religion could be legally limited. Does this sound a little familiar, like school prayer in public school? So if an aspect of being a Christian is to obey the command "to make disciples of all nations" in order to spread the gospel, this religious mandate can now be legally restricted in the name of the greater rights of the collective. Now, what happens if the world becomes a federation of global states, whether loosely or tightly structured?

Under the banner of human rights, we have seen a line of reasoning that has been a supremely effective device in curtailing religious freedoms. This argument is tailor-made for a pluralist and globalist situation. If we suddenly submitted to the decrees of the United Nations General Assembly as law, then America would operate very much like our example of the extended public school. We would submit to doing this "for the benefit and out of respect for all world citizens."

In 1973, many famous and influential people signed the Humanist Manifesto II as a virtual collective of academics, lawyers, financiers, and politicians whose names read like a *Who's Who*. They declared:

> We deplore the division of humankind on nationalistic grounds. We
> have reached a turning point in human history where the best option is
> to transcend the limits of national sovereignty to move toward the build-
> ing of a world community . . . a system of world law and world order
> based upon transnational federal government.

What does the United Nations provide for world citizens desiring religious rights? If you consider the following, George Orwell could not have done a better job had he included the following in his novel *1984*.

In the 73rd plenary meeting of the 36th General Assembly, on November 25, 1981, among the resolutions adopted by the Third Committee was "The Declaration on the Elimination of All Forms of Intolerance and of Discrimination Based on Religion or Belief." Should the world's nation-states come under the umbrella of the United Nations, this will become inviolable law. Under Article 1, Sections 2 and 3, it states:

> 2. No one shall be subject to coercion which would impair his freedom to have a religion or belief of his choice.

> 3. Freedom to manifest one's religion or belief may be subject only to such limitations as are prescribed by law and are necessary to protect public safety, order, health, or morals or the fundamental rights and freedoms of others.

These same words have appeared in another context. In the United Nations Covenant on Human Rights, Article 15, Section 3, it states: "Freedom to manifest one's religion or beliefs may be subject only to such limitations as are prescribed by law."

Some years ago George Orwell wrote a brilliant satire on twentieth-century collectivism entitled *Animal Farm*, the story of a revolution staged by animals on Farmer Jones' place. As with all revolutions, there were leaders and there were followers. In this case, the pigs became the leaders since they were, through no fault of the others, a little smarter than the rest.

One of their first official acts was to draft a statement of seven principles which were then painted on the back wall of the barn for all to see. These principles became the basis of the new order and were designed to protect the animals from any future injustice or infringements on their rights. There were noble pronouncements as "No animal shall drink alcoholic beverages;" "No animal shall sleep in a bed;" and "No animal shall kill another animal." But the greatest and wisest of these was, "All animals are equal."

As the months became years, however, the "workers" were working twice as hard and eating half as well as they had when they were "exploited" by Farmer Jones—all of them, that is, except the rulers, the pigs, who were now drinking Jones' ale and sleeping in his bed. When the puzzled workers tried to figure out how things turned out this way, they went to the rear of the barn to see if there was not something in the seven great principles prohibiting this kind of injustice. They found, instead, that the principles were now worded slightly differently. Indeed, just a few words changed here and there completely changed the picture: "No animal shall drink alcoholic beverages . . . to excess;" "No animal shall sleep in a bed . . . *with sheets*;" "No animal shall kill another animal . . . *without cause.*" But by far the worst shock of all came when the poor creatures turned with hope to the seventh principle guaranteeing their rights but which now declared, "All animals are equal . . . *but some animals are more equal than others.*"

Let us again remember the resolution from the above United Nations declaration: "Freedom to manifest one's religion or belief may be subject *only to such limitations as are prescribed by law and are necessary to protect public safety, order, health, or morals.*" With enough legalese, word games, and elastic redefinitions of concepts, the above limitations could be instituted at the drop of a hat. Christians, should they ever fall under the United Nations World Court, might well look to the back of the barn one day and ponder these words.

The Iron Hand of Peace

New words are constantly being written on the back of today's international barn, as rules and ideas shift constantly. Globalists trying to pull off "the planetary bargain" continue to push ahead to find a spiritual unified field theory that resolves apparent differences among religions. This is what Teilhard de Chardin initially offered at the altar of the earth and what Bishop Swing is pursuing with the United Religions. "Some wastage" may happen in the event of those not willing to go along with the "peace plan."

When receiving the Norman Cousins Global Governance Award in October 1999 from the World Federalist Association (WFA), Walter Cronkite echoed, as a faithful talking head, what the elite over him believe, "We need a system of enforceable world law – a democratic federal world government—to deal with world problems."[23] Cronkite has been rewarded with huge material assets for his faithfulness and obedience, this crypto globalist with such a believable "patriotic" face.

To pave the way for Leviathan, Teilhard de Chardin's planetary faith is ideally suited to leaders and statesmen of the industrial world. It is a creed for the Family of Man, which fits in perfectly with the agenda of the United Nations as well as the New World Order.

Robert Muller, former Assistant Secretary General of the United Nations, is a perfect example of a high ranking UN leader who is an unabashed disciple of Teilhard de Chardin. Muller is dizzyingly optimistic about Teilhard's vision of the "confluence" of forces towards World Government and the "convergence" of faiths into a World Religion. And like Teilhard, Muller does not for a moment entertain the possibility of things ever going wrong with centralized power. Like many of his peers at the top of UN leadership, Robert Muller embraces the idea of a strong centralized government. And no wonder, because when Muller's mentor, Teilhard de Chardin, was in China, during the rise of Mao Tse Tung, he enthusiastically read *Red Star Over China* by his friend Edgar Snow, as well as the writings of Karl Marx. Teilhard saw in communist socialism the germ of world government:

> Teilhard seems to have admired any form of totalitarianism simply because it seemed to prove his theory of 'convergence,' whether it was Hitler or Stalin or the early Mao Tse-tung did not seem to worry him very much.[24]

Globalists have already been monitoring the forced bussing of the cultures of the world while closely watching new resistances appear. Melting pot nations like America and Great Britain provide a test run for synthesis, using various methods of mass socialization based on conformity and intimidation. Rule one is that there is shrinking room for individualists, especially those with strong convictions who they demonize as "fundamentalists."

For the rest, new norms have been instituted such as multiculturalism, unity-in-diversity, inclusiveness, and political correctness, which are pushed relentlessly on all levels of culture. The new human family is portrayed inevitably as a mandated cross sample of ethnic quotas, especially in the omnipresent media. TV news teams, roundtable discussions and town hall meetings, quiz shows, right down to the crew members of Star Trek, all embody the new ethnic constellation of the human family.

Those who come out of the mold of today's rigid socialization, not only do not feel as strongly about their religions as their parents, but feel apologetic about their religions or anything else that might make them look prejudicial or exclusivist with their peers. They are already ripe for a New World Order, as easy to mold as soft jello. No strong convictions or great strength of character will beleaguer them with hard and costly choices. These are the minions that totalitarians dream about. It's the gifted individualists, the resistors, who may have to be crushed.

The planetary paradigm is that the few can be sacrificed for the preservation and well-being of the many. "Surrender or be destroyed for the sake of the Earth," could become the choice given to separatist sects by the

Leviathan of the New World Order. This was true in ancient Rome, as recorded by Tacitus and Pliny, when Christians knew that it was a lie and a betrayal of their true Lord to offer worship Caesar as a god. And so when they refused, they were executed, martyred.

New Age globalist and URI insider Barbara Marx Hubbard has foreseen this same dilemma for resistors. She projects that for planetary transformation to take place, up to one quarter of the inhabitants of the earth will have to be excised like a cancer. She doesn't say how this will be done. She merely comments on the destruction of the resistant group in the manner an evolutionist describes the extinction of a species.

> This is a universal law: Only the good evolves — "good" meaning that which is capable of aligning with the whole emerging systems, by attuning to its overall design. A Quantum transformation is the time of selection of what evolves from what devolves. The species known as self-centered humanity will become extinct. The species known as whole-centered humanity will evolve. The goal of evolution is the emergence of beings in the image of the Creator. God is creating godlike beings through the evolution of worlds in the universe without end. Amen.[25]

Barbara Marx further adds:

> We are now in a sorting-out phase. Those who elect to transform are now being magnetized by their attraction to the next phase. Those who do not elect to transform are being turned off by their repulsion to the next phase. By attraction and repulsion the selection is being made.[26]

Many other New Age leaders, have echoed similar statements about the fate of those unable or unwilling to go along with the paradigm shift of planetary transformation. Elimination seems to be the only option.

The Soviet experiment eliminated up to 60 million people, mostly Christian farmers in the Ukraine who resisted Bolshevism. If that can happen within throwing distance of history, it can happen again in a New World Order.

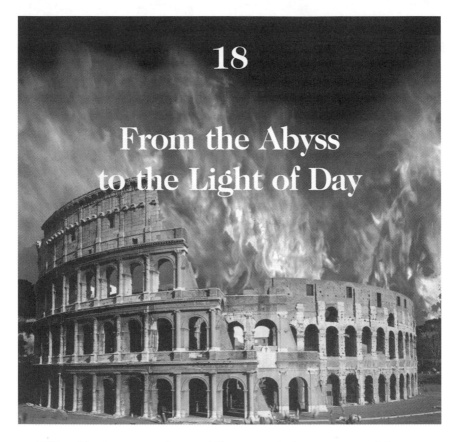

18

From the Abyss to the Light of Day

I could not escape the terrible screen before my eyes. No matter what, I had to keep looking on as I pressed myself down into the thick burgundy chair in horror. Vivid impressions of the ancient Roman world penetrated my five-year-old mind. The horrifying scenes before me depicted real events, true history, and that was the shocker.

I looked on helplessly from the balcony of one of Washington's grand old cinerama movie theaters as the colossal power of the emperor Nero was being portrayed. In his eyes was a perverse cruelty, a concentrated evil given to arbitrary whim. He seemed a law unto himself as he played with people like a bored child plays with helpless insects, cutting off this and that bit to see what happens. This emperor was so hard that no pleading would get through to him. The fact that such a dehumanized figure could exist baffled my young mind. What power could bend such a soul so grotesquely? How could someone choose evil over good? He was a human monster without an atom of sensitivity, goodness, or compassion, and he ruled the entire world! There was a reality behind this that I would learn of much later in life. Nero, in truth, was a vehicle for something else. He was a representative and a type among a very select group.

Contrasting with this terrible figure was another group of people who stuck in my mind as the supreme embodiment of good—they were his exact opposite. In one scene they were in the center of Rome's huge Colosseum. They were being persecuted because they would not pay homage to Nero. They were loyal to Christ alone above any state or emperor, and for that they would die. The crowds in the Colosseum roared. They wanted entertainment. Christians by the hundreds were spread across the arena. Nero was outraged, for rather than begging for mercy, renouncing their Christ, or running in terror, they sang these powerful hymns to their God while looking skyward. Peace radiated from their faces. Nero could not stand it. Finally he gave the thumbs down. Huge iron gates into the arena opened as scores of lions entered the stadium. The lions left some of the Christians alone as they sang and stared fearlessly into the crowds and at the emperor. Others were mauled while still singing. In the end, all died with dignity, leaving the Circus Maximus in an eerie silence. The emperor's desire for a blood orgy was completely frustrated, but only for the time being.

My terror increased as I saw the city of Rome all ablaze. The face of Nero grinned as it flickered with a scarlet light radiating from the enor-

mous flames. Perhaps he was punishing his subjects—mere insects to him—or seeking new forms of entertainment. He sang mad, intoxicating songs as massive crowds wailed in the background, running in helpless terror to escape falling columns and collapsing buildings. Nero ranted and laughed. How did he of all people end up with so much power? Why this evil creature among men?

After the fire of Rome, Nero blamed the Christians. Waves of persecution rolled on even more grotesquely. It was an affront to everything I instinctively felt, to see that evil and falsehood could hold such power. This situation cried out to be judged. As the mobs of Rome went wild in the streets looking for Christians, believing their emperor's lies, the powerful figure of Paul the apostle reassured the believers in the catacombs of Rome of ultimate hope. Nothing could quench

their hope or their goodness. I sensed something far mightier in the
Christian martyrs than the despotic evil that Nero embodied. I recall ask-
ing my parents to take me out of the movie theater. I had reached my limit.
This triumph of evil was too much.

Three decades after seeing this movie as a child, I was able to glimpse
this era once again through the eyes of such ancient contemporary historians as Pliny, Tacitus, and Suetonius, whose eyewitness records of the
Roman era were brought to vivid life in a course by Dr. Bruce Manning
Metzger, a famed Princeton professor who was one of my advisors. Bruce
Metzger, a man with five Ph. D.'s and one of the world's most brilliant
Christian scholars, was a key reason I was at Princeton during the last
years of his tenure. There was no question that the Neronic persecution
was real history—that this all happened in Rome. Indeed, the mortar of
the early church was persecution. Out of the fire came an unstoppable witness.

It was incredible what the ancient Christians suffered—and did so time
and again without God invisibly removing them from the scene! That is
history.

Like their Christ, they, too, suffered martyrdom, and they expected no
less. Christ himself had told them: "If they persecuted me, they will persecute you" (John 15:20 RSV); "Blessed are you when men revile you and
persecute you and utter all kinds of evil against you falsely on my account."
(Matthew 5:11 RSV); and "If any man would come after me, let him deny
himself and take up his cross and follow me" (Mark 8:34 RSV). Paul had
followed suit, saying, "When reviled, we bless; when persecuted, we
endure; when slandered, we try to conciliate" (1 Corinthians 4:12,13 RSV).
And Paul knew from experience what this was like. Paul was stoned at
Lystra; he and Silas were beaten by a mob in Philippi, then with lacerated
backs sang hymns to God; he had experienced the near-lethal 39 lashes on
various occasions; and he had a long imprisonment in Caesarea, was later
sent to Rome as a prisoner, and died a martyr. He says to some of the slow-
witted believers in Corinth: "Five times I received from the Jews the forty
lashes minus one. Three times I was beaten with rods, once I was stoned,
three times I was shipwrecked, I spent a night and a day in the open sea, I
have been constantly on the move" (2 Corinthians 11:24,25). Paul's litany
of trials goes on and on.

If God could allow such trials to happen to the apostles and early
Christians without removing them from the scene, should modern and
postmodern Christians expect any less? The wrath of man should not be

underestimated. As we see in the Roman era, it can seem almost as bad as the wrath of God from the receiving end—almost.

The ancient Roman historian Tacitus, who, like most of his contemporaries, did not sympathize with the Christians, describes what he saw after the great fire of Rome in his *Annals, XV, 44*:

> Therefore to scotch the rumor [of his starting the fire], Nero substituted as culprits, and punished with the utmost refinements of cruelty, a class of men loathed for their vices, whom the crowd styled Christians. Christus, from whom they got their name, had been executed by sentence of the procurator Pontius Pilate when Tiberius was emperor; and the pernicious superstition was checked for a short time, only to break out afresh, not only in Judaea, the home of the plague, but in Rome itself, where all the horrible and shameful things in the world collect and find a home. First, then, those who confessed themselves Christians were arrested; next, on their disclosures, a vast multitude were convicted, not so much on the charge of arson as for hatred of the human race. And their death was made a matter of sport: they were covered in wild beasts' skins and torn to pieces by dogs; or were nailed to crosses and set on fire in order to serve as torches by night when daylight failed. Nero had offered his gardens for the spectacle and gave an exhibition in his circus, mingling with the crowd in the guise of a charioteer or mounted in his chariot . . . it was felt that they were being sacrificed not for the common good but to gratify the savagery of one man.

This happened in A.D. 64, around the time that the apostle Paul was martyred.

Sixty years later, Pliny, governor of Bithynia in A.D. 112, wrote the emperor Trajan describing his manner of dealing with the Christian problem. By then, the church had endured well over 60 years of persecution. Pliny tells the emperor in his *Epistles of Pliny, X, 33 & 34*:

> So far this has been my procedure when people were charged before me with being Christians. I have asked the accused themselves if they were Christians; if they said "yes," I asked them a second and third time, warning them of the penalty; if they persisted I ordered them to be led off to execution. . . . An anonymous letter was laid before me containing many people's names. Some of these denied that they were Christians or had ever been so; at my dictation they invoked the gods and did reverence with incense and wine to your image, which I had ordered to be brought for this purpose along with the statues of the gods; they also cursed Christ; and as I am informed that people who are really Christians cannot possibly be made to do any of those things,

I considered that the people who did them should be discharged.

Pliny's letter to the emperor Trajan describes the reality of emperor worship and the very real fact that Christians lost their lives for refusing to engage in this brief act.

One wonders how many Christians of today could face death with anything approaching this degree of raw courage and faith. The governor knew of no true Christians who had tried to spare their lives by resorting to this brief idolatrous act—no exceptions! Imagine instead the well-earned image of so many modern Christians, who, to the world, are a great host of butterballs and couch potatoes sitting at their TV sets and flipping through channels to view their modern "Christian" leaders. And who do modern Christians follow? People whose faith has been borne out by suffering, whose purity and strength of character have shone through even to the death? Unfortunately, not at all. They remain the ignorant faithful even after these leaders have been caught repeatedly with prostitutes, homosexual lovers, and after they have built up private, luxurious estates with expensive cars and mansions from good-faith money.

What would these modern "Christian" leaders of today do in the face of the emperor Nero or Trajan? I believe they would do anything to hold onto their lives and estates. They would jump through any hoop—including burning incense to an altar and uttering a quick one to the emperor. They have already done as much to stay on TV. All these voices would beg the emperor just like they beg their TV audiences.

They never seem to stop and wonder whether they might be among that massive crowd of false believers who hear the stinging sentence of Christ uttered after they implore him, "Lord, Lord, did we not prophesy in your name, and in your name . . . perform many miracles?" And Christ will respond, "I never knew you. Away from me, you evildoers!" (Matthew 7). Rather than awe or reverence, they tout God's name with the cheap flippancy of game-show hosts.

What is incredible is that "Christians" would dignify them with even a moment's air time. Paul had well warned the Ephesian elders at the port of Miletus, on his third missionary journey, that the church would be inundated with false Christians throughout the ages, coming both from within and from outside the church. The epistles warn that such false teachers would ply people for money, exercise their secret lusts, introduce false doctrines, and seek personal glory.

The condition of the church today reflects this spiritual cancer. The church is bloated and unprepared. If the contemporary church were somehow able to change places with the early church, it would bail at the first moment of discomfort, long before it got even within earshot of Rome's Colosseum.

Had the apostle John, who saw and recorded the Book of Revelation, been sitting by my side when I saw Nero in action on that movie screen, he would have told me that I was sensing the spirit of Antichrist filtering through this Roman emperor. John wrote in his first epistle to those under his leadership that the spirit of Antichrist who will come in the end was already at work in the world of that day (1 John 2:18).

Like mounting refrains in a symphony, Nero foreshadowed the climax. He was but one of many types of antichrists. John lived to see Nero. By the time John recorded the Book of Revelation in A.D. 92, Domitian sat on the throne of the Roman empire. By then, great numbers of Christians had been martyred and the imperial cult of emperor worship was fully enforced. The caesars, who were considered to be "vehicles" for the Roman gods, by the time of Domitian's reign claimed to be fully god incarnate. Until that time they were given the title of gods posthumously.

The line between life and death for early Christians was the following: In public ceremonies before altars of Caesar across the empire, subjects were to proclaim Caesar as Lord and offer incense to his likeness at the altars. Subjects referred to Domitian (A.D. 81-96) with the words *dominus et deus noster*: "our Lord and God." Those who refused this test of loyalty to the state were seen as "haters of the human race," a term we saw in the account of Tacitus. Josephus and others revealed that Jews, as subjects under the empire who had a long-established religion, were exempt from this. Not so with Christians. It was before these Roman altars that Christians were rooted out repeatedly. Christ was their Lord, not Caesar. They could not, with integrity, utter the words *Kaisar est Kurios*, "Caesar is Lord," while offering incense to an idol of Caesar. They recognized what spiritual powers of darkness worked through this system of tyranny, where the emperor sat in the seat of godhood demanding to be worshiped by his subjects—an ancient theme that would reappear at the end of history between the first and second advents of Christ, but this span would not endure forever. God had placed an upper limit on it.

The Bible spoke emphatically of a final day. Evil would have its ultimate unleashing in a shocking escalation at the end of history. The final denouement of evil would be so great that God himself would have to intervene in the affairs of the world.

When asked about the world conditions before his return, Christ told his apostles that these future days would be more wicked than the days of Noah. How evil were those days? They were sufficiently wicked for God to send a global flood! The biblical record in Genesis mentions that virtually the entire human race mocked and defied God. Whatever perversities and occult-sexual practices they embraced in their hedonistic feeding frenzy, the lid had been blown off. They had passed the point of no return.

The picture we get of Noah's day is that all moral restraint was broken. "The Lord saw how great man's wickedness on the earth had become, and that every inclination of the thoughts of his heart was only evil all the time" (Genesis 6:5). Like Sodom, it required a total purge.

Such was the antediluvian world before the flood. Interestingly, New Agers believe that an advanced occult civilization named Atlantis in prehistory was totally destroyed, leaving only a handful of survivors. Now they believe its secrets are being rediscovered. How ironic if myths of Atlantis are in reality Noah's age.

Christ spoke of many antichrists that would come. Some would be miracle workers claiming to be divine, like Sai Baba, whom I was under in India. They are described in Matthew 24:24: "For false Christs and false prophets will appear and perform great signs and miracles to deceive even the elect, if that were possible." Their effect would be to delude and deceive masses of people, counterfeiting themselves as the Messiah. The concluding climax would be the ultimate counterfeit messiah, the final Antichrist—one figure over the entire earth, similar to his predecessors, the Roman emperors. He would be an eschatological personage, not a collective symbol (as the Reformers viewed the papacy), though he would have human forerunners, other antichrists. To the world he appear as the Messiah.

In the Old Testament, Daniel describes the Antichrist at the close of his vision of future events. Daniel 11:36,37 (KJV) gives the profile:

> And the king shall do according to his will; and he shall exalt himself,
> and magnify himself above every god, and shall speak marvellous
> things against the God of gods, and shall prosper till the indignation be
> accomplished: for that which is determined shall be done. Neither shall
> he regard the God of his fathers, nor the desire of women, nor regard

any god: for he shall magnify himself above all.

He will "honor the God of forces" (v. 38)—or Satan. Paul, many centuries later, focuses in on this same eschatological personage described in his second letter to the Thessalonian church:

> Now concerning the coming of our Lord Jesus Christ and our assembling to meet him, we beg you, brethren, not to be quickly shaken in mind or excited, either by spirit or by word, or by letter purporting to be from us, to the effect that the day of the Lord has come. Let no one deceive you in any way; for that day will not come, unless the rebellion comes first, and the man of lawlessness is revealed, the son of perdition, who opposes and exalts himself against every so-called god or object of worship, so that he takes his seat in the temple of God, proclaiming himself to be God (2 Thessalonians 2:1-5 RSV).

The early church knew that the church era existed during the period between Christ's first and second advents ("the last days"). They learned from Paul that a general apostasy—a falling away or rebellion—needed to come first before the Lord would return. Evil would increase, while the scaffolding of the nominal church-at-large would collapse. The world would rebel against God and his truth. They also knew that the final Antichrist had to come not as a collective symbol, but as a man, "the man of sin or lawlessness." Paul reveals the source of the Antichrist's power: "The coming of the lawless one will be in accordance with the work of Satan displayed in all kinds of counterfeit miracles, signs and wonders, and in every sort of evil that deceives those who are perishing" (2 Thessalonians 2:9).

The Antichrist or "The Beast"

As we have seen, the Antichrist has been called the "man of sin," the "son of perdition," and "the lawless one." In the Book of Revelation, he is also called "the beast." The apocalyptic imagery shows the outrageous reality of one who uses the body of a man, but who is far more than a man. This ageless spiritual power—the power from the Abyss—is possessing a human body to fulfill a deadly agenda centuries in the making.

Why is "apocalyptic language" used? It is needed when mortal minds are grappling with aspects of reality that go far beyond the senses, especially the spiritual dominions. If they happen to be operating in the distant future, the challenge becomes far greater. Apocalyptic language is the only conceivable medium to communicate these realities.

For instance, God, using the apostle John as his instrument, would not invent some Aramaic or Greek word for "holographic laser scanning" that by its own future context would not any meaning for 2000 years. John the apostle could not say, "Oh yes, it was a laser operating at a billion joules of power," or "After they achieved nuclear fusion . . ." or, "Particle beam weaponry in advanced satellites . . ." He could only describe things with available imagery in the ancient world—thus enabling it to be meaningfully transmitted—but imagery that the mind could use to make the leap. Even in this century direct terms like "the central processor was operating at a gigahertz" would have been meaningless before the past decade. As recently as the early seventies, people would have been baffled by, "My IBM crashed using Windows 95 and an older Pentium."

Now imagine suddenly being able to glimpse into the far future from the ancient world, then being told to describe that utterly different world 2000 years ahead. Add to this an ability to discern spiritual realities at work, and the job of communicating this to contemporaries and others across history is titanic. Only God can find a linguistic medium to do this—apocalyptic language: visual and symbolic metaphor that describes spiritual and concrete realities intersecting and acting in concert. There will be lessons in apocalyptic descriptions applicable to any era, such as the ageless struggle  between good and evil, but only when outward conditions approximate the time of the prophecy do things really come into focus. God set it up that way, and that is why Luther and Calvin almost gave up on the Book of Revelation!

When Daniel asked God the meaning of his baffling vision of the future, God responded: "Go thy way, for the meaning of these things will not be shown until the time of the end." So, too, with the Book of Revelation, which unfurls like a massive blueprint as the calendar of world events progresses.

Undoubtedly, the Book of Revelation had a message to the early believers of its day about the real powers at work behind Rome and the caesars.

It provided a context for their persecution, spiritual insight regarding the source of this adversity. It encouraged the efforts of the early church to maintain the faith against immense opposition. All this helped the church survive this first wave of persecution (the preterist view).

Revelation also portrays the rising and falling tides across history, the patterns and interplays between good and evil, the kingdom of God versus the principalities and dominions of Satan (the idealist view).

Many suggest that Revelation also shows the shifting stages of church growth versus church decay and apostasy throughout history (the historicist view).

Most believe that the Book of Revelation shows those events immediately before Christ's return (the prophetic futurist view). It is there to make sense of the end of history when times could mirror those of the ancient world. It portrays ultimate hope no matter to what heights evil arises. It also predicts the end of linear history with its grand conclusion as well as its cyclic movements. We see that history is indeed "his story"—it is God's Story, and nothing can thwart the unfoldment.

What does it say about "the beast" who is to come in the final days before Christ's return. Revelation 13, describes this future reality:

> The Dragon [Satan] gave the beast his power and his throne and great authority. One of the heads of the beast seemed to have a fatal wound, but the fatal wound had been healed. The whole world was astonished and followed the beast. Men worshiped the dragon because he had given authority to the beast, and they also worshiped the beast and asked, "Who is like the beast? Who can make war against him?"
>
> The beast was given a mouth to utter proud words and blasphemies and to exercise his authority for forty-two months. He opened his mouth to blaspheme God, and to slander his name and his dwelling place and those who live in heaven. He was given power to make war against the saints and to conquer them. And he was given authority over every tribe, people, language and nation. All inhabitants of the earth will worship the beast—all whose names have not been written in the book of life belonging to the Lamb that was slain from the creation of the world (vv. 2-8).

Then another powerful figure emerges two verses later:

> Then I saw another beast, coming out of the earth. He had two horns

like a lamb, but he spoke like a dragon. He exercised all of the authority of the first beast on his behalf, and made the earth and its inhabitants worship the first beast, whose fatal wound had been healed. And
he performed great and miraculous signs, even causing fire to come
down from heaven to earth in full view of men. Because of the signs he
was given power to do on behalf of the first beast, he deceived the
inhabitants of the earth. He ordered them to set up an image in honor
of the beast who was wounded by the sword and yet lived. He was
given power to give breath to the image of the first beast, so that it
could speak and cause all who refused to worship the image to be
killed. He also forced everyone, small and great, rich and poor, free and
slave, to receive a mark on his right hand or his forehead, so that no
one could buy or sell unless he had the mark, which is the name of the
beast or the number of his name. This calls for wisdom. If anyone has
insight, let him calculate the number of the beast, for it is man's number. His number is 666 (Revelation 13:11-18).

The beast, or Antichrist, and the second beast, or false prophet as he is
sometimes described, form an awesome power. They are directly empowered by Satan himself, who is called "the dragon" in the Book of
Revelation. Satan gives a human agent his throne and his powers for the
first time in history.

John previously revealed in Revelation 12:9, that "The great dragon
was hurled down—that ancient serpent called the devil or Satan, who leads
the whole world astray. He was hurled to the earth, and his angels with
him." It is the same dragon that establishes the beast. In chapter 13, the
chapter about the Antichrist, the dragon initiates the process: "And the
dragon stood on the shore of the sea. And I saw a beast coming out of the
sea." (the sea being the endless masses of humanity)

And the soul of the Antichrist? This is another deep mystery. Those
who have read my book *Riders of the Cosmic Circuit* will see far more completely the dynamics of demonic possession. After two years
in India, I personally felt these ancient forces trying to invade
my soul. My guru at the time—who claimed to be God in the
flesh—had himself undergone a possessive transformation.
As with all "enlightened" masters, we used the term "there's
nobody home" inside the shell of the body. We assumed it
was God inside. But it turned out to be something else.
Compared to the One to come, this was merely a preview—I am convinced of this.

We now discover that the soul of the Antichrist has another origin. In

Revelation 11:7 it says: ". . . the beast that comes up from the Abyss . . ."
The abyss is that shaft of infinite darkness which is the holding place and
gateway of the demonic powers and principalities. The beast is in a state
of total possession. Most likely Satan himself enters the body of the beast.
Finally Lucifer briefly walks the earth as "the god of this world."

What God prevented from happening at Babel when the world spoke
one language—a unified world system under an earlier prototype of the
Antichrist, Nimrod—is finally allowed to happen.

In the Book of Revelation we gain an interesting glimpse of the
Antichrist. He is inspired and empowered by Satan while the hidden powers and kingships of the earth provide the floor plan for his emergence.
The kings surrender to him their dominions. Unlike Rome's dominion,
this will truly be worldwide.

One highly placed international banker remarked to an acquaintance
that a shadow government of ten or twelve men in international finance
would be the true rulers of United Europe, EC. One could almost think
of them as the true invisible kings, the banker kings, who would pull
strings while almost no one would know who they were. Perhaps the
2000-year-old Book of Revelation continues to unfurl. But only God
knows the timeline.

The beast will be in the control seat of an awesome power: the world's
military arsenal. This will give him direct powers over life and death—the
life of every citizen on the earth. He will be feared the way the Roman
emperors were feared. We see this with the words, "Who is able to make
war with the beast?" The rhetorical answer is clearly, "No one on earth."

U. N. leaders since Alger Hiss have talked of a global military force
policed by the United Nations. Leaders in high places, such as Brzezinski,
who wrote *Between Two Ages*, have spoken of a simultaneous surrender and
merger of American and Soviet military powers to enforce world peace. It
would be run by a third force, a "neutral" force. This has been a long-term
goal of the Trilateral Commission, the Bilderbergers, as well as the
Council on Foreign Relations (the CFR), among a number of elitist
groups. This shadow government, in
place for some time, will be waiting in
the wings for the switchover and surrender of powers to take place. These
are the real movers and shakers of history. Once the global police force is in
place, there will be no turning back,

Echelon

no divvying back the chips to once-sovereign nations.

Picture, therefore, a global umbrella of Star Wars technology—satellite-linked supercomputers communicating in gigabytes, total-eye satellites, lasers, particle beam weapons platforms, ICBM's or whatever else is on hand that we don't even know about now—once the merger of Soviet, European, and American military arsenals has taken place. Orwell's Big Brother, portrayed in the novel *1984*, did not approach this kind of power.

Think now of this. What better imagery could the apostle John—2000 years ago and a thousand years before the Dark Ages—use to describe the reality of some futuristic laser and Star Wars technology than the descriptive phrase that "he could make fire come down from heaven?" No better metaphor was available in the ancient world. For good reason they will ask, "Who can make war on the beast?"

I will speculate more. The beast and his false prophet are empowered directly by Satan. The latter is able to work deceiving miracles. The beast is at the axis of the world's new religious system, which in reality is a revival of what the Book of Revelation terms *Mystery Babylon*. The beast is to be the messiah of a mystery religion, receiving worship from the inhabitants of the earth who "will worship the dragon."

The third global domain that the beast has total control over is the world's banking and economic system, which is now finally centralized. He is the mystery banker as well as the messiah. This reality has been foreshadowed by the Roman emperors whose images appeared on ancient coins accompanied by words proclaiming their deity. The imperial cult and commerce were interlinked. This ancient link will be forged once again. A surviving structure of this has existed in recent centuries in the Masonic orders where commerce and an occult brotherhood form a secret link.

But there is yet another detail that alarms us. It is a prophetic detail that comes to us from 2000 years ago. Keep in mind that computer chips did not hit the world scene till the 1970s, and Norbert Weiner at the Massachusetts Institute of Technology (MIT) did not talk about cybernetics till our era. Yet the apostle John describes a reality that has only recently come into focus: global banking, laser scanning, and the universal computer bar code. As was recounted earlier, John recorded the following 2000 years ago on the island of Patmos: "He also forced everyone, small and great, rich and poor, free and slave, to receive a mark on his right hand or on his forehead, so that no one could buy or sell unless he had the mark, which is the name of the beast . . ." (Revelation 13:16,17).

It is a tiny step to go from using a Visa card or a bank card on the Plus System and other ATM machines, in which the electronic strip is attached to the card, to putting that same information on or in the human body so that it can be laser scanned. This has already been done with implanted microchips. It is only since the advent of networked supercomputing that the hardware is now in place to easily track economic and other profiles of every citizen on earth. Again, what better descriptive term could John have found in the ancient world than "the mark," which would enable every citizen to buy or sell who had it? The building blocks for a one-world economic system are already in place—colossal power in the hands of a few.

Applied Digital Solutions (NASDAQ:ADSX) announced at the close of the millennium that it had acquired the patent rights to a miniature digital transceiver—which it has named "Digital Angel."™ With Digital Angel, you can track every living person on earth! The company noted:

> In some of its applications, the tiny device is expected to be bonded closely to the body or implanted just under the skin. The Company believes Digital Angel will be able to send and receive data and be located by GPS (Global Positioning System) technology.

Stop and take a breath. This is now real history. Commentators who speculated about "the mark" in the mid-twentieth century had no computer hardware, bar codes, satellites or anything else to envision the process.

In the ancient Book of Revelation, the beast is the military commander of the world, the messiah and object of worship of the world's unified mystery religion, and the supreme banker. These three headships (or heads)—military, religious, and economic—give him undisputed military, religious, and economic powers over a one-world system. Finally "somebody gets it all," and it is the beast. The unrealized dreams of Alexander the Great, Julius and Augustus Caesar, Napoleon, Stalin and Hitler—plus countless others through the centuries—are finally achieved. The world hands him the souls of the masses on a platter as all nations surrender their sovereignty like Esau selling his soul, his birthright, for a meal—and this taken to cosmic proportions.

As under Orwell's Big Brother in *1984*, there is barely freedom to think. The mind dares to move beneath the surface, but that is all. In the end, all who differ with this agenda will be found out and exterminated. Like the pogroms of 60 million in Russia, or the millions of political prisoners killed in Cambodia, or the tens of millions in China, or the millions and millions of "political" prisoners killed during our present era, so, too,this genocide—which is by no means too fantastic to conceive of since such things have already happened—will happen on a global scale. At least that seems to be the plain meaning of the text of Revelation.

Martyrs, once again, become a reality as the Christian holocaust expands. In the words of Revelation 13:7, "He was given power to make war against the saints and to conquer them"—but only for a brief season. One factor that affects the timing of the Second Coming, by my understanding, is the martyrdom of God's saints.

The Beast's aim will be to usurp God with the full powers of the world under his dominion. To achieve this, he will try to totally abolish any evidence of the true God from the face of the earth, starting with destroying the knowledge of God to finally destroying God's people. The knowledge aspect of the attack is not new (*Time* lavishing the Jesus Seminar, Media specials on Christ to deconstruct Christianity in a kind of endless gnawing process, plus other options like the United Religions, ad infinitum). Truly, if there have been emperors before in the flesh, they can come again. If God came in the flesh as Christ, so can Satan come to eclipse and possess the Antichrist in the form of a man. It would make sense then that there would be a mystery religion based on the divinity of man. If gurus and teachers can be divine, surely this figure will be—only more so!

When I saw Nero on that movie screen as a small child, it was little wonder that my skin crawled and that I felt horror in the pit of my stomach. Perhaps I was sensing the spirit of Antichrist which was at work even in the apostle John's day. Something far more foreboding than the celluloid images pierced my soul. I didn't know then that I would one day be under an Antichrist myself for two years in India, nor did I know that a far greater one could be on the way—from out of the abyss and into the light of day.

19

The Great Lie

A single thought has danced as a whirling dervish across history, seducing millions in its path. Indeed this very thought seduced the highest created intelligence in the universe. It was also great enough to cause the fall of the entire human race. It has invaded culture after culture, each time captivating the hearts and minds of the people. People find it infinitely desirable and beautiful, its promises irresistible, as it seems to hold such great promise. This thought seems to answer our greatest hopes and longings, our deepest struggles with our identity in the cosmos, and our quest for ultimate meaning. It is the Great Lie. It is the foundation stone of Hinduism, Buddhism, Sufism, Jainism, Sikhism, Taoism, the Kabbala, the Greek Hermetic and Eleusinian Gnostic beliefs, Neoplatonism, all the occult creeds from Theosophy and the Masonic orders to the Rosicrucians, as well as too many cults to mention. It is the central foundation stone of the New Age movement.

The tenets of the Great Lie have been chanted on the banks of the Ganges since time immemorial. Weather-beaten sages have uttered secret syllables and mantras in caves to invoke its powers. Modern meditators have sought to plumb its secret depths as they have gathered in intimate meetings from MIT to Esalen, from Greenwich Village to Marin County, from the west bank of the Seine to Cambridge, England.

The Great Lie is quite simply the belief *that man is God*, that his true identity is the immortal self that is ageless and eternal, and that *as God, he will never die*! Death is merely a veil through which we pass—it is not real. Sin and depravity are, therefore, illusions since this inner divinity is at man's core. Sins and imperfections are passing blemishes clouding the effulgence of the eternal Atma. The outward drama of the world can be used to beckon us back to our ultimate self if we know the secret wisdom.

The Great Lie promises delicious temporal rewards. Oh, to be divine and do anything we want, whenever, wherever! To sin and do it divinely, to paraphrase Rajneesh. What outrageous freedom! It is behind the knowing smile at the Rainbow festival. It is behind the body language of the outrageous and autonomously defiant Berkeleyite cruising down Telegraph, or the straight yuppie in the corporate world waiting to run a line of coke and then go to a wife-swapping party cum seance. Now all those wild little desires can be acted out without real risk because it is God playing the game with himself. The Hindu term for this is *Maha-lila*. One can sin without consequence since it is all a cosmic game of hide-and-seek anyway. In mainline Hinduism this does not apply, for karma hangs over the head like a mountain. But many Westerners use the guru's argument from the *Bhagavad Gita:* that any action is permissible if done in the right consciousness, even killing. Rajneesh cites this all the time.

Thus part of the Great Lie involves blotting out the reality of the consequences of our actions. People hate to acknowledge them anyway. It is like the odd defiance, the turning against reality that we witness in the homosexual underworld now that AIDS has killed millions. Now many are even more profligate, swapping partners like they are on a merry-go-round. Yet the whirlwind of self-destruction follows along behind—as real as a tornado uprooting a Texas ranch house.

Genesis 3 recounts the fall of man through the Great Lie. Satan, speaking through the serpent, promised Adam and Eve that they would become like God. In the same breath he assured them that there was no death—that death is an illusion. " 'You will not surely die,' the serpent said to the woman. 'For God knows that when you eat of it, your eyes will be opened, and *you will be like God*, knowing good and evil'" (Genesis 3:4,5). Here it is: "You will not surely die" and "You will be like God." It is a direct contradiction to what God had told them and what Adam and Eve knew in their consciences. In Goethe's masterpiece *Faust*, the question is asked Mephistopheles, "What is the fastest thing in the Universe?" The answer is that it is a thought, "when the will turns from good to evil." How great the plunge! Adam and Eve fell for it and fell from a vast summit, taking all of the human race with them. It was a cosmic event.

Originally Adam and Eve were exemplars of everything we long for. At the height of their created powers, these federal heads of the human race had the full capacity of immense intellects and clear consciences—without taint of original sin. They had original righteousness. Their senses were razor-sharp. This was human potential at its best; nothing dulled their vital intimacy with their Creator. If we believe the biblical record, these two foundational heads of the race were created perfect. With all their faculties operant, living in paradise, the ideal environment, experiencing deep fellowship with the living God, they still fell for the Great Lie! It was the unhindered human will without the environmental argument of: "I grew up in a poor family in Detroit and was abused as a child, and that's why I did it." There were no excuses. The will alone was accountable—the naked will. Under these conditions they chose evil, and their choice flew in the face of both reason and reality. That alone illustrates both the potency of the lie and the human vulnerability centering around the self, the "I." We are like vampires running through a blood bank with sin in our veins. That is the post-Fall biblical revelation of the state of man.

The issue is this: If our two perfect federal heads of the race succumbed by their wills, can we be so confident that we ourselves won't fall as they did?—we who have so much less than Adam and Eve and are but blemished images of these original paragons. If they fell in paradise, how are we supposed to fare in a corrupt world inundated with evils of all kinds? You can only appreciate grace once you see the full perspective of the dilemma. The human condition doesn't need a Band-Aid, it needs a miracle.

In God's great salvation plan, only the doors of grace can free us, and such grace can only come through the mystery of the Messiah's atoning act. God's counter offer of grace has been on his terms, not on the serpent's. Unfortunately, multitudes have opted for the latter's offer because it has felt good, and seemed right. Playing God with their own wills, many have declared the serpent's path to be the more desirable choice.

But the Great Lie did not originate in Eden. It goes further back. It came through one cosmic being far superior in capacity to the two perfect humans who were later seduced. The most endowed created being ever, who witnessed the creation of the physical cosmos before time began, wanted to become God and ascend above the throne of God. Isaiah 14:12-14 (KJV) recounts this pivotal cosmic event:

> How art thou fallen from heaven, O Lucifer, son of the morning! How art thou cut down to the ground, which did weaken the nations!

> For thou has said in thine heart, "I will ascend into heaven, I will exalt my throne above the stars of God; I will sit also upon the mount of the congregation, in the sides of the north; I will ascend above the heights of the clouds; I will be like the most High."

The fall of Lucifer heightens the issue of what took place in Eden. In deep heaven, the will embodied in Lucifer existed in the most exalted spiritual regions, unlike Adam's physical existence. For in the midst of heaven-ly splendor, bathed in the love of God, the unimaginable *Viseo Dei*, free of any possible influence or pull of physical existence (the Gnostic excuse), and with the most lucid of intelligences imaginable, the will still chose evil.

Cambridge philosopher Austin Farrer pinpoints Lucifer's perversity of choice as that of "preferring the sterile satisfaction of pride and self-will to the inexhaustible wealth of a participation in the life of God." This becomes the most monstrous of imaginable sins. To Farrer, this incident depicts "without obstruction what perversity is—the perversity expressed in any and every sin." Human perversity "can do all the devil can do in mak-ing an absolute beginning of evil; this at every moment in time."[1]

Lucifer fell and became Satan, the father of lies. The very pride that ensnared him—the desire to become God—Satan in turn used against the human race as a snare. When absolute greatness corrupts and then falls, its evil is beyond estimation. Satan became the spiritual equivalent of a black hole. His evil became all-consuming and his hostility to God, after he transformed, became total. No *Star Wars* imagery can depict this complex and fallen being. His footprints, however, can be seen across time, across human history, as the great adversary of God and architect of the Great Lie, and the secret mystery religions upon this lie rides.

The almost 2000-year-old Book of Revelation, the last book of the New Testament, summarized and distilled over 1500 years of biblical prophecy in its far-reaching vision of ultimate one worldism. Brooks Alexander com-ments on this future global empire involving economic, political, and mil-itary forces under an occult *gnosis* which appears in a single unified system of oppression and delusion known as *Mystery Babylon*. Ten years before the term "New Age" appeared, Brooks Alexander wrote in the early seventies: "The Bible gives us a clear, if unpleasant picture: in the last days of history as we know it, our race will be brought together in a common expression of cosmic humanism. This coming great world religion will offer itself to us as the ancient wisdom and hidden truth underlying all the religious forms of history."

Why "Mystery" Babylon? Something is a mystery as long as it remains secret and hidden from public disclosure. Yet the Book of Revelation says that the mystery will finally be revealed. The public proclamation of the mystery only takes effect when the prophecy becomes activated at the crit-ical historical moment. As Brooks Alexander notes, "Mystery Babylon is a spiritual system that is founded on the widespread public disclosure of pre-viously concealed information." Keep in mind that Hinduism has both exoteric and esoteric knowledge. There is a polytheism-pantheism for the general masses, and there is a high level "advaitic" monism for the higher initiate. Tantra has always been extremely secret, though gurus like Rajneesh popularized it in ever-widening circles.

Why does the Book of Revelation pinpoint Babylon? What can we glean from Babylon-of-old if its mystery is to be revealed?

Isaiah warns God's people of Babylon's deadly delusion. God reminds them, "I am the Lord, and there is no other. . . . I did not say to the offspring of Jacob, 'Seek me in chaos' [or the formless void]. I, the Lord, speak the truth, I declare what is right" (Isaiah 45:18 RSV). God is the great "I AM." He is transcendent. He is not the impersonal Brahman of Hinduism or the void of Mahayana Buddhism. Only He claims the title of the "I AM." But what of Babylon? Did it not seek the divine within while living by the hedonistic pleasure principle? Again, that same pattern keeps appearing—a society given over to the hedonistic pleasure principle, shattering moral laws, while teaching the divine within. That was Babylon-of-old, and it seems to be resurrecting in our day—in Europe and America as well as other places.

In Isaiah 47, God exposes the spiritual realities of the Babylonian religion as he addresses Babylon: "Now, therefore, hear this, you lover of pleasures, who sits securely, who say in your heart '*I am and there is no one besides me*' . . . [God's judgment] shall come to you in a moment . . . in full measure, in spite of your many *sorceries and the great power of your enchantments*. You felt secure in your wickedness, you said, 'No one sees me'; your wisdom and your knowledge led you astray, and you said in your heart, 'I am and there is no one besides me' " (Isaiah 47:8-10).

Babylon embraced the Great Lie. Its inhabitants claimed the title of "I AM" and identified the human self with God. They were also earmarked by their sorcery and their hedonism—that was the essence of Babylon. Their occult practices, such as astrology and channeling, undergirded this. God was not denying that such occult pursuits gave them experiences and powers. After all, God said "in spite of your many sorceries and the great power of your enchantments." But the root source of this occult power was the Dragon himself, never God. God abhorred these practices. Israel was warned with drastic words to stay away from Babylon's occult practices, the way a parent warns a child to avoid an electric power line that has fallen and could kill the child with a touch. The presumed wisdom, like the child with the parent, is that God knows some things that mortals don't. His warnings then were against the same occult practices that are surfacing today. They could equally apply to every New Age holistic fair where hundreds of booths are selling crystals, pyramids, and so forth while live channelers are opening the doors to the void. Apart from a miracle, it is hard to deny that *Mystery Babylon* is resurrecting again.

What does God say about the Babylonian channelers as he warns Israel to avoid contamination? And what do we gather about the "familiar spirits" that work through their human vessels? God by no means denies the reality of "familiars" or "familiar spirits," but we learn that they are demonic and not to be trusted—that these spirits teach the Great Lie, just as they are doing in our time through channelers like Helen Schucman.

God, from the beginning, warned of the Babylonian, Canaanite, and Chaldean sorceries with clear scriptural admonitions of the great danger. God is like a parent warning a child to stay away from a downed power line arcing thousands of volts:

> And when they say to you, "Consult the mediums and the wizards who whisper and mutter," should not a people consult their God? Should they consult the dead on behalf of the living? (Isaiah 8:19 NASB).

> There shall not be found among you any one who burns his son or his daughter as an offering, any one who practices divination, a soothsayer, or an augur, or a sorcerer, or a charmer, or a medium, or a wizard, or a necromancer. For whoever does these things is an abomination to the Lord (Deuteronomy 18:10-12 RSV).

> Regard not them that have *familiar spirits*, neither seek after wizards, to be defiled by them: I Am the Lord your God (Leviticus 19:31 KJV).

> If a person turns to mediums and wizards, playing the harlot after them, I will set my face against that person, and will cut him off from among his people (Leviticus 20:6 RSV).

> A man or a woman who is a medium or wizard shall be put to death; they shall be stoned with stones, their blood shall be upon them (Leviticus 20:27 RSV).

To put it simply, the Babylonian occult arts were such an abomination that they were a capital offense among the Israelites. Those who played with this occult fire died.

Remember Jane Roberts and her pluralistic entity, Seth and Seth II, recounted in our first chapter of contacts? How would that fit into the rubric of biblical explanation? We see a perfect example of a pluralistic entity when Christ confronts the Gadarene, who when asked his name responded that it was "Legion." Why was that his name? The demons in the man responded "for we are many" and then they begged not to be sent into the abyss when they were exorcised.

As an illustration of the concrete reality of these demonic possessing spirits, Christ sent them into a large herd of pigs nearby. The pigs charged off a cliff and into the sea, killing themselves—not at all normal behavior for a pig. The man "Legion" had in his possessed state exhibited a sufficient range of superhuman and paranormal feats to scare everyone away. Among other things, he had the physical strength to snap heavy chains. But when Christ appeared, the demons trembled in horror.

Legion was demon-possessed. After he was exorcised, his countrymen were awed when they found him fully clothed and in his right mind. Somewhere in his past he had opened the door for these "familiar spirits."

Paul reveals still yet another mystery—that these spirits can even stand behind idols, like the idols of ancient Babylon or of modern India. Paul says, "Do I mean then that a sacrifice offered to an idol is anything, or that an idol is anything? No, but the sacrifices of pagans are offered to demons, not to God" (1 Corinthians 10:19,20). He calls them "elemental spirits."

Paul also says, "Now the Spirit [of God] expressly says that in later times some will depart from the faith by giving heed to deceitful spirits and doctrines of demons" (1 Timothy 4:1 RSV). Such was the story of Jane Roberts, who fell away from the faith to pay heed to doctrines of demons. Channeling is by no means new at all. As we plainly saw in the Old Testament, it came right out of Babylon.

Babel of Old

The Tower of Babel, Babylon's founding edifice and spiritual center, observes Brooks Alexander, "was an astral temple representing the structure of reality. As the 'cosmic mountain,' it tied heaven and earth together. It was the all inclusive image of the totality of the universe." Alexander adds that "in the ritual act of ascending the astral altar, the priests acted out the stages of god-realization and the inner meaning of mankind's oneness with the cosmos. The Babylonian monarch was the focus of the occult power channeled through the activities of the priesthood. He was regarded as a divine being, a god-man."

The monarch was also the one through whom the gods spoke. He was the initiate who could travel to the realm of the gods. He was the mouthpiece for the gods and goddesses of Babylon. The secret wisdom of

Babylon is a direct ancestor of India's mystical system, from its hidden wisdom of man's inner divinity and its priestly class, to its gods and goddesses. Pantheism fuses with polytheism, just as in India.

How did Babylon's mystery religion suddenly appear in the ancient world? The Book of Genesis informs us that before the great flood, the world was in a frenzy of "wickedness." God's wrath fell, while a remnant was preserved in the ark.

But scarcely had the waters of the great flood abated when, sure enough, the Great Lie appeared again. Nimrod founded Babylon centered on the tower, which was a temple of man rising to the stars. He appointed himself as its godman and messiah, and again the mystery religion rose from out of the floodwaters. If some sorcerized hedonism had caused the whole earth to fall away from God, bringing on the flood, then that handful of survivors would have been very aware of it. Nimrod's father Cush was a son of one of Noah's sons (Genesis 10:8). Thus, within a generation of Noah, the same spiritual bane was again being resurrected on the earth in the post flood world of Babylon.

Noted English archeologist and antiquarian Alexander Hislop says:

> The Babylonians, in their popular religion, supremely worshipped a goddess mother and son [Semiramis and Tammuz]. From Babylon, this worship of the mother and child spread to the ends of the earth. In Egypt, the mother and child were worshipped under the names of Isis and Osiris. In India, *even to this day*, as Isi [or Parvati] and Ishwara [The Indian God Ishwara is represented as a babe at the breast of his own wife Isi, or Parvati]. . . . [Hislop says] . . . the Hindu mythology, *which is admitted to be essentially Babylonian, could not have been subdued*.[2]

The mystery religion of Babylon is the root of all mystery religions, the secret initiations, the exalted priesthoods and, above all, the secret knowledge. It promises the keys to the tree of life, immortality, as well as divinity. India has been the place where the mystery religion has taken root unhindered. It has distilled over the centuries into a refined wine—the Chateau Rothschild of religious wines. Revelation reports that the whole world becomes drunk on the wine of Babylon.

20

The Hidden Aristocracy

As the massive pieces of this emerging global order lock into place, it becomes increasingly clear that we are not just dealing with airy "spiritual" projections of mere dreamers. Very tangible forces have been at work beneath the opinion shaping machinery of our time. These powerful engines of change, largely out of view, are all the more effective because of their invisibility.

Gears and levers of history have been moved and adjusted, and a large-scale game of Monopoly has been played, with real currency and real assets shifting hands—a game with very real winners and losers. It is not at all out-of-the-question that such "players" would finance the new spiritualities through their publishing and broadcasting monopolies for the religious arm of the plan. But that is merely one dimension.

Indeed, the New Age piece of the puzzle may indeed have served its purpose by seducing America to go along with the globalist plan in its search for a mystical heaven on earth. But European nations are more likely to be swayed by tangible programs of State provided welfare services than any New Age vision. The seduction of a world takes supreme pragmatism. People operating out of self-interest do not surrender their freedoms and heritage unless they are persuaded that there is something for them better ahead.

If it takes communism to get the Eastern bloc and Asia to fall in line, fine. If it takes some variation of socialism for modern Europe, fine. If America needs a New Age bromide, no problem. The meshing of the net of steel to capture the world has been a quiet undertaking out of public view. Its big events, as we shall see, have taken place at quiet meetings where an elite few move enormous amounts of capital. The superrich and the super brilliant have teamed up while the masses watch television and eat at McDonald's. Their small, dull, prosaic worlds never embrace the truly colossal perspective around them. And should one among the masses look up for a second, there is always an army of experts and skeptics to ridicule any suspicions of some "conspiracy" among the elite. Spin artists can use the "complexity of life" argument tied in with the "random forces of history" argument to further numb a public preoccupied with their own immediate problems of day to day living.

It seems the world has had an elite few operating in the shadows of history and far from public view. These insiders have avoided the spotlights flooding the main stage of history. Other actors have been thrust onstage, but the ones directing the drama have remained shrouded. This fractional minority of people can only activate their plans of power and affect billions of lives if they remain out-of-view and beyond suspicion. It is a dangerous and risky undertaking, for they are vastly outnumbered. Secrecy is critical. You don't want to awake the sleeping giant.

To someone who is an atheistic materialist, the idea of a long range plan that might take centuries seems preposterous. People have but one life to live, so what would inspire loyalty in or sustain any participant in some grand-scale conspiracy to take over the earth, if those who finally benefited were not even on the scene for another few hundred years? How could anyone, fired with ambitions for the moment, be made to sacrifice his life for a complex and deliberate plan spanning centuries?

Apart from the obvious immediate material rewards, the supernatural dimension is the one that gives the puzzle real meaning. If there is a spiritual dimension guiding the insiders, a messianic plan, if you will, then it makes sense. One becomes a player in an invisible war spanning centuries and heading to "utopia," along with other intensely loyal team players whose private allegiances are far stronger than the most fired up old world patriot! Like a chess player seeing 30 moves ahead, the present sacrifice of a pawn or a rook makes perfect sense in light of the coming checkmate. Wars involve risk. Each player in the game can feel the the nudge towards victory when he manages to reach some remote crank or dial and turn it while out of public view. He becomes a cosmic player in history. He might even feel as if he is in the body of some corporate messiah. He can feel a kind of transnational allegiance to a higher cause as well as reap the extremely generous temporal rewards of wealth and prestige he will accrue for being a player—riches, power and prestige sufficient for the most ambitious of lives.

A Masonic Revolution

Over 200 years ago, in 1797, one of the most respected scientists in the world wrote a book entitled *Proofs of a Conspiracy* (London: Creech, Cadell, Davies Ltd., 1797). John T. Robison, the author, was Secretary General to Scotland's prestigious Royal Society and professor of natural philosophy at the University of Edinburgh. He was considered to be one of the truly great intellectuals of the day. Science then was called "natural philosophy." Robison was also a high-degree Mason. Whenever he traveled to Europe from Scotland, he always attended the Grand Orient Masonic Lodges. But when Robison had recently been in Europe on a sabbatical, he detected a new element in the Grand Orient Lodges. Adam Weishaupt, the founder of this new elite group now penetrating the lodges, approached Robison to get him to join an inner circle known as *Illuminism*. It was the quiet flame that burned in the French intelligentsia such as Voltaire, Robespierre, Mirabeau, and the Duc D'Orleans.

The Illuminist plan was to unseat the present powers of hereditary aristocracy and replace them with an intellectual aristocracy, using a staged revolt of the masses to do this. This, indeed, was exactly what the French Revolution appeared to be—key people catalyzing great numbers of people.

James Robison, loyal to the royal family of England, warned them that hidden powers were pulling strings and that the French Revolution was not an historical accident happening by whim, but that it was manipulated by brilliant and powerful men who had their own agenda. Robison published his book to warn England that it could undergo a revolution similar to what was happening in France, thus unseating the Royal Family and changing life in England as they knew it. One genius in particular, Adam Weishaupt, was the visionary of Illuminism, and like Karl Marx, was of Jewish descent, though he had temporarily joined the Jesuit Order. Later Weishaupt got into league with some powerful German merchants who were initiates in the occult. Adam Weishaupt was a professor of canon law at the University of Ingolstadt. He started the Order of the Illuminati on May 1, 1776. His plan was to use the Grand Orient Lodges of Europe as a means to screen out talent and build a hierarchy of inner circles. Only the real inner circle could be trusted with the true purpose of the Order.

The true purpose of the Illuminati, according to Professor Robison, was world hegemony: a world order ruled by an elite pretending to represent the common man, an elite who had penetrated every aspect of society from the arts to politics and law while shaping public opinion with more subtlety than the average citizen was able to detect. Weishaupt's plan involved a communistic order outlined a full seventy years before Marx came on the scene.

Weishaupt was exposed in 1785, when the Bavarian government stepped in and seized his papers. An unknown variable had caused his exposure. The hidden hand was forced to come out of the shadows for a moment. The horseman, named Lanze, carrying various secret papers and plans to France, was struck and killed by lightning in Regensberg. The local police handed the papers over to the Bavarian government. When the Bavarian government questioned four professor colleagues of Weishaupt, they testified to the conspiracy. On historical record is the attempt of the Bavarian government to warn other European governments in an official document entitled *Original Writings of the Order and Sect of the Illuminati*. Four years after lightning struck the horseman, the French Revolution rocked Europe.

Rumor remained that the Illuminati then shifted locations to Italy, calling itself "the invisible 40." By the early 1800s, Weishaupt and his conspiratorial Illuminists were mentioned in the correspondence of George Washington, Jefferson, Madison, and John Quincy Adams. They did not want this plan infiltrating America any more than Robison wanted to see it in England. They had seen the ruthlessness of France's "Reign of Terror."

George Washington wrote in 1798: "It is not my intention to doubt that the doctrine of the Illuminati and the principles of Jacobinism had not spread in the United States. On the contrary, no one is more satisfied of this fact than I am."[1] That was 200 years ago, and, indeed, a connecting thread existed through the 1800s. It had to do with merchant bankers and occultists, as well as other invisible players.

200 Years Later

Today, the power of a certain group of bankers is colossal according to Harvard and Princeton professor emeritus Carroll Quigley, who confessed to being an insider and confidant of this elite group. Professor Quigley's *magnum opus* was entitled *Tragedy and Hope: A History of Our Time*, and rocked those who saw it when it came out in 1966. This 1300-

page book named major insider power groups attempting to manipulate a world socialist order.

Quigley ardently *supported* the plan, but said that it should no longer be done under cover. His book was a triumphalist announcement of the inevitable, since the plan had virtually reached completion. Quigley had been among the intellectual brain trust, rubbing shoulders with the insiders. The problem was that he had said too much. The Macmillan first edition of 1966 suddenly disappeared almost overnight, even from public libraries, during the time professor Quigley was at his final academic post at the Georgetown University School of Foreign Service.

One of professor Quigley's students at Georgetown in the 1960s was William Jefferson Clinton, future Rhodes Scholar (with Quigley's recommendation) and president of the United States. During his acceptance speech at the Democratic National Convention, Bill Clinton reverently mentioned Carroll Quigley, his mentor, as being one of the two people most to influence his life! When I heard this admission on the radio as I crossed the Richmond San Rafael Bridge from Berkeley to Marin County, I was stunned and wondered how many in the audience—including readers of the first edition of this book—had any idea what Clinton had just revealed.

Doubtless, Clinton was eager to meet the same powerful insiders Quigley knew. With such backers, how could he fail to meet with destiny (his and theirs)! And, indeed,, it seems he has served them well, nudging America towards the globalist goal while melding his ambitions with theirs!

When I eventually got a copy of Carroll Quigley's book, *Tragedy and Hope*, printed in Taiwan (an exact copy of the original Macmillan edition), I was amazed. Professor Quigley had, indeed, let too much out of the bag. Quigley showed in 1300 pages of detail that there were indeed elite insiders manipulating world events behind the scenes. It also made sense of America's strange descent downward—as though people in power were trying to destroy and undermine the very nation they had been elected to protect and represent!

It was all more incredible than an Ian Flemming novel or Robert Ludlum's *Matarese Circle*. I was seeing tangible evidence of insiders who were so well-versed at removing their own fingerprints that they slipped detection. Evidence had previously come in faint traces here and there; certain names kept cropping up. When author Ian Fleming, who for years had been a member of the British Secret Service, wrote about

James Bond combating such secret conspiratorial groups as Smersh and Specter, one wondered whether he was indulging in more than just fiction and showing insider's knowledge thinly veiled. According to Quigley, such hidden groups most certainly exist and remain far from public view. The average person would not think twice as their stretch limousines with dark tinted windows might glide down Wall Street or "the City" of London.

Harvard professor emeritus Quigley divulges the following about this "international network" in *Tragedy and Hope*:

> This network which we may identify as the Round Table Groups, has no aversion to cooperating with the Communists or any other group, and frequently does so. I know of the operations of this network because I have studied it for twenty years and was permitted for two years, in the early 1960s, to examine its papers and secret records. I have no aversion to it or to most of its aims and have, for much of my life, been close to it and to many of its instruments.[2]

In the next sentence, Quigley differs on only one point with the insider network: "It wishes to remain unknown." Other sources have led me to believe that though Quigley went very deep, there are levels far deeper.

Quigley summarizes the insider's grand plan: "Their aim is nothing less than to create a *world system* of financial control in private hands able to dominate the political system of each country and the economy of the world as a whole. The system was to be controlled in a feudalistic fashion by the *central banks of the world acting in concert*, by secret agreements arrived at in frequent private meetings and conferences."[3] This is almost a perfect description of the secret international meetings of the Bilderbergers: "secret agreements arrived at in frequent private meetings. . . ."

One fact that Quigley and others reveal is that the banking houses owned by the great family dynasties are also the banks behind the International Monetary Fund, as well as The World Bank. The same names keep cropping up. They are king makers and nation breakers. The goal is a global central bank—once national banks have been established and conditions are right.

So far, the central banking system projected for Europe is a major milestone to this goal. No small part of this same gradualist agenda is America's very own central bank, the Federal Reserve Bank. National debt is highly in their favor. The trillions of dollars now owed to them by the United States, as they wear the outer attire of the Federal Reserve Bank, gives this inner circle of select banks yearly interest payments of hundreds of billions of dollars.

Elections and stock markets can switch directions overnight with a directive from the Federal Reserve. Alan Greenspan, the visible chairman of the Federal Reserve, could change the prime lending rate and cause a panic, a recession, indeed, a depression with a single word. The politician who does the bidding of the insiders gets in the door. It is always good policy to justify substantial loans from these banks. The rhetoric is irrelevant and has been for a very long time—just watch one president after another promise to balance the national debt, then watch it quietly climb off the graph. The debt will soon equal the sum total assets of the nation.

Ruben & Greenspan

How do banks and money barons manipulate conditions?

According to Harvard economist John Kenneth Galbraith, Winston Churchill was shown an interesting object lesson by New York banker and industrial magnate Bernard Baruch in 1929. Baruch, of the lineage of the money changers, was an advisor to President Woodrow Wilson at the Treaty of Versailles, beside that other great advisor "Colonel" Mandel House. Baruch also advised Roosevelt and was a member of his brain trust. When he was chairman of the War Industries Board during World War I, Baruch made hundreds of millions of dollars from lucrative contracts in the war and munitions industry. He was at the right place at the right time. According to Harvard economist Galbraith, Baruch walked Sir Winston Churchill out on the floor of the New York Stock Exchange the very morning it fell.[4] Churchill was brought to witness the crash firsthand on October 24, 1929, because it was desired that he see the power of the banking system at work. This presumes plenty of lead time for Winston to take the ship from England to the United States, hang out for a while, maybe start the day with a good breakfast at the Waldorf, and make it there in time to see the floor open up. This is

insider knowledge that would pale Simon Boesky's. We will see later why
Baruch gave Churchill this object lesson.

The American market collapsed that day of 1929, and so did the world
market not long after. Economic conditions for the next world war were
set up, greatly aided by America's Great Depression. Billions of dollars
shifted hands overnight. Some had gotten out in time—the big hitters—
while scores of the wealthy were destroyed. Then, after the crash, when
railroads and industries plummeted, the big hitters came back on the
stock market floor and bought industries at whim for a dime on the dollar. One such "fortunate speculator" was Bernard Baruch who had boasted to Churchill that he had liquidated his stock holdings when the market was at the top and bought bonds and gold, while retaining a huge
cash reserve. Now he could buy companies like pieces on a Monopoly
board. And he was not the only one.

Millions of lives were wrecked, and America suddenly needed a "New
Deal" in the form of social welfare. The Great Crash created another
precedent for free America: gradual socialism, as the Fabians had been
doing in England. Why would any banker or insider be the least bit
attracted to socialism? Because the idea that socialism is a share-the-
wealth program is strictly a confidence game to get the people to surrender their freedom to an all-powerful collective. It is a means to con-
solidate and control wealth. Once this is understood, it is no longer a
paradox that the superrich promote it. Here is another riddle: Once the
central banks become "socialized" as in Britain, the ownership remains
the same. Rothschild still controls the Bank of England, and the Bank of
England is still a private bank. As a central bank, it is literally above the
law.

While wars and revolutions have been useful to international bankers
in gaining or increasing control over governments, the key to such control has always been control of money. You can control a government if
you have it in your debt. A creditor can demand special privileges from
the sovereign. Money-seeking governments have granted monopolies in
state banking, along with natural resources, oil concessions, etc. But the
monopoly that the international bankers most covet is control over a
nation's money. The famed quote of Lord Rothschild to his friend
Benjamin Disraeli, England's first Jewish prime minister, was, "As long
as I control a nation's currency, I care not who makes its laws." Disraeli's
novel *Coningsby*, a thinly veiled story that involved Rothschild, contained
the following interesting quote: "The world is governed by very differ-

ent personages from what is imagined by those who are not behind the scenes."[5] This is true.

International bankers, as private companies, actually own the central banks of the key European nations. The Bank of England, Bank of France, and Bank of Germany are not owned by their respective governments, as most people imagine, but are privately owned monopolies that were granted by the heads of state. That is precisely why the *London Financial Times* of September 26, 1921, revealed that even at the time, "Half a dozen men at the top of the Big Five Banks could upset the whole fabric of government finance by refraining from renewing Treasury Bills."

Disraeli

But Professor Quigley revealed that these visible heads at the top of the Big Five Banks were only front men, the *agentur* of the invisible international bankers. Again, it was imperative that the shadow figures stay in the shadows and work behind front men. Quigley directly addresses the issue of the front men of the state banks of Europe:

> It must not be felt that these heads of the world's chief central banks were themselves substantive powers in world finance. They were not. Rather, they were the technicians and *agents* of the dominant investment bankers of their own countries, who had raised them up and were perfectly capable of throwing them down. The substantive financial powers of the world were in the hands of these investment bankers (also known as "international" or "merchant bankers") who remained largely behind the scenes in their own unincorporated private banks. These formed a system of international cooperation and national dominance which was more private, more powerful, and more secret than that of *their agents* in the central banks.[6]

Such a front man was Montagu Norman who was governor of the Bank of England. He suddenly came to America the year of the Great Crash, in February of 1929, to confer with Andrew Mellon, the Secretary of the Treasury. *The Wall Street Journal* on November 11, 1927, had already referred to Norman as "the currency dictator of Europe." Wrong. He was the front man for Lord Rothschild, the true currency dictator of Europe. Norman, a close friend of J. P. Morgan, had said of himself, "I hold the hegemony of the world," according to Dr. Quigley. John Hargrave who wrote the biography about and entitled *Montagu Norman*, cited the dream of this titular head of the Bank of England:

President Roosevelt and Bernard Baruch

"that the Hegemony of World Finance should reign supreme over everyone, everywhere, as one whole supernational control mechanism."[7] Norman was parroting someone else's view behind the scenes.

The Fabian Society of Britain, another of Quigley's inner circle round table groups who were present at Versailles, had worked up the gradualist agenda for the spread of socialism. Americans needed the backdoor approach. So after the crash, which, in turn, started the Great Depression, in came the Trojan horse of socialism in its first small increments as Roosevelt was cast in the light of the savior of the people with welfare and government programs. Not far behind were his liberal advisors, including Bernard Baruch who had also advised President Woodrow Wilson (Baruch contributed generously to both Wilson's and Roosevelt's campaigns). Take note that within a decade of Churchill's object lesson on the floor, he became one of Britain's greatest prime ministers. His bid as prime minister had failed repeatedly, but with the right support, he was elected.

Creating America's Central Bank

How did America finally get a central bank like its European cousins? Let's look back again. There were numerous attempts in the 1800s to create a central bank in America—most of these attempts point back to the Rothschilds.

The Rothschilds had their invisible hands in many of the early major American banking houses. One banker was August Belmont, a superstar of Birmingham's *Our Crowd* (whose original family name was Schoenberg). He used to put ads in the New York paper advertising himself as Rothschild's agent. He became incredibly wealthy. In the South, Rothschild had the Erlangers.

It is interesting that both the original American banking houses that represented Rothschild—August Belmont and the Erlangers—funded the North and the South respectively during America's Civil War. Rothschild sent August Belmont to the United States during the Panic of 1837 and empowered him to buy government bonds. Right then the Civil War started. Whichever side won owed its respective banker for the victory. Could the goal be monopoly of capital?

It seems Abraham Lincoln saw the power play behind this masquerade as one bank was seemingly played against the other. The invisible hand underneath was never seen by the multitudes. Lincoln did see it, for he had resisted the pressure to create in America a central private bank that would print its money. He also spotted the "divide-and-conquer" movement where the North was pitted against the South with both sides financed by the same money elite.

Abraham Lincoln battled for the right of Congress and the Treasury to preserve the legitimate power that the outsiders were after—the power of coining money. He knew that to surrender this power to private banks was ultimately to surrender the sovereignty of America. Adams and Jefferson had already warned of this danger of giving the power of coining money to outside interests. Defying the hidden bankers, Lincoln issued the greenbacks. Interestingly, Lincoln was soon assassinated.

J. P. Morgan

Forty years later there was another pivotal event: John Pierpont Morgan created the Panic of 1907 and was amply rewarded. He gained numerous holdings, as well as his bid to be the Rothschild's number-one American agent. J. P. Morgan's real feat and service to Rothschild in the Panic of 1907 was that he created a mood in

America that was receptive to finally getting a central bank—to be known as the
Federal Reserve Bank. Morgan's own
bank, The Morgan Guaranty Trust, was
allowed to be among the inner circle of
primary owners of the Federal Reserve. It
is interesting that Morgan had spent five
months in Europe right before the 1907
Panic, shuttling between London and
Paris. He was gaining an inside look at
Europe's central banks.

Solomon Loeb

The New York Times, October 26, 1907,
noted in connection with J. P. Morgan's
actions during the Panic of 1907: "In conversation with The New York
Times correspondent, Lord Rothschild paid a high tribute to J. P. Morgan
for his efforts in the present financial juncture in New York. 'He is worthy of his reputation as a great financier and a man of wonders. His latest action fills one with admiration and respect for him.'" This is the only
time a Rothschild praised another banker outside his own family. A few
decades later, The New York Times dropped another nugget. On March
28, 1932, during the Great Depression, The New York Times noted:
"London: N. M. Victor Rothschild, twenty-one-year-old nephew of
Baron Rothschild, is going to the United States soon to take a post with
J. P. Morgan & Co., it was learned tonight."

Soon after J. P. Morgan had created the Panic of 1907, the American
people were finally at a point to believe that
a central bank would prevent such a panic
from occurring again. When the moment
was right, Senator Aldrich—who later married into the Rockefeller family when his
daughter Abbey married John D.
Rockefeller, Jr.—was in place to push
through the Federal Reserve Act. That delicate moment was during a lame duck
Senate, right before the Christmas break on
December 22, 1913. Immediately before
that, Aldrich, representing the Rockefellers,
with Paul Warburg, who represented the
Rothschilds as well as the Kuhn Loeb Bank

Otto Kahn

of New York, had gone to Jeckyl Island, Georgia, in a sealed train, away from the press, to iron out how they would present the Federal Reserve bill to the House and Senate. Paul Warburg was the banking genius who understood the labyrinthine structure of the Federal Reserve Bank, and Aldrich was the public relations man in the Senate.

Warburg had some interesting connections. Paul Warburg had come to America ten years prior, in 1902, from his family's bank, the Warburg Bank of Germany. He married Nina Loeb, daughter of Kuhn Loeb founder Solomon Loeb, while his brother, Felix Warburg, married Frieda Schiff, the daughter of Jacob Schiff, who was the ruling power of Kuhn Loeb. Both Paul and Felix Warburg were made full partners of Kuhn Loeb, and Paul was finally paid an annual salary of half a million dollars (then!) to enlighten the public on the need for a central bank. His father-in-law, who paid him this colossal salary to set up the Federal Reserve, was Jacob Schiff. Stephen Birmingham writes in his authoritative bestseller *Our Crowd: The Great Jewish Families of New York*, "In the eighteenth century the Schiffs and Rothschilds shared a double house in Frankfurt." Jacob Schiff reportedly bought his partnership into Kuhn Loeb with Rothschild money—hence, the Kuhn Loeb connection with Rothschild.

Once Senator Aldrich had gotten the Federal Reserve Act through the Senate, Woodrow Wilson, under the nod from "Colonel" Mandel House, signed the Federal Reserve Act. Among the international financiers who contributed heavily to Woodrow Wilson's campaign were Jacob Schiff, Bernard Baruch, Henry Morgenthau, and *New York Times* publisher Adolph Ochs. Insider banker Bernard Baruch was later made absolute dictator over American business when President Wilson appointed him chairman of the War Industries Board, where he had control of all domestic contracts for Allied war materials, hence his war

Senator Aldrich

industries profits of over two hundred million dollars.

Yale professor Charles Seymour, whose collection of secret papers of Colonel Edward Mandel House are at the prestigious Beinecke Rare Books Library at Yale, revealed in his book *The Intimate Papers of Colonel House*, that "Colonel" (who was never in the military) Edward Mandel House was the "unseen guardian angel" of the Federal Reserve Act. His

father, Thomas House, reportedly a Rothschild agent during the
era of the Civil War, made millions of dollars running supplies
through the blockades. Then he
retired to Texas and sent his son
Edward to Europe to be educat-
ed. "Colonel" Edward Mandel
House almost never left Wilson's
side.

After President Wilson signed
the Federal Reserve Act, none
other than Paul Warburg became
the first chairman of the Federal
Reserve Bank. Naturally he had
to temporarily give up his partnership of Kuhn Loeb. Paul
Warburg remained chairman of

Edward House and Woodrow Wilson

America's new central bank until it was revealed that his third brother,
Max Warburg, who was still in Germany, headed the Central Bank of
Germany! It just seemed too much of a coincidence. Paul's brother Max
Warburg, by World War II, also headed up German Secret Intelligence,
which has baffled many of their fellow Jews—as has the fact that some of
Hitler's major funding came through the Warburgs, who controlled the
Mendelsohn Bank of Amsterdam through which they sent loan money.

Once America had a central bank in place from which to borrow
money, World War I suddenly arrived just in time for America to take
some substantial war loans and get into the action. Versailles was the
urban renewal after the "war to end all wars." The goal was the League
of Nations: guaranteed peace through world unity—again, "world
unity."

The Challenge of Sovereign States

While Europe was ready for the League of Nations, America was
not. So those insiders meeting at Versailles after World War I
now had to regroup to get America ready for globalism. The coming
Crash of '29 would help. Meanwhile several semisecret groups were
formed. According to Professor Quigley, they were round table spawns.

One in America was named the CFR, or Council on Foreign

Relations, a boringly neutral name. But try to become a member or walk through the door! The founders included many of those who had been at the signing of the Treaty of Versailles after World War I,

1920- Moritz Warburg & Sons (Paul & Max far L & R)

including Colonel Edward House and Walter Lippmann. Finances for the CFR came from: J. P. Morgan; John D. Rockefeller; Bernard Baruch; Paul Warburg; Otto Kahn; and Jacob Schiff.

The CFR was established on July 29, 1921, in New York City. Its building is on the west side of fashionable Park Avenue at 68th Street.

The Council on Foreign Relations (CFR)

Facing it today is the Soviet Embassy to the United Nations on the opposite corner.

The flame for the League of Nations had to be kept alive at all costs, and the best and the brightest had to be tapped as members of these groups. One of these groups, the CFR, traditionally divulges almost nothing about its aims and purpose, but something did leak out once. The CFR's *Study No.* 7, published November 25, 1959, openly declared its true purpose: ". . . building a New International Order [which] must be responsive to world aspirations for peace, [and] for social and economic change. . . . an international order [code for world government] . . . including states labeling themselves as 'Socialist.' "

The roster of CFR members is thoroughly impressive—so are the power groups who have representatives in it.

International banking organizations that currently have men in the CFR include Kuhn, Loeb & Co; Lazard Freres (directly affiliated with Rothschild); Dillon Read; Lehman Bros.; Goldman Sachs; Chase Manhattan Bank; Morgan Guaranty Bank; Brown Bros. Harriman; First National City Bank; Chemical Bank & Trust; and Manufacturers Hanover Trust Bank. The CFR is totally interlocked with the major foundations (Rockefeller, Ford, Carnegie) and the so-called think tanks (Rand, Hudson Institute, Brookings Institute).

According to Article II of the CFR bylaws, no minutes are to be taken

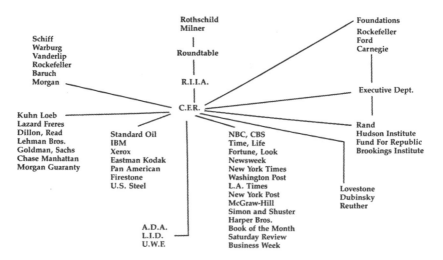

The CFR

and no member of the CFR is to divulge the content of any of its top secret meetings. If a member should do so, he is to be expelled immediately. One former member to do so was Rear Admiral Chester Ward (USN ret.). Though there is an elite of high military in the CFR, Chester Ward was a patriot. They misjudged him. The former rear admiral went public about the CFR warning:

> The most powerful clique in these elitist groups have an objective in common—they want to bring about the surrender of the sovereignty and the national independence of the United States.

> A second clique of international members in the CFR . . . comprises the Wall Street International bankers and their key agents.

> Primarily, they want the world banking monopoly from whatever power ends up in the control of global government.

> They would probably prefer that this be an all-powerful United Nations organization; but they are also prepared to deal with, and for, a one-world government controlled by the Soviet Communists if U.S. sovereignty is ever surrendered to them.[8]

Less than 20 years after the CFR was founded, World War II had arrived. Once that war had ended, America was now ready to join "the League of Nations," now incarnating as the United Nations. America sat down in San Francisco with Alger Hiss and joined the United Nations, the successor to the League of Nations. Hiss was a charter member of the CFR and his sympathy with communism can no longer be denied. The CFR's long time chairman was David Rockefeller. The United Nations' 18 acres of prime Manhattan land was donated by the Rockefeller family. The United Nations charter and constitution is a thin paraphrase of the Soviet model from which Alger Hiss borrowed when he co-authored it. The UN constitution is therefore a Marxist socialist paradigm. According to Quigley, this is

Lenin and Trotsky (side right)

anything but an accident. World socialism, communism and bankers could actually fit together!

There was always the Communist question. Bankers kept cropping up in this area as well, which is odd—unless one understands the logic of Hegelian synthesis: the logic of propping up two counterforces who are to oppose one another until they merge. It is also a great way to run up national debt— weapons systems that take billions to create, that through a disarmament treaty are then trashed. This has happened again and again. Did the bankers have goals for Russia? These are shrouded historical facts.

Jacob Schiff

Jacob Schiff, head of Kuhn Loeb, had given Trotsky (born in the Ukraine as Lev Davidovitch Bronstein) $20 million in gold bullion in 1917 and sent him to Moscow to trigger the Bolshevik Revolution with his 275 comrades (now bearing new Russianized names) from the lower East side of Manhattan. When this long roster of names entered the United States Congressional Record, many saw a pattern that took the full weight of the Antidefamation League to silence further discussion. *The New York Journal-American* of February 3, 1949, cited Jacob Schiff's grandson in observing, "Today it is estimated by Jacob's grandson, John Schiff, that the old man sank about $20 million for the final triumph of Bolshevism in Russia." But there was a brief embarrassment. Trotsky and his 275 comrades on the S. S. *Christiana* were held in Halifax, Canada— their first port of call. World War I was going on and Canada was suspicious. Trotsky spent five days in jail in Canada, but certain powers-that-be soon persuaded the Canadian government not to interfere. Trotsky, along with the $20 million in gold bullion and his 275 comrades, was, again, back en route to Russia. What happened?

The British, through Kuhn Loeb partner Sir William Wiseman, and the United States, through "Colonel" House, put the heat on Canada. Trotsky even got an American passport

Trotsky

out of the deal. William Wiseman, who had also been sent by British intelligence to help bring the United States into the war, was amply rewarded for his services. After World War I ended, he stayed in America as a new partner in the Jacob Schiff and Paul Warburg-controlled Kuhn Loeb Bank.

William Wiseman

While Jacob Schiff was sending Trotsky on his way, the German Warburgs independently gave Lenin five million dollars and sent him through Germany in a sealed train. The world was distracted by World War I. Lenin was installed, and by the end of the war, the Communist takeover of Russia was well in effect. Loans to Russia continued. World War II solidified things even more. By then, Stalin had come to power.

After World War II came Yalta, where Churchill and Roosevelt gave Stalin all sorts of concessions as they drank gallons of whiskey and ate pounds of Beluga caviar. Stalin was handed 11 nations on a platter including East Germany, Albania, Latvia, Lithuania, Hungary, Bulgaria, Estonia, Rumania, and other satellite land holdings. Soon enough, Stalin got Poland and Czechoslovakia through unhindered invasion. Roosevelt had held Patton back from finishing the war against Germany and marching right into Moscow. Had Patton been allowed to do what he had wanted to do and continue his march, which moved without obstruction, there would be no Russian occupation of East

Lenin & Stalin

Germany and countless other satellite countries. After World War II, the Communist bloc was far more solidified. Nations and power groups were being shuffled like cards in a deck, with decisions as weighted as gambling casino odds.

Now another irony: Russia still apparently needed the capitalists. This has been clear in the ten books by Antony Sutton, a British scholar and former member of

Stanford University's Hoover Institute. Sutton wrote *Wall Street and the Bolshevik Revolution*, tracing all kinds of capital flowing from Wall Street into Russia. Sutton also wrote *National Suicide: Military Aid to the Soviet Union* (New York: Arlington House, 1974) about how one military secret after another was leaked out of America and into Soviet hands—how we keep giving them our secrets after spending hundreds of millions of dollars on research to get that edge which we lose almost instantly. Several news leaks stated that in one day the plans for the cruise missile disappeared from a Pentagon desk and went out the door somewhere. They were very top secret. Just an innocent mistake! Months later, Russia had its own version of the cruise missile—so, too, with Polaris submarines. Sutton cites volumes of "coincidences." In the Clinton era, at least as many defense secrets found their way into China.

But there were earlier precedents for leaking secrets. Oddly enough, it was Alger Hiss' friends Julius and Ethel Rosenburg who shared with the Stalin government the secrets from the Manhattan Project on how to build the atomic bomb. Close to the Rosenburgs was Communist sympathizer and genius of the Manhattan Project, Robert Oppenheimer.

Till recently, billionaire Armand Hammer, owner of Occidental Petroleum (and the original benefactor of Senator Gore, Sr.), could arrive in Moscow and get any dissident he wanted freed, including the Jewish Nobel-prize-winning physicist Sakharov, builder of the Tokamak linear particle accelerator. Armand Hammer was of that very group whom the Russians "persecute," yet he gets special treatment. Why? Is there something we are missing? What about other super capitalists visiting this bastion of communism?

What about the trip to Russia in October 1964 of David Rockefeller, the chairman of the CFR and the Chase Manhattan Bank? What an odd place for a money superbaron to go—a capitalist, no less. And what about the coincidence that happened after Rockefeller left Russia? A few days after Rockefeller ended his only vacation to Russia, the head of Russia, Nikita Khrushchev, was recalled from a vacation at a Black Sea resort to learn that he was no longer premier of the Supreme Soviet. He had been fired—Khruschev who pounded his shoe on the desk at the United Nations General Assembly, the killer from the Ukraine who said to the capitalists, "We will bury you." He was fired after David Rockefeller's visit—amazing. Also of interest was the low-key reporting of these "coincidences" by the press, until you examine the interlocking boards of directors of the CFR and the New York media: publishing, radio, and television. Then it is not so incredible, nor is it amazing when very powerful publishing houses push bestsellers and create hot topics. *Avant-garde* and *chic* is always in. Traditional values are always out. Some topics are strictly taboo—Christian bashing, unfortunately, is not one of the taboos.

The Rockefeller empire took off at the beginning of this century. Today it is colossal, though it is sometimes hard to see where their ownership ends and that of other bankers begins—and that includes the Rothschilds. Yet staggeringly, compared to the Rothschilds of Europe, who have been in the banking business for over

John D. Rockefeller

200 years, the Rockefellers are mere country squires, upstarts. But let us look at these country squires for a minute. Seeing the panorama of their holdings is like trying to photograph a mirage—things shift in and out of view.

In the 1970s, a report was sent to Congress by two University of California professors revealing the extent of the Rockefeller empire. The findings were reported in January 1975 in the *Intelligence Digest* of the United Kingdom. According to the findings:

At that time, 15 members of the Rockefeller family were directors of 40 corporations which had assets of $70 billion. The boards on which the Rockefellers served had interlocking directorates with 91 major U. S. corporations controlling combined assets of $640 billion. The Rockefellers have more than 200 trusts and foundations where tremendous deposits of wealth are placed.

The Rockefellers' first business is the oil empire of Exxon with its 300 subsidiaries and affiliates worldwide, and secondly, the banking empire— the Chase Manhattan bank, Citibank, and Chemical Bank. Closely related to these banks are three gigantic insurance companies—New York Life, Equitable Life, and Metropolitan Life—which have interlocking boards of directors. More than these main banks and insurance companies, the Rockefeller investments account for about 25% of the assets of the 50 largest commercial banks and 30% of all the assets of the 50 largest life insurance companies in the USA. Similar influence holds true for their holdings in major corporations, including Mobil Oil, Marathon

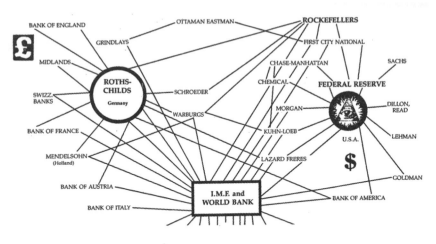

A Part of the International Banking Framework

Oil, IBM, Westinghouse, Boeing, Xerox, Avon, TWA, Eastern, United, National, Delta, Northwest Airlines, Penn Central, Safeway, General Foods, Allied Chemicals, Anaconda Copper, Shell, Gulf, Union, Continental Oil, American Motors, and so on. And keep in mind the above holdings was true twenty-five years ago when a dollar was worth much more than today's inflated dollar.

The main homestead of the Rockefellers has been the occasional meeting place for the secret meetings of another round table group of global elites known as the Bilderbergers. This homestead is the palatial mansions at Pocanto Hills in upstate New York. It is more than 4,000 acres in size, with 70 miles of private roads. In 1929 it had 75 buildings. No expense has been spared. Some rumor that it makes Buckingham Palace seem like a barn. It has underground archives to store family records that cost almost five million dollars to build. Among them, the Rockefellers have about 100 residences internationally, with palaces, estates, and plantations from Ecuador to Rome, from Hawaii to Manhattan.

But again, compared to certain other banking dynasties, the Rockefellers are *nouveaux riches*, mere upstarts of this century. There exist powers within powers that they have only tapped. The grand directors—the illumined seers—are in other drawing rooms—older, grander, and more palatial drawing rooms way out of public view.

The Moneychangers and the Temple

After Christ had cast the money changers out of the temple, they went out into the greater marketplace of the world and, in time, captured it. They did this colossal feat through "money changing" in all its aspects. The greatest international banks on the face of the earth now belong to them.

The following are the international banking aristocracies of the earth, those temple moneychangers who have resurfaced as international bankers. They include the banking dynasties of Rothschild (in the five pivotal nations of Europe), Warburg (Germany and Holland), Sassoon (cousins of the Rothschilds operating in the Far East), Lazard Freres (France), Mendelsohn (Amsterdam), Israel Moses Seif (Italy), Kuhn Loeb (New York), Goldman Sachs (New York), and Lehman Brothers (New York). All but one of the above are among the select "primary owners"/class A stockholders of the Federal Reserve Bank of the United States that collects over a $100 billion of interest a year from the United States government on America's national debt to them. (Note: The primary banks alone participate in the profits, not the hundreds of associate member banks protected by the Federal Reserve. The secrecy of the primary banks has been so great that from 1914 until now only certain insiders even knew who they were.)

There is a primary member of the Federal Reserve Bank who is not from among the lineage of the money changers. It is the Rockefellers of the Chase Manhattan and CitiBank of New York. Though the Rockefeller's Chase Bank had already merged with the Warburg's Manhattan Bank to become the Chase Manhattan Bank. Each of the above dynasties presides over multiple banks, and many of them have interlocking directorates.

Most of these banks are private partnerships, family-run dynasties. As partnerships, they are free from auditing. Those that are central banks of nations are especially free of auditing. They loan to nations as well as major corporations and individuals.

Lincoln made the following interesting observation about conditions around him, an observation that equally applies today: "When we see a lot of framed timbers, different portions of which we know have been gotten out at different times and places and by different workmen, and when we see these timbers joined together and see that they exactly make

the frame of a house or a mill, all the lengths and proportions of the different pieces exactly adapted to their respective pieces, and not a piece too many or too few, not omitting even scaffolding, or if a single piece be lacking, we can see the place in the frame exactly fitted and prepared to yet bring such a piece in; in such case, we find it impossible to not believe that they all understood one another from the beginning, and all worked upon a common plan or draft drawn up before the first lick was struck."

Fifty years after Lincoln's statement, America finally did get a central bank. The blueprint for that was the one used by the same architects who established the central banks of Europe. Now

the building materials for the grand pyramid—hewn, polished and assembled—finally stands ready to form the grand structure of the supreme Master Masons.

This project is to be ultimately overseen, as always, by the "all-seeing-eye" poised above the missing capstone—the same all-seeing eye, mind you, as the one portrayed on the back of the Federal Reserve one-dollar-note and called "the Great Seal"—the pyramid and the floating eye printed on a banking note. The moneychangers have indeed reentered the temple. It is the temple of the pyramid and the all-seeing eye, commercial and occult Babylon.

21

Summoning the Dark god

In the Book of Revelation, a vast number of the inhabitants of the earth reject God and willingly embrace Satan's system and living embodiment. Preparing the way—perhaps for centuries—are the merchants and kings of the earth. This wealthy and powerful elite is depicted in Revelation as worshipping the Dragon (ie. Satan) while preparing the world for the Dragon's dark messiah. When the Dragon-empowered despot named the Beast arrives, the global merchants and kings, "being of one mind" [a conspiracy], throw their vast fortunes at his feet.

> These [kings] have one mind, and shall give their power and strength
> unto the beast. (Rev 17:13)

This apocalyptic picture is about as far removed from the naturalistic worldview as one can find. The supernatural dimension makes no sense to those who have rejected anything beyond the five senses. But others in the younger generations have been more receptive to the possiblity of the super-natural. Most of them would have little trouble accepting the possibility of some group practicing ancient occult rites or that some amongst them might foreshadow these merchant kings.

A powerful contemporary portrayal what such people might be like—albeit through a fictional lens— has been done by two of the most famous directors of our time, Stanley Kubrick and Roman Polanski. Both directors in their own way may have stumbled into this dark international cabal, perhaps taking risks to warn of this reality (or conditioning the public to accept this eventuality). There has been some speculation that Kubrick, at one point, got a glimpse of this secret world. Perhaps he wanted to be included and was rejected. But if anyone were in a position to rub shoulders with members of such an elite, or at least know about them, it would be Stanley Kubrick. We may never know the nameless group of witnesses who might have come forward—perhaps servants or visitors at such estates who saw more than they bar-

Stanley Kubrick

gained for—pleading for an audience just to be believed, then reported in the papers as being dead soon after.

Stanley Kubrick's *Eyes Wide Shut* is like a final telegram to the world. It was completed just two weeks before he died a mysterious and untimely death. The famed director had filmed most of his final opus under absolute secrecy in England.

It is not about sex; it is about power, a very specific and very frightening kind of power. It is also about hidden realities that escape the common man (whose eyes are wide shut). Like other Kubrick films so far ahead of their time (as with *2001* and *Clockwork Orange*), Kubrick's final film has left audiences baffled and in shell-shock. Critics have been intent on down playing it either as a satire or as a flop. The message is too threatening for self-satisfied and urbane materialist-agnostics secure in believing that there really is no devil.

In *Eyes Wide Shut*, an ambitious young Manhattan doctor, Doctor William "Bill" Harford, played by Tom Cruise, manages to walk in on a massive midnight gathering at a vast gated palatial estate on Long Island (perhaps suggesting the even larger Rockefeller estate in nearby Upstate New York). It is a chillingly sober event with an unnerving sinister power.

Gathered in masks and wearing black robes with hoods are a hundred or so of "the most powerful people in the world." The young doctor has entered a deadly serious ritual—a hidden rite—shrouded from the masses. As Cruise strolls into the huge hall, one cannot help wondering who are behind the masks: perhaps a statesman on the evening news that night, addressing the public with a message of humanitarian compassion? Another, perhaps on Wall Street that day brokering a merger

between two of his corporations with a third corporate giant? Public figures like Kissinger, Rockefeller, Greenspan?

The young doctor, attired as the others and hidden behind his mask, watches the ceremony as he stands near the walls of the palatial ballroom. But he is being watched. His mask does not hide him. The leader, or host of the event, whose mask suggests a captain on the deck of a ship, stands in the upper balcony. With an aura of terrible, probing intelligence he looks down at the intruding doctor as if he were an insect.

The unholy rite is led by a masked ringleader holding a stave and censor, standing in the middle of a circle of masked semi-nude women. The event suggests a Satanic mass. A strange, indecipherable chant that sounds French overlays the haunting and dark organ music in the background. If anything, the sound—done with the complex layering of a Moog synthesizer—is anti-erotic and threatening. An orgy comes after the religious ceremony, extending throughout the estate. Moral barriers of the outside world are broken in contempt, for the god of forces does not honor the rigid morality of the holy God.

The young doctor is frustratingly naïve as he wanders through this dark, forbidden world, oblivious to every sign of danger before him. He is no different than the vast majority of men who are clueless about this dark nobility in the upper reaches of society. He tries awkwardly to blend in as he explores various anterooms and halls, voyeuristicly looking in on masked orgies. But he is being watched everywhere he goes until he is finally singled out and sum-

The Ceremony

moned. Publicly exposed, the doctor is told to undress before the huge reassembled group as he stands before them and an all-powerful masked potentate. His death might be as pleasurable to this group as the orgies.

What saves Cruise from possibly becoming that evening's human sacrifice is the rescue effort of a woman whose life he recently saved at a lavish Manhattan party put on by billionaire Victor Zeigler, a member of the cabal. The former beauty queen stands at the uppermost balcony and volunteers herself in place of Cruise, using the protocol of prescribed ritual. Cruise does not have a clue what price she is about to pay. Earlier, when Cruise had been wandering about, she had been trying repeatedly to warn him that he was in great danger, and that if he did not leave, that there would be terrible retribution. He was in way over his head and did not have a clue what kind of world he had just entered.

Kubrick's message was direct and to the point: *THEY EXIST.* Other activities were window dressing around this one central statement.

The terrible reality that the doctor encountered is portrayed as being so shocking and contrary to the mindset of the average man on the street that the normal

The council comes into session.

consciousness rejects it outright and tries to forget it as quickly as possible. That was precisely Kubrick's point when he had his real-life friend Sydney Pollack, playing Victor Ziegler, gambling on the same common mindset to persuade the young naïve doctor that:

Cruise is told to unmask and undress.

because we know such things don't exist, what you thought you saw was really something else. "So just forget it. Walk away and pretend it never happened. Oh, and the woman's dead body found the next day, well that was just a 'suicide.'" Pressed by Cruise's resistant idealism, Ziegler's next level of argument was calculated to get the doctor to back off before he got really hurt. "You really don't want to mess with this group. They are the most powerful people in the world, organized, ruthless, and can change your life in ways you don't want to even think about."

Another lesson: if you enter Satan's domain and the mind rejects it outright saying, "this is impossible," you are not protected, but are in the most vulnerable position imaginable (picture someone nude and blindfolded stumbling about in front of a King Cobra ready to strike). Your eyes are wide shut, sealed in blindness, just like the agnostics of our day who deny the Devil exists because they cannot conceive it. A world of naturalists and materialists turns out to be the best of all possible worlds for the Devil and his dark elite to operate. They have almost unlimited freedom of movement in a society blinded by its unbelief. The same point was made by Polanski.

Victor Zeigler talks to the young doctor.

Rosemary's Baby

Roman Polanski's powerful occult classic, *Rosemary's Baby*, was filmed three decades earlier at the Dakota House, in Manhattan's fashionable Central Park West, where John Lennon and Yoko Ono lived a decade after the film was made. This was also where John Lennon was eventually shot and killed.

Polanski took a varied approach to the same theme as *Eyes Wide Shut*: that a dark, hidden cabal at the highest reaches of society operates virtually undetected—due to unbelief—controlling huge sectors of the world from a hidden vantage point. These cunning internationalist devil worshippers blend in with the rest of society, outwardly looking harmless. They could raise people to stardom, as they did with Rosemary's aspiring-actor husband Guy, in payment for his offering her up as the coven's midwife to Lucifer; or they could utterly destroy those who got in their way. Rosemary's ambitious husband, brilliantly played by John Casavettes, suddenly got the part when the main actor trying out for the Broadway play, suddenly went blind (courtesy of the coven). Yet they had a deeper agenda. Like the merchants of Revelation, their plan was to prepare the earth for Satan and his Messiah.

Rosemary, naïve and therefore utterly defenseless, was the perfect foil for Polanski to give his dark tale a riveting momentum through countless scenes crafted in stunning detail. One of many insights from the dark side came when the coven's leaders, the elderly couple in the apartment next door to Rosemary and Guy, were hailing a cab outside Saks 5th Avenue. They were

en route to Paris and attired in the brightest muted pastels; she in a strawberry and cream dress, and matching hat, he in a lime colored suit—all in one brilliant cinematic moment of cloaking—as he intoned season's greetings to a passing acquaintance. It

is a revelation about the propensity of evil to camouflage itself: that in a layered reality, things are often not what they seem.

One prominent member of the Cabal, Doctor Abraham Saperstein, the world's premier gynecologist, constantly used the prestige of his international reputation and his most soothing bedside manner to repeatedly neutralize Rosemary's natural gut sense that something was terribly wrong both in her life and inside of her. Saperstein fed Rosemary various potions needed by the satanic fetus gestating within her while he coaxed and goaded the expectant mother to feel good about it all.

As in the Kubrick film, the point is made about the naïve modern mind being out of its depth with no reference points when coming up against the

realities of supernatural evil. Rosemary is yanked about like a fish on a hook. Even knowing they are a coven, all she can do is flail about, inevitably ending up in the same trap as she comes up against an unbelieving world time and again.

At one point, wise to the cabal and determined to escape, Rosemary sneaks out the foreboding residence and calls some ordinary doctor from a pay phone's yellow pages. She wants to take a cab to his office for a second opinion. Rather than gaining weight like most normal pregnant women, she is getting thinner and more run down by the day.

After she arrives, the doctor queries her about who her physician is. When he hears the name of the renowned Dr. Saperstein, his face drops and her fearful accusations look preposterous. Rosemary's desperation can only be pregnancy related paranoia. The idea of Saperstein being a Satanist is completely over the top. Then Saperstein arrives, hat in hand, to Rosemary's

horror. Rosemary realizes that the lesser doctor had secretly alerted the renowned physician. Looking mildly inconvenienced, but understanding, Dr. Saperstein proceeds to escort Rosemary home. She melts in impotent dread seeing the lesser doctor's ready dismissal of her pleading. She realizes the ground rules of this invisible war and that she has a losing hand. No one will believe her about this group of Satanists next door. No one, that is, but another Satanist.

Polanski uses dread and paranoia to make an important point about one's helplessness in a closed system. If society does not believe that certain realities exist, those encountering them have no recourse but to go within or hide. By the end of the film, the Cabal triumphed and broke Rosemary's spirit. She passively accepted her fate. There was no hope of escape for her in a world of sophisticated skeptics to whom such evil could not exist and where there was no God given as an option. In such a setting, evil was unrestrained and reigned uncontested. The film either exposed the blinding power of unbelief or, on a deeper level, was a paean to Satan's power.

Soon after the film was released, Charles Manson targeted Polanski's famous wife, Sharon Tate, and the Manson gang invaded their Hollywood home (while Polanski was on the road committing adultery) and hacked her to bits in one of the most notorious murders of all time.

Bohemian Grove

Some speculate that Stanley Kubrick was once a guest at the elite Bohemian Grove's annual gathering. The French-and sounding chant during the ritual in *Eyes Wide Shut* suggests the inscription on the gate at Bohemian Grove.

For two weeks at Bohemian Grove, a virtual who's who of over 2,000 of the worlds most influential and wealthy gather on the 2,700-acre grounds, their corporate jets streaming in to local airports. Gourmet food, drugs, sex, and expensive

Bohemian Grove Entrance

wine are plentiful. Security is so tight during this two week event, starting on July 15, that almost no one has been able to penetrate the tightly guarded grounds until Alex Jones, a journalist, somehow got in with a camcorder (infowars.com) long enough to record one of the ceremonies. His footage was played in England on BBC 4's *World of Wonder*.

Bohemian Grove is hidden deep in the redwood forests of Northern California close by the hamlet of Monte Rio (population 1,200) on the Russian River near Guerneville, a coastal town on the Pacific. When a close friend of mine and I were driving through the area one summer we decided to see if we could get in. I figured that if anyone could talk us in at the sentry gate, it would be my close friend Dan Meyer, a former Yale University student body president with GQ looks. But even Dan's gracious manner and aristocratic demeanor didn't budge the well armed sentry. We were told to leave immediately. Armed guards patrolled the area, and with High fences and towering redwoods, the place looked impregnable.

Members watch the ceremony.

The Orlando Weekly, from August 31 to September 6, 1995, reported on Bohemian Grove when the founder of *USA Today*, Al Neuharth, and Newt Gingrich were among the speakers:

> Al Neuharth spoke at Bohemian Grove, the all male encampment in Northern California where much of America's government and corporate elite gathers each summer for two weeks of speeches and activities like mock-Druid fire rituals. The official program described Neuharth's topic as "a look inside media newsrooms and boardrooms."

Political posturing of "left" versus "right" becomes meaningless at these elite gatherings, overshadowed by a deeper unity which transcends these public differences. *The Orlando Sentinel* revealed:

> Neuharth was among 2,200 men who heard an address by House Speaker Newt Gingrich. And what did Gingrich have to say? "I'm sorry," Gingrich staff writer Robert George told us. "We do not have a copy of that speech, and it will not be transcribed. The Bohemian Grove events are basically private functions."

... A week later, former President George Bush spoke at Bohemian Grove. In fact, every Republican president since Coolidge has been a member. In modern times, participants have included secretaries of state Henry Kissinger, George Shultz, and James Baker; Jimmy Carter, William Randolph Hearst Jr., Walter Cronkite, David Gergen and David Rockefeller. Notables have also included the presidents of CNN and the Associated Press.

Occasionally, shadow impressions of these elite gatherings surface. At Bohemian Grove, for example, members can be seen lighting torches, wearing black robes with hoods during midnight ceremonies. Druids march in procession chanting

Stone Owl five stories high & altar

to the Great Owl (Moloch) before a
funeral pyre with "corpses." It is the
"Cremation of Care" ritual, in which the
club's mascot is burned in effigy. "A
harmless Canaanite cult?" But why go to
such trouble if it is all just a meaningless
ritual? "Male bonding?" That can happen at the golf club or duck hunting.

Some ask if the entire assembly is

Hooded men escort "corpse" to burning altar.

composed of practicing Satanists? Of course not! But that does not exclude
the possibility of an inner-circle monitoring events, which is usually the case
in secret societies where neaphytes are being evaluated and recruited (several recruits have fled Bohemian Grove reporting people disappearing in the
woods as well as ritual human sacrifices—*Santa Rosa Sun* July 1993).

Ambitious newcomers may find the rituals exciting, especially as a "harmless" means of greater inclusion within a global elite with incredible privileges and rewards—a seemingly a small price to pay. But at some point, a few
of them will face a hard choice. Those who make the inner-circle, as C. S.
Lewis pointed out in his address at Oxford entitled "The Inner-Ring," will
have to pledge their very souls. At some point they, too, will begin sum-
moning the dark god.

It brings to mind the various rationalizations Satan, asking to be wor-
shipped, might have presented to Christ during the temptation in the
wilderness. "Look, the act of worship means nothing in itself. It's only a brief
ritual—over in seconds—and is only symbolical. Besides, I will give you the
kingdoms of the world in return." The obvious question is: how could such
an act really be valueless if such truly staggering rewards are given in return?
It would seem that the rewards give the game away? Christ told his disciples,
"For what is a man profited, if he shall gain the whole world, and lose his
own soul?" (Matthew 16:26).

Then there's the other question: why do these rituals always return to the
same dark enactments that go back to time immemorial? Perhaps the
rewards give them away! Ambitious and amoral people find the Devil's bargain irresistible, and belonging to an exclusive inner-
circle is delicious beyond words -- while it lasts.

22

When the Last
Piece Fits into Place

John's vision on the Island of Patmos, spanning millennia, revealed the final denouement of world history with a one-world system (religious, economic, military, and political) which would begin with intoxicating claims but end as a cruel tyranny ruled by a despot. The world system is referred to as *Mystery Babylon*, doubtlessly linked to its ancestor, Babylon in the ancient world, but this time returning with fierce power.

Today we see commercial Babylon has been progressively unfolding, even for centuries. The political powers of unity have made great strides in the past fifty years, while a general corrupting process has infected Western culture at a remarkable rate. No one really knows when this Babylonian system will emerge. It could be ten years, fifty years, or more. But the New World Order must be in place before the

United Europe Poster with Tower of Babel

"man of sin," the final Beast of Revelation, ascends to power. Inevitably, there is more to the pattern that will unfold that we cannot see from our perspective (did anyone in the '50s anticipate the worldwide web?).

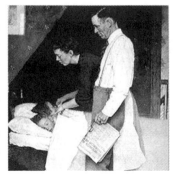

The knowledge of God must be obscured, then abolished. At some point the inhabitants of the world, having rejected the knowledge of God, will embrace the One energized by the Dragon.

The changes have been all too rapid. In the 1940s and 1950s, a stone's throw back in history, Norman Rockwell's paintings summed up the soul

of mainstream America with depictions of the happy American family sitting in a country church or at the family dinner table. They were the majority then, and the cultural ideal was the strong, stable, and loving father who was seated at the head of the table offering grace after the mother humbly and affectionately served the family dinner. The kids were gracious and respectful. Each was comfortable and secure in their own roles in a family that had stability, security, and love. They went to church and were loyal patriots who treasured a free America where they could live

unsupervised lives and where Horatio Alger was the ideal—in which the future offered unlimited possibilities to those diligent, honest and hard working.

But today, these wholesome folk, whom Norman Rockwell portrayed, have all but vanished with the buffalo. Today's liberated and politically correct consensus mocks the values of this straight generation.

If one of these conservative families could somehow be lifted out of rural America of the 1940s to appear on the Howard Stern Show,

it would be a delicious triumph of public degradation. Howard Stern, sensing a rare opportuni-
ty as a shock jock, might put a condom on his
nose, slide in between them at the dinner table in
his underwear, arms around each, as he tongues
the husband and wife in the ears while offering
them the latest high-tech sexual novelties to
fire up the marriage bed. By then a transsex-
ual stripper would be writhing near the husband as two gays in chains winked at the kids.
The audience would roar while the straight
couple sat in shock. The kids would be crying
in horror and shame at the far end of the dinner table on stage.

Of course, Howard Stern and Jerry Springer have
benefitted from decades of media deconstruction.

Past talkshow hosts like Phil Donahue used to
concoct a passionate tone of moral outrage, inform-
ing the occasional old-fashioned family that Dad
should be a "house husband" as Mom goes out to
drive a big rig while Johnny gets to experiment with
open sex-role options like leotards, jelly slippers, and
stick-on nails. He would intone this with his hands
outstretched, pleading to his audience the obviousness of what has become
the conventional wisdom.

In the late seventies, it was with great pride that Phil Donahue introduced his television audience to a family he could get excited about,
applauding their "courage." The husband and wife had gone to John
Hopkins Medical Center to have extensive surgery to reverse their gen-
ders. They were true transsexuals. The dad was now the wife, and she was
now the husband—right down to prosthetic penis and breasts. No, there
was no feeling in "the act" anymore (neither emotional nor physical—just
nerve-less pseudo organs flopping back and forth). The one who was once
the father was now experimenting with strong feelings for men. Donahue
beamed at them with admiration.

At the annual dinner of the American Press Association in 1914, John
Swinton, editor of the *New York News*, which later became the *New York
Times*, summed up the reality behind the media even in those early years:
"There is no such thing as an independent press in America. . . . Not a man

among you dares to utter his honest opinion. . . . We are the tools and the vassals of the rich behind the scenes. We are marionettes. These men pull the strings and we dance. Our time, our talents, our lives and our capacities are all the property of these men—we are intellectual prostitutes." This took courage, and I am sure Swinton headed for early retirement. Can you see Dan Rather, CFR member, sacrificing a multi-million dollar annual salary to give this type of confession? Now think of what the media has done since Swinton's era of 1914. It has worked miracles on changing America. Clinton's Marxist hero Antonio Gramsci was totally right about cultural change as being the effective route for socializing the West (over staged revolution).

By the 1980s, an American Civil Liberties Union (ACLU) legal victory enabled the courts to take a ten-year-old boy from his Christian mother (described in court as "fanatic and bigoted") to be placed into a more suitable household. The boy was awarded by the courts to his divorced homosexual father dying of AIDS and living with a gay lover—obviously a better environment for a growing boy than a Christian one. The judge was a lesbian.

Indeed, little Johnny has come a long way since the era of Norman Rockwell! By the 1980s, he was living with his divorced homosexual father whose live-in lover was a man. In Rockwell's era, Johnny was reading *Dick and Jane* in the family living room. Now he could read about Dick and James, learning all about sodomy. Johnny would be able to come home from fourth grade while the dad and his gay lover were wandering about arm-in-arm. Or if Johnny were alone, he could slip in one of their videotapes—not old Walt Disney films to be sure, but movies like *Heavy Bondage* with men wearing leather masks sodomizing, "fisting," (it's also called "anal justice") and torturing each other. And rather than Monet on the wall, Johnny would see photos by Robert Mapplethorpe.

All of this because the ACLU really cares about Johnny, right? Their very efforts prove that they have an agenda: to destroy the old America for the new. But most of them on the road to serfdom will absorb these changes as long as they are not bumped too painfully en route.

If you time-grafted today's youth culture next to the era of the fifties, no one would believe it. Who would have ever thought that God, goodness, and virtue would be so quickly despised by so many? Try talking about the old values in today's high school cafeteria. You can bet on getting incredulous hostility or mockery the minute you mention God and Country. But if you talk about the next all-night rave party or Marilyn Manson concert, you get the old Satan sign.

In the 1950s, a fellow with long hair, a dyed pigtail, wearing a bit of eye shadow, with maybe one big earring in his ear or nose would not be well-received showing up for gym class at Oklahoma State. For the average girl in the fifties with pretty long hair, a stylish dress, and a feminine demeanor, a freak was exactly what is now "in"—namely, a woman with a crew cut or flattop and a hard look in the eyes, wearing boots, jeans, and anything else to look masculine. This butch and her

**The Rolling Stones
Bridges to Babylon tour.**

colleague-in-arms would be an object of derision, shock, and disgust 30 years ago—reactions that are healthy, by the way. Now they are "in"—an ugly turn of events.

There is a timeless observation about rebellion as Paul described "the last generation" to Timothy. It is a description that seems to be getting closer everyday. The apostle Paul says:

> But mark this: There will be terrible times in the last days. People will be lovers of themselves, lovers of money, boastful, proud, abusive, disobedient to their parents, ungrateful, unholy, without love, unforgiving, slanderous, without self-control, brutal, not lovers of the good, treacherous, rash, conceited, lovers of pleasure rather than lovers of God (2 Timothy 3:1-4).

A Dark Vision

The New World Order will be different from anything the world has ever seen and will have elements that will surprise all of us—things we cannot foresee.

I have had what I think are glimpses of forces behind this emerging reality—spiritual forces. I believe, but cannot prove, that these glimpses were given to me as discernments after I left India. I was a young Christian recuperating in my parents' London house in Kensington. Dad, a diplomat, had retired in London. I was still battling serious intestinal problems from living in the wilds of South India for two years. A dream is a dream, but what I experienced was something more like an Imax—it was massive full color, panoramic, and bigger than life. I was present within the dream-experience with all of my faculties. I knew it was not just another dream but something, perhaps instructional, to prepare me for a future time.

I am a difficult person to scare. I used to go to horror films alone even when I was seven and was completely unfazed. But in the darkness of 5 A.M. after the panoramic experience was over, I was in a cold sweat, breathing heavily. I was certain that it was not just another dream—I had spent years gear-shifting to different levels of altered consciousness. This was unique. Now that I was a Christian, it felt as though the Holy Spirit impressed this direct connection with a certain reality right into my soul.

A few years later, I recounted this experience to a number of close college friends (among other things, AIDS hit national headlines about ten years after.).

The Main Dream Vision: It is the Place De Canon in downtown Brussels, the city of my father's final diplomatic post. It is the large medieval cobblestone square surrounded by impressive regal buildings. A terrible inhuman laughter fills the air. As I round the corner, I see a huge canvas canopy covering a throne.

A huge swollen leg, maybe 20 feet long, rests on a ramp emerging from this grotesque gigantic humanoid creature sitting on the throne. It is the source of the mocking laughter. I almost do a demonic mind meld with its thoughts. I cannot begin to describe the hideous cascade of direct feeling. I suddenly realize that this image represents the reality behind the triune Antichrist. One head is astoundingly intelligent, maybe an IQ of half a million, and another head swings around flopping on its chest and is insane beyond belief. The third head is entirely sinister, pure evil. It wants to destroy everything in creation. It is the source of many embodiments. I recognize India's Siva, who I once meditated on, as being one outward type of this creature. (Note: The dream event is near one of the future headquarters for United Europe that resembles three heads and a ramp).

The being knows I am watching and that I have some understanding of its real mission—to unify and possess the human race, to penetrate every

Berlaymont building, Brussels: Economic headquarters for United Europe

soul. Satan himself has entered this creature. A bent and mythologized history of the cosmos emerges with every hideous screaming laugh. It is trying to unmake God. It is trying to keep out the knowledge that the holy God in fury will consign this creature to the lake of fire. It wants to destroy God's people in particular—the future Christian martyrs.

I notice hundreds of hypodermic needles sticking in the creature's distended leg. Then I notice people in some kind of trance approach the leg. This is the moment they are to lose their souls through a kind of pollution. They idly play with the hypodermics, forcing polluted blood to go in and out. A slurping sound is emitted. Then they plunge the needles into their arms, co-mingling their blood with that of the creature. I can see their consciousness changing the minute the blood has entered them—there is no turning back. The dazed lack of awareness of the brainwashed subjects is terrible beyond belief. They seem unreachable as they walk away. The wailing cackle becomes distant.

I sit up in bed and look out into the black early morning of London through the window of my bedroom. This mood haunts me the whole day. No, it's not just another dream—almost ten years later, AIDS appeared in headlines. But blood can have other contaminants, from heroin to cocaine, and who knows what else awaits down the road? Just a dream? I'm not so sure. I feel it was a glimpse at a spiritual reality operating behind the scenes.

Some of the great writers have tried to see into the future to glimpse this invading global reality. Aldous Huxley saw the manipulated masses in his

Brave New World as being reduced to trivial hedonists, living for the moment, enthralled with designer drugs, with no purpose for living beyond the next shallow thrill. These drugged subjects were putty in the hands of the state. They had no will, no character—they could not fight the system even if they wanted to. But they were not the gray masses living on

Euro Millennium Party, Berlin

the edge of absolute poverty that George Orwell envisioned in his tyrannical world order in *1984*.

Orwell, like Ian Flemming, had been a member of the British secret service during the Second World War. In some ways his book is the blueprint of a terrible plan. In the forties, when Orwell wrote *1984*, he envisioned a collective semi-global system in which the populace had been reduced to slaves of the State without hope, dignity, or free will. They were the brainwashed masses who had no concept of history, since all books were destroyed. And what passed the State's "Ministry of Truth" had been rewritten to fit the confines of permitted thought. History was skewed with new interpretations yearly.

The populace of *1984* were surrounded by Doublethink slogans that constantly assault-

1884—Winston confesses thoughtcrimes

ed the natural gut sense as well as the conscience. Orwell's "antisex league" brilliantly foresaw the antisexism leagues of today—that liberal collective who have invaded college campuses with their nonsexist and antifamily agenda. In the world of *1984*, there was not a moment to think in privacy. "The individual is only a cell." Reality is in "the collective Mind, the Mind of the Party, collective and immortal." Even one's son or daughter could be an informer to the ever-present central control.

1984—the crowds listening to Big Brother

Orwell's two-way telescreen anticipated the host of technological breakthroughs of today that could be used to end privacy. The goal was to invade and take over wanton parts of the individualist mind that might engage in "thoughtcrime." No private thought could escape the all-seeing eye of Big Brother. The science of behavior could even turn to the most elaborate forms of torture, in Room 101, to flush out anything it wanted and remake the mind in any fashion it so chose. Room 101 was deep in the massive gray structure known as "the Ministry of Love," where thoughtcriminals were "cured." Today, our gentler slope is "sensitivity training"

"Power is tearing human minds apart and putting them back together by your own choosing." Winston, the lone individual in the collective, was being made an example: an "unperson." He was told by the Ministry of Truth: "We will lift you clean out of history. You will be annihilated in the past and in the future. But first we will make you perfect. Your mind will be perfectly remade, and only then, destroyed." It's a vision of total dehumanization—an apt portrayal of the system of Antichrist.

In Orwell's future world, there were no families, and sex roles had been obliterated. Intimacy and trust between the sexes had all but vanished. Tenderness was gone. Innocence and vulnerability were gone. Love between men and women was abolished forever. Rather, men and women were neutered in drab uniforms. A member of the Party told a rally of the brainwashed that "unorthodox loyalties lead to thoughtcrime; that the family leads to unorthodox loyalties," encouraging "ownlife." Therefore "the introduction of 'artsem' [artificial insemination] combined with the neutralization of the orgasm will render impossible the family until it becomes impossible to conceptualize." Even the memory of the family will be blotted out of history.

In the end, all human passion and genius is destroyed in Orwell's world. The free-thinking individual has become anathema. The state has become

God and is ruled by an invisible elite who can live as gods. George Orwell was a secularist, so it is natural that he would omit the metaphysical and spiritual dimension. Far worse than Orwell's Big Brother is the Antichrist.

But there is another difference between Orwell's future world and biblical reality. The vision in Room 101 for the human race is: "Picture a boot stamping on a human face forever." The biblical picture does not permit this. The prophetic picture is simple and final—God intervenes and ends the conflict that has spanned ages of human history.

The God of history absolutely forbids the final triumph of evil, and what he does to the powers of evil and their system is horrifying beyond imagining, should you happen to be on the wrong side. Wrath explodes from the all-powerful God who is great enough to create the galaxies with a single word. He demolishes those who hated and destroyed good, those who terminally rejected God and wrenched others' souls apart, and those who chased God's saints to the ends of the earth, persecuting and destroying the church. It is for a good reason that the Second Coming of Christ has been called the "Blessed Hope." Indeed it is for God's people, for the pure-hearted and the innocent who await His Coming. But for the enemies of God, this moment is the terror of judgment. He who they believed in their delusion they had defeated and unmade has now come in great power.

The one whom the dark rulers and their anti-God subjects thought they could erase from the universe suddenly cracks the sky apart. His light floods the souls of those who thought they could mythologize him out of existence. The faulty cement of the New World Order comes unglued, and this brief global experiment ends. The global banking fraternity watches helplessly. The economic spell ends as the cleverest plans are laid waste. The apostle John on the Isle of Patmos describes this moment when commercial and occult Babylon falls.

> Fallen! Fallen is Babylon the Great! She has become a home for demons and a haunt for every evil spirit, a haunt for every unclean and detestable bird. For all the nations have drunk the maddening wine of her adulteries. The kings of the earth committed adultery with her, and the merchants of the earth grew rich from her excessive luxuries (Revelation 18:2,3).

> 'Woe! Woe, O great city, O Babylon, city of power! *In one hour your doom has come!*'

> The merchants of the earth will weep and mourn over her because no one buys their cargoes any more—cargoes of gold, silver, precious

stones, and pearls . . . and the bodies and souls of men. (Revelation 18:10-13).

Commercial Babylon is destroyed in a single hour—impossible but for future technologies far removed from John's ancient world. Yet the Apostle John saw it all a thousand years before the Dark Ages! Think about it—a system that could only be possible with post twen-  tieth century technology, and John describes how the world economy collapses in a single hour. Already we see the New York, London, and Tokyo stock exchanges affecting one another in a matter of hours. But a fully unified system, a true global economy, could really fall in a single hour. A downed computer system has frozen mega corporations, bringing them to their knees.

John Lennon, in *Imagine*, sums up the one-world dream in this song of the century. . . "When The World Will Be As One." He paints a picture of utopian egalitarianism, but it rings hollow.

Lennon tell us, "You may think I'm a dreamer, but I'm not the only one." One pauses to reflect on his ascent from Liverpool obscurity to becoming the greatest rock legend of all time.  He was given every instrument needed to broadcast this messianic message to the world. It is easy to imagine something else: that Lennon entered even larger drawing rooms than the ones in Buckingham Palace, and met those who might not just be imagining, but actually pulling the levers for *the world to be as one*.

But John Lennon's utopian dream of *Imagine* will last but a season. It cannot endure because its foundation stone is hewn from the great lie. The promise of perfection and egalitarian harmony will become something else.

A planet in catastrophe cannot be utopia. The Book of Revelation, near the end of history, pictures the earth as a tortured planet suffering vast ecological damage that only a post-Industrial age could create in tandem with vast natural disasters, including an asteroid. The earth's oceans are poisoned, its sea life dying, water has become undrinkable, weather and seasons are in upheaval, the atmosphere is heating up to agonizing temperatures causing boils and skin cancer to break out on the earth's inhabitants.

What better description of an asteroid could come from 2000 years ago than a mountain on fire plummeting into the sea. Read the ancient scripture:

> And the second angel sounded, and as it were a great mountain burning with fire was cast into the sea: and the third part of the sea became blood;
>
> And the third part of the creatures which were in the sea, and had life, died; and the third part of the ships were destroyed.
>
> And the third angel sounded, and there fell a great star from heaven, burning as it were a lamp, and it fell upon the third part of the rivers, and upon the fountains of waters;
>
> And the name of the star is called Wormwood: and the third part of the waters became wormwood; and many men died of the waters, because they were made bitter. (Rev. 8:8-11)

God finally allows the cause and effect cycle of human rebellion to bring on catastrophic consequences. Man's hatred of God, his embracing of a demonic system, can only bring planetary judgment in the end. The vials of wrath in the Book of Revelation portray realities that could not possibly apply to the ancient world of John's day. It certainly was not the end of history. The global catastrophies John described had not happened and nor had Christ returned. Such cosmic events still lie ahead in our uncertain future.

The Gathering Storm

Lennon's utopian world described in *Imagine* will not be heaven on earth by any stretch of the imagination. In a technologically omnipotent World Order, there will exist the full-blooded potential for bringing to pass exactly what is described, not only by some New Age strategists and globalists, who use Darwinian language about excising the human race by a third, but by the Book of Revelation—the mass martyrdom of Christians and destruction of others on an unthinkable scale, surpassing the time of Nero and Domitian.

> And when he had opened the fifth seal, I saw under the altar the souls of them that were slain for the word of God, and for the testimony which they held:

Revelation's asteroid portrayed in the film Apocalypse

> And they cried with a loud voice, saying, How long, O Lord, holy and
> true, dost thou not judge and avenge our blood on them that dwell on
> the earth? (Revelation 6:9-10)

The biblical view of history is linear. History progresses from the Fall,
in which evil enters the world, to the end of history, in which evil needs a
final remedy. It was never God's plan that evil continue throughout all eternity. It is on a limited timeline, while sin and human rebellion are an ever
present constant that fluctuates. Christ's first advent is as the ransom sacrifice of Isaiah 53, the Suffering Servant, who takes on the sins of the world.
His Second advent is as king and judge. Most have understood the Second
coming to be one of judgment; and that presumes, not peace on earth in a
spiritual golden age, but a saturation point of depravity, when human apostasy and evil is incorrigible. God's timetable is fulfilled at that point, and
the Son of God comes to resolve human history.

One of the things that completes the final stages of this timetable is the
martyrdom of God's people, especially under the final despot who is
referred to below as "that Wicked." It will not be some New Age Christ
declaring the New Millennium from the United Nations General
Assembly or some podium in modern Jerusalem. Rather, the real return of
Christ will bring planetary judgment.

> And then shall that Wicked be revealed, whom the Lord shall consume
> with the spirit of his mouth, and shall destroy with the brightness of his
> coming: (2 Thess. 2:8)

If God's saints have been martyred, the returning Christ will greet the
perpetrators with the relentless fire of judgment.

> And shall not God avenge his own elect, which cry day and night unto

him, though he bear long with them?

I tell you that he will avenge them speedily. Nevertheless when the Son
of man cometh, shall he find faith on the earth? (Luke 18:7-8)

Far from celebrating with the intoxicated optimism of the Cosmic
Millennialists, with their brash declarations of triumph about a liberated
Family of Man, we should, as a nation, be kneeling in tears before a Holy
God whom we have offended with our arrogance, apostasy, and perversion.
In God's eyes, we are blind and naked. The shadow of judgment, in the
form of delusion, is rising by degrees in our midst daily.

In this condition, who but one deluded would dare dream of beating our
drums down Wall Street in an ecumenical pan-religious revival to celebrate the advent of some Cosmic Christ. Rather:

But the day of the Lord will come as a thief in the night; in which the
heavens shall pass away with a great noise, and the elements shall melt
with fervent heat, the earth also and the works that are therein shall be
burned up.

Seeing then that all these things shall be dissolved, what manner of persons ought ye to be in all holy conversation and godliness,

Looking for and hastening unto the coming of the day of God, wherein
the heavens being on fire shall be dissolved, and the elements shall melt
with fervent heat? (2 Peter 3:10 -12)

What sort of world will it be when He appears? Certainly not a spiritual golden age as some Christians and most New Agers believe. We are told
it will be like the time of Noah, the only time God sent planetary judgment
on the earth—a flood—destroying all human civilazation but for a human
remnant in the ark. To bring this kind of judgment, something had to have
gone terribly wrong.

But as the days of Noah were, so shall also the coming of the Son of
man be.

For as in the days that were before the flood they were eating and
drinking, marrying and giving in marriage, until the day that Noah
entered into the ark,

And knew not until the flood came, and took them all away; so shall
also the coming of the Son of man be. (Matt. 24:37-39)

The antediluvian world of Noah that God destroyed in its entirety had
the sort of evils that brought not just local judgment but planetary judgment. Similar evils are predicted to reappear by the Lord's final coming.

We can only guess what the particular evils were in Noah's day (Tantric witchcraft? Incest? Murder for pleasure? Worshipping Satan?). This distant world had the moral equivalent of AIDS that could no longer be healed or salvaged, only purged from the earth. The flood was a purge, nothing less. The destruction of Sodom and Gomorrah was another example of a judgmental purge, where the moral depravity was so full scale as to be beyond salvaging.

When Christ returns, the world will be in moral chaos. Strong Delusion will run head long into Reality—The Son of God who is the Alpha and the Omega. He is the One whom Colossians tells us "Through Him all things were created."

The dazzling empire that came in like a rainbow will be no more. The despotic and tyrannical global system will be blotted out, replaced by the New Creation. At minimum, the world will be remade. For only God can remake the universe and its planets—not with the glue of human or diabolical cunning, but with a single divine act.

The End

Notes

Introduction-The New World Order
1. The Utah Independent, Sep. 1977.

Chapter 1—Contact
1 Jon Klomo, "Channeling," in *The New Age Journal*, Dec. 1987, p. 37.
2 Ibid., p. 34.
3 Whitley Strieber, *Communion* (New York: Avon Books, 1988), p. 16.
4 Ibid., p. 100.
5 Ibid., p. 123.
6 Ibid., p. 21.
7 Ibid., p. 245.

Chapter 3—Opening the Third Eye
1. Tal Brooke, *Avatar of Night* (New Delhi: Vikas Publishing, 1982), pp. 9-13.

Chapter 5—Higher Guidance
1. J.D. Salinger, *Nine Stories* (Boston: Little, Brown, and Co., 1951), pp. 287-88.

Chapter 6—Voices from Out of the Rainbow
1. John Randolph Price, Planetary Commission Update, Aug. 1986, p. 4.
2. Ken Wilber, *The Atman Project* (Wheaton: Theosophical Publishing House, 1980), p. ix.
3. Peter Russell, *The Global Brain* (Los Angeles: Tarcher Publications, 1983), pp. 210-11.
4. Robert Muller, *New Genesis* (Garden City: Doubleday & Co., 1984), p. 100.
5. Russell, *The Global Brain*, p. 231.
6. Note: The list of New Western Hybrids was put together with the aid of Robert Burrows.
7. Alice Bailey, "Externalizing the Mysteries," Part I, The Beacon, Nov./Dec. 1975, p. 171.

Chapter 7— The Eye of the Earth
1 Doe, John, *Report From Iron Mountain on the Possibility and Desirability of Peace* (NY, Dial Press, 1967).pp. viii-ix; emphasis in the original.
2 Brooks Alexander, " The View From Iron Mountain, planning global eco-war," *The SCP Journal* 17:3, 1992, p. 42
3 Sanders, Franklin, (1992) "The Three Legs of the Beast" Moneychanger, January, 1992, p.4.
4 *Report From Iron Mountain*, p. 67.
5 Ibid., pp 66-67.
6 URL = http://www.igc.apc.org/habitat/agenda21/rio-dec.html
7 *Los Angeles Times*, May 8, 1997
8 http://www.gci.ch/GreenCrossPrograms/earthcharter/
9 The Earth Charter Project, "The Green Cross Earth Charter Philosophy," Internet document, http://www.gci.ch/greencrossprograms/earthcharter/earthcharterphilosophy.html; p. 5
10 "In their own words." eco-logic, May/June, 1996, p.20f.
11 James Garrison, "Toward a New Civilization," Internet document; http://www.arq.co.uk/worldforum/program/news.htm; cited below as Document 97
12 "About the Forum: Mission Statement," Internet document; http://www.arq.co.uk/worldforum/about_the_forum/mission.htm; cited below as Document 102
13 Mikhail Gorbachev, "Toward a New Civilization," September 27, 1995, State of the World Forum; Internet document; http://www.well.com/user/wforum/transcripts/keynote/gorbachev1.html; p. 1

Chapter 8— Entering the Mind
1 Lattin, Don, "The Need to Cry Out," *Common Boundary*, May/June 1991, p. 21
2 Brooks Alexander, "Recovery's Family Tree," *SCP Journal* Vol 18;3, 1993. P. 41
3 Barbara Ehrenreich"The Psychology of Growth," *Mother Jones*, April 1983.

4 William Kirk Kilpatrick, *The Emperor's New Clothes* (Westchester: Crossway Books, 1985), p. 27.
5 Ibid., p. 28.
6 Ibid., p. 28.
7 Ibid., p. 36.

Chapter 9—Wiring The Earth
1 Philip Elmer-Dewitt, "Welcome to Cyberspace," *Time* Special Issue, Spring, 1995.
2 Philip Elmer-Dewitt, "Cyberpunk!" *Time*, Oct 15 1993
3 George Gilder, "Scoping Out the Data Highway," (interviewed by Mary Eisenhart) *Microtimes*, July 25, 1994.
4 Ibid.
5 Philip Elmer-Dewitt, "Cyberpunk!" *Time*, Oct 15 1993
6 Victor Keegan, "The Guardian", London Dec. 12,1994.
7 Robert Wright, Mitch "Kapor, Data Highway Guru. The New Democrat From Cyberspace," *Wired*, May 7, 1993.

Chapter 10— The Educational Droidworks
1 "U.S. Teens rank Low in World Tests," by Nanette Asimov, *San Francisco Chronicle*, Feb 25, 1998, front page.
2 Eackman, *Educating for a New World Order*, (Portland: Halcyon House) 1991. p. 12-13.
3 William Kilpatrick, *Why Johnny Can't Tell Right from Wrong* (New York: Touchstone/Simon and Schuster, 1992). pp. 14, 55, 76
4 Marilyn Ferguson, *The Aquarian Conspiracy*, (Los Angeles: Tarcher Publ.) 1981. p. 283.
5 Francis Adeney, "Educators Look East," *SCP Journal*, Vol 5, #1, 1981, p. 29.
6 The Society for Accelerated Learning, "New Dimen- sions in Education-Confluent Learning," San Francisco, Apr. 25, 1980.
7 Felix Frankfurter, "The Supreme Court and the Public," *Forum* magazine, June 1930, pp. 232-33.
8 Connecticut Citizens for Constitutional Education, Jan. 22, 1980.
9 Jack Canfield and Paula Klimek, "Education in the New Age," *The New Age Journal*, Feb. 1978, p. 27.
10 Ibid., p. 28.
11 Ibid., p. 30.
12 Ibid., p. 36.
13 Ibid., p. 39.
14 Ibid., p. 39.
15 *The Washington Times* , "Provincetown Preschoolers to Learn ABC's of Being Gay," August 21, 1997
16 Ibid.
17 *Eagle Forum* , "Gay Lesbian Caucus Flaunts its Influence", August 1996.
18 Supplied personally by Dr. Paul Cameron, Family Research Inst. Colorado Springs, Co.
19 Clinton, Hillary Rodham, *It Takes a Village*, (New York, Simon & Schuster, hardback) 1996, p. 32
20 Hillary's Global Village by William Norman Grigg, The New American, March 4, 1996.
21 "Cradle to Grave" OBE The New American,Volume 11, Number 15 July 24, 1995, p.41 *By William F. Jasper*
22 http://www.thewinds.org/, "Restructing Society Through Education."

Chapter 13—Erasing God from the Universe
1. William Barrett, *Irrational Man* (Garden City: Doubleday, 1958), p. 217.

Chapter 14—Letting Mr. Gumby Control the Universe
1. Henry Thoreau, *Walden* (New York: New American Library, Signet Classic, 1960), p. 67.
2. Walter Pater, *The Renaissance* (New York: Mentor Books, 1977), pp. 157-58.
3. Ibid., p. 158.

4. Alan Bloom, *The Closing of the American Mind* (New York: Simon and Schuster, 1987), p. 141.
5. Diogenes Allen, *Philosophy for Understanding Theology* (Atlanta: John Knox Press, 1985), p. 265.
6. Gunther Stent, *The Coming of the Golden Age: A View of the End of Progress* (Garden City: Natural History Press, 1969).

Chapter 15—Bridges to the New Consciousness
1. James Webb, *The Occult Underground* (La Salle: Open Court Publishing, 1974), p. 86.
2. Ibid., p. 101.
3. Ibid., p. 101.
4. M.K. Neff, *Personal Memoirs of Helena P. Blavatsky*, p. 244.
5. Ibid., p. 291.
6. Madame Helena P. Blavatsky, *The Key to Theosophy* (Chicago: Theosophical Publishing House, 1930), p. 111.
7. Madame Helena P. Blavatsky, *Collected Writings*, Vol. 8, p. 277.
8. Madame Helena P. Blavatsky, *The Secret Doctrine* (Los Angeles: Theosophy Co., 1925), Vol. 3, p. 386.
9. Ibid., Vol. 2, p. 132.
10. Ibid., Vol. 3, p. 246.
11. Ibid., Vol. 3, p. 376.
12. Blavatsky, *The Secret Doctrine*, Vol. 4, p. 52.
13. H.T. Edge, *Theosophy and Christianity*, p. 52.
14. Ibid., p. 37.
15. Ibid., pp. 85-90.
16. Ibid., p. 168.

Chapter 16—The Reality of Evil
1. Malcolm Muggeridge, "The Death Wish of Western Civ." Eternity magazine, Apr. 1972.
2. John Whitehead, *The Stealing of America* (Westchester: Crossway Books, 1983), p. 53.
3. John W. Whitehead, *The Stealing of America*, pp. 43-44.
4. Walker Percy, *Lost in the Cosmos: The Last Self-help Book* (New York: Simon & Schuster, 1983), p. 44.
5. Ibid., p. 44.
6. H.J. Blackham, *Humanism* (London: Penguin, 1968), pp. 13, 19.
7. Henry Miller, *The Tropic of Cancer* (New York: Grove Press, 1961), p. 232.
8. Soren Kierkegaard, *Fear and Trembling* (Princeton: Princeton University Press, 1941), p. 30.

Chapter 17—The Coming World Religion
1 Teilhard de Chardin, *Human Energy*, (New York: Harcourt, Brace, Jovanovich, 1970), p. 37-38.
2 King, Ursula, *Towards a New Mysticism: Teilhard de Chardin and Eastern Religions*, (London: Collins, 1980), p. 98.
3 Ibid., p. 172.
4 Alice A. Bailey, *The Externalisation of the Hierarchy*, 1957, Lucis Publishing Company, New York, ISBN 0-85330-106-9, p 510; the "wise prophecy" of Blavatsky appears to be the statement that "In Century the Twentieth some disciple more informed, and far better fitted, may be sent by the Masters of Wisdom to give final and irrefutable proofs that ... like the once-mysterious sources of the Nile, the source of all religions and philosophies now known to the world has been for many ages forgotten and lost to men, but is at last found." (Blavatsky, *The Secret Doctrine*, Vol. 1, p. xxxviii, http://www.theosociety.org/pasadena/sd/sd1-0-in.htm)
5 Alice A. Bailey, *The Externalisation of the Hierarchy*, 1957, Lucis Publishing Company, New York, ISBN 0-85330-106-9, p. 202
6 Alice A. Bailey, *The Destiny of the Nations*, Lucis Publishing Company, New York, 1949; p. 152
7 Alice A. Bailey, *Problems of Humanity*, Lucis Publishing Company, New York, 1st ed. 1947; rev. ed. 1964, p. 159
8 Robert Muller, *My Testament to the UN: A Contribution to the 50th Anniversary of the United*

Nations, World Happiness and Cooperation, P. O. Box 1153, Anacortes, Washington 98221; ISBN 1-880455-07-2, p. 4

9 Robert Muller, *2000 Ideas And Dreams For A Better World*, Idea 126, 13 November 1994, http://www.lsw.org/ideas/RMideas.html

10 United Religions Initiative, "Questions: What is the URI," http://www.united-religions.org/questions/question_1.shtml

11 United Religions Initiative, "72 Hours," http://www.united-religions.org/newsite/index.htm, p. 1

12 Richard Scheinin, "Interfaith ceremony promotes world peace," *San Jose Mercury News*, June 26, 1995

13 Don Lattin, "Religions of World Celebrated With Prayers to Dozen Deities," *San Francisco Chronicle*, June 26, 1995, pp. A1 and A11, front page section

14 Bishop William Swing, *The Coming United Religions*, United Religions Initiative and CoNexus Press, 1998, ISBN 0-9637897-5-9; p. 63

15 Bishop William Swing, "Opening Address" to the 1997 URI summit conference, http://www.united-religions.org/youth/welcome/swingspeech.htm, p. 2

16 Dennis Delman, "Bishop Swing Preaches at Cape Town Cathedral: Urges 'New Day and New Way of Peacemaking', *Pacific Church News*, February/March 2000, p. 25

17 Transcribed by Lee Penn from URI-provided tape of URI forum at Grace Cathedral, held on 2/2/97

18 Lucis Trust, "Transition Activities: The United Religions Initiative," *World Goodwill*, vol. 1, 1999, http://www.lucistrust.org/goodwill/wgnl991.shtml, pp. 21-22; Lucis Trust, "Invoking the Spirit of Peace," *World Goodwill*, vol. 3, 1999, http://www.lucistrust.org/goodwill/wgnl993.shtml, pp. 2, 3

19 Neale Donald Walsch, *Conversations with God: An Uncommon Dialogue, Book 3*, Hampton Roads Publishing Company, Inc., 1998; ISBN 1-57174-103-8; p. 287

20 Neale Donald Walsch, *Conversations with God: An Uncommon Dialogue, Book 2*, Hampton Roads Publishing Company, Inc., 1997; ISBN 1-57174-056-2; p. 141

21 Neale Donald Walsch, *Conversations with God: An Uncommon Dialogue, Book 2*, Hampton Roads Publishing Company, Inc., 1997; ISBN 1-57174-056-2; pp. 195-196

22 Neale Donald Walsch, *Conversations with God: An Uncommon Dialogue, Book 2*, Hampton Roads Publishing Company, Inc., 1997; ISBN 1-57174-056-2; p. 205

23 World Federalist Association, "Walter Cronkite's Remarks to WFA – United Nations, New York – October 19, 1999," *News and Announcements*, January 2000, http://www.wfa.org/news.htm, p. 3

24 Zaehner, R.C., *Zen, Drugs, and Mysticism*, p. 181

25 Hubbard, *Revelation* (Document 62), cited above, pp. 101-102; also, Hubbard, *Revelation/Hope*, cited above, p. 111

26 Hubbard, *Birth Day*, cited above, p. 41

Chapter 19—The Great Lie
1. Austin Farrer, *Love Almighty and Ills Unlimited* (New York: Doubleday and Co., 1961), p. 126.
2. Alexander Hislop, *The Two Babylons* (Neptune, NJ: Loizeaux Publ., 1916), pp. 20, 78, 96.

Chapter 20—The Hidden Aristocracy
1. *The Writings of George Washington*, published by the U.S. Government Printing Office, 1941, Vol. 20, p. 518.
2. Carroll Quigley, *Tragedy and Hope* (New York: The Macmillan Company, 1966), p. 950.
3. Ibid., p. 324.
4. John Kenneth Galbraith, *The Great Crash, 1929* (New York: Time Inc., 1954), p. 102.
5. Benjamin Disraeli, *Coningsby*, p. 233.
6. Quigley, *Tragedy and Hope*, pp. 326-27.
7. John Hargrave, *Montagu Norman* (New York: Greystone Press, 1942).
8. Rear Admiral Chester Ward, Review of the News, Apr. 9, 1980, pp. 37-38.

End Run Publishing

"To provide an end run around..."

The publishing giants keep producing books that fit within certain narrowly prescribed politically correct & secularist views, thus keeping from publication books that challenge their views, regardless of how well written. Free speech is thus effectively defeated at the editorial & marketing gateways of these 70-story monoliths. Today's high-tech revolution—digital short run printing, powerful computers, & the Internet—may eventually level the playing field (How many publishing giants started as humble two room bookbinders in Brooklyn at the turn of the century?). Stay tuned for more titles.

Tal Brooke has written numerous books on diverse subjects. His most popular book in the West, *When The World Will Be As One,* was a 100,000-copy bestseller marketed to a very limited audience. He has written seven other books, including *Riders of The Cosmic Circuit,* which came out in Europe. Keep your eyes out for these and other titles being considered.

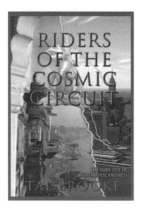 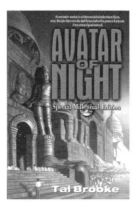

**Tal Brooke, President of SCP, is on the Web at the
SCP Web Site: http://www.scp-inc.org/
Check out the in-depth Journals and Newsletters that SCP
(Spiritual Counterfeits Project) has published over the years.
Or phone the SCP offices at: 510-540-0300**

END RUN PUBLISHING
1442A WALNUT STREET, PMB 387, BERKELEY, CA, 94709

End Run Publishing

The Indian Bestseller was released in December of 1999 and is the most complete version ever published.

Avatar of Night, The Millennial Edition, by Tal Brooke

As Woodstock and the Apollo moon landing lit up the skies of history, Tal Brooke flew to New Delhi, quickly becoming immersed in the vast subcontinent of India as he pursued a radical pilgrimage of consciousness. After quickly exhausting the 'Grand Tour' of landmarks popularized by the spiritual tourists of the West, Brooke plunged into wilderness India, and the journey shifted into high gear.

From their first meeting, Brooke was heralded by Sai Baba, India's greatest miracle-working godman, as the inner-circle disciple who, like Oppenheimer at Los Alamos, would help trigger the explosion of India's ancient mystical tradition into the Western world. Within Baba's enchanted realm, Brooke saw and experienced things that seemed to obliterate all Western conceptions of reality as his journey vectored further into an alien universe. What had appeared as the prized state of godlike enlightenment, which seemed just within reach, became a precipice—not of enlightenment—but obliteration, even possession. Brooke was becoming a captive soul of an ancient inner transformation, while Baba's outward divinity concealed a timeless, demonic presence.

After two years of surrender to a Being who claimed to be God on earth, something remarkable happened. The end-game of spiritual powers ensnaring one man's soul turned abruptly and miraculously. Poised on the edge of a precipice, Brooke was rescued from above.

With hauntingly vivid images, unexpected humor, and a profound passion for truth, Brooke lays bare the powerful reality of good and evil and of things beyond the familiar realm of the senses, in a book that will not be easily forgotten.

Avatar of Night: ISBN: 1-930045-00-X
406 pages, 180 photographs and graphics

To Order End Run Books

ONE WORLD
&
AVATAR OF NIGHT

1. For Toll-Free Credit Card Orders—Dial: 800-266-5564 and ask for either title for immediate Priority Mail shipment.

2. Phone SCP Inc. at: 510-540-0300 in Berkeley California and they will take credit card orders over the phone and ship immediately by Priority Mail or Internationally via Global Priority (this ranges from $9-$12).

SCP Web Orders: You can also order via secure shopping cart on the SCP web page at: www.scp-inc.org/

3. Berean Bookstores have started to stock both End Run books. So check with your nearest Berean store.

4. Amazon.com. Do an author search for Tal Brooke. Amazon.com carries the books but are very slow and, at the moment, only ship books in 4-6 weeks. Much slower than Barnes and Noble.com.

5. Barnes and Noble.com. Do an Author search for Tal Brooke. Barnes and Noble.com have a 24 hour turnaround **when the book is in stock**. Otherwise the web page states the book is unavailable till supplies arrive at their warehouse—an archaic system. B&N web services are very uneven and we have had numerous complaints.